The Melancholia of H. P. Lovecraft's "The Music of Erich Zann"

James Goho

H. P. Lovecraft's "The Music of Erich Zann" (1922; *CF* 1.280–90) is an early expression of the melancholia of the modern age. Severe depression characterizes modern cultures, according to Elaine P. Miller, who calls it the modern "malady of the soul" (1), after the work of Julia Kristeva. Lovecraft's story exhibits melancholia in both of his main characters: Erich Zann and the unnamed student, who narrates this first-person perspective story. The story illustrates the experience of depression in all its bleak despair and terrifying perceptual and cognitive dissonance. Kristeva's notion of melancholia[1] (a form of narcissistic depression) suggests that a primary symptom of depression is the loss of the ability to communicate at a symbolic level. Communication regresses to signs. In part, Kristeva views depression as paralysis at the verbal level of expression. This is the public face of depression. A causal or risk factor for falling into depression for Kristeva is a figure of loss, which is how George E. Haggerty[2] phrases it. Here persons with depression lament a lost Thing, a loved object they cannot em-

1. Melancholic depression is a form of a major depressive disorder. The American Psychiatric Association no longer recognizes it as a distinct disorder; now it is categorized as a subtype of a depressive mood disorder. Symptoms of depression include: deep feelings of despair, sleep disruptions, isolating oneself, weight loss, and thoughts of death or suicide. Some suggest depression is primarily a physiological illness, characterized by an imbalance of brain bio-chemicals. But there are many possible causes of depression. Psychoanalysis hunts for the roots of depression in our experiences and memories, both conscious and unconscious.

2. Haggerty argues that Gothic fiction can be understood, in part, through the figure of loss, which often involves an unusual eroticism (3, 21–44).

brace or be embraced by any longer. According to Sigmund Freud, mourning for a dead friend or relative is healthy, but melancholy is pathological. Both mourning and melancholia involve a lost loved object, but in melancholia a person cannot let go of the loved thing, and over time it becomes an unconscious loss (Freud 155). At a primal level Kristeva's narcissistic melancholy arises from the loss of an archaic, unnamable pre-object.[3] This longing for the lost Thing creates a search to re-embrace that Thing, to find it again, but this fails. It cannot be recovered. And the individual becomes trapped in the chaos of the unconscious, which, Kristeva claims, "is not structured like a language" (*Black Sun* 204). Kristeva's concept of melancholia will form a structure for my interpretation of Lovecraft's story, which paints a deep, multileveled, and disturbing portrait of melancholia.

"The Music of Erich Zann" was one of Lovecraft's favorite stories (*SL* 3.402), second only to "The Colour out of Space" (*SL* 3.379)—the two stories he felt were "worth saving" (*SL* 5.338) later in life (1936). But he also wrote at that time that the story had a negative value for him; he liked it for what it "*hasn't* than for what it *has*" (*SL* 5.348 [his emphasis]). Lovecraft adjudged the story expressed "the horror of the grotesque and the visionary" but was not, "as a whole, a dream" (*SL* 1.166–67). Yet he said it had a "dream-like" narration (*SL* 3.193). Maurice Lévy says the dreamlike setting "reactivates the primordial anguish that in Lovecraft is always tied to the past" (47). But Lovecraft also wrote that the story exhibited "febrile doubt & apprehension inherent in an imperfectly glimpsed vista" (*SL* 3.212). This suggests that Lovecraft saw the story illustrating how nervousness and anxiety over an awful thing that might occur could affect the perception of one so afflicted.

The story was widely reprinted. Lovecraft noted its fifth printing in 1933 (*SL* 4.188). Commentators have interpreted the story in diverse ways.[4] S. T. Joshi argues that the story leaves the denouement too nebulous. Yet the tale has an uncanny power with

---

3. The primal theoretical "inaugural *loss*" (Kristeva, *Powers of Horror* 5 [her emphasis]) is an archaic memory of identity with the mother prior to the unavoidable emotional separation.

4. These include Daniel R. Burleson, Henrik Harksen, Maurice Lévy, James Manchin, Robert M. Price, and Brad Tapas.

THE LOVECRAFT ANNUAL

Edited by S. T. Joshi — No. 12 (2018)

Contents

The Melancholia of H. P. Lovecraft's "The Music of Erich Zann" 3
James Goho

Feminine Powerlessness and Deference in *The Case of Charles Dexter Ward* 13
Cecelia Hopkins-Drewer

Ravening for Delight: Unusual Descriptions in Lovecraft 21
Duncan Norris

Where Lovecraft Lost His Telescope: His Kingston and the Towns around It 35
Robert H. Waugh

Why Michel Houellebecq Is Wrong about Lovecraft's Racism 43
S. T. Joshi

"Whaddya Make Them Eyes at Me For?": Lovecraft and Book Publishers 51
David E. Schultz

Two Centenaries: H. P. Lovecraft and Elsa Gidlow 66
Kenneth W. Faig, Jr.

2001: A Lovecraftian Odyssey 75
Michael D. Miller

That Fool Olson 90
Bobby Derie

A Placid Island: H. P. Lovecraft's "Ibid" 105
Francesco Borri

Lovecraft, Aristeas, Dunsany, and the Dream Journey 136
Darrell Schweitzer

H. P. Lovecraft—Beacon and Gateway 144
Donald Sidney-Fryer

The Void: A Lovecraftian Analysis 149
Duncan Norris

Howard Phillips Lovecraft: Romantic on the Nightside 165
Jan B. W. Pedersen

How to Read Lovecraft 174
A Column by Steven J. Mariconda

Reviews 180

Briefly Noted 12, 34, 104, 148

Abbreviations used in the text and notes:

AT	*The Ancient Track* (Hippocampus Press, 2013)
CE	*Collected Essays* (Hippocampus Press, 2004–06; 5 vols.)
CF	*Collected Fiction* (Hippocampus Press; 2015–17; 4 vols.)
LL	*Lovecraft's Library: A Catalogue*, 4th rev. ed. (Hippocampus Press, 2017)
SL	*Selected Letters* (Arkham House, 1965–76; 5 vols.)

Published by Hippocampus Press, P.O. Box 641, New York, NY 10156
www.hippocampuspress.com

Cover illustration by Allen Koszowski. Hippocampus Press logo designed by Anastasia Damianakos. Cover design by Barbara Briggs Silbert.

Lovecraft Annual is published once a year, in Fall. Articles and letters should be sent to the editor, S. T. Joshi, % Hippocampus Press, and must be accompanied by a self-addressed stamped envelope if return is desired. All reviews are assigned. Literary rights for articles and reviews will reside with *Lovecraft Annual* for one year after publication, whereupon they will revert to their respective authors. Payment is in contributor's copies.

ISSN 1935-6102
ISBN 978-1-61498-229-6

its mood of age, gloom, and despair, grounded in a sense of dread expressed through the continued manic playing of a viol. Part of the story's appeal is Lovecraft's rewriting of original Gothic trappings. For example, the Gothic castle is reborn as an ancient boarding house. There is no tower, but there is a high garret room. A mysterious paralytic runs the house. Everyone is old, as if we have stepped back into the past. Robert M. Price sees the Rue d'Auseil as a road into the past. There is no underground maze, but there is a labyrinthine street leading to the ancient house. And no maiden flees, as Isabella runs through the "long labyrinth of darkness" (26) away from Manfred in Horace Walpole's *The Castle of Otranto* (1764), but the narrator does flee from the house in the closing paragraphs of Lovecraft's story.

That unnamed narrator is a student of metaphysics attending an unnamed university in an unnamed city, presumed to be Paris. The story starts and ends with the narrator lamenting that he has not been able to find again the Rue d'Auseil. It is a reminiscence of loss by that student reflecting back on an odd encounter in that ancient boarding house with Erich Zann, a viol player. In his reflections, the student exhibits characteristics of a person suffering from depression. For example, he obsesses over his experience. He searches repeatedly for the Rue d'Auseil. He "examined maps of the city with the greatest care, [. . .] delved deeply into all the antiquities of the place," and "explored every region, of whatever name, which could possibly answer to the street." While residing in that ancient house, it appears the student did not attend any classes. None of his acquaintances visit him at the house. He does not sleep well in the old house. The student, himself, admits he is a "victim of physical and nervous suffering."

The first stage in the student's journey to the boarding house is crossing a dark river, along which it "was always shadowy." Freud wrote that the "shadow of the object" (159)—that is, the lost love object—falls upon the ego of a person suffering from depression. This shadow haunts Lovecraft's characters in the story. The student follows the Rue d'Auseil to the ancient, "tottering" boarding house through a labyrinth of steep, narrow streets past houses leaning "crazily" in all directions. Some of the houses touch above the street and blot out the sunlight. The street paving is "irregular," with the bare earth patches marked with "struggling greenish-grey vegetation." The aged, the ailing, and the physically challenged occupy the house. The inhabitants are very old ("old" is the most frequent non-common or non-proper word in the text). As previously noted, the proprietor of the boarding house is a paralytic. Erich Zann is mute. It is a world of damage and disorder where everything is perceived by the student to be distorted, dark, and ancient. The student always describes the street and the house and its rooms as lacking light or being very dark.[5] This feeling of darkness is associated consistently with depression, according to Lisa Conti. Individuals suffering from depression often describe themselves as trapped in a dark hole and view their world as a dark, inescapable place. Andrew Solomon writes that depression can be spoken of only through such metaphors. He uses "the abyss" (27, multiple other pages), which is often described as a place of "darkness" (28). The main title of William Styron's depression memoir is *Darkness Visible* (1990), referencing Milton's description of hell in *Paradise Lost.* Lewis Wolpert describes the feeling of depression coming as like a "dark cloud, somewhere, waiting, to descend" (165). Those "seething abysses of clouds" in the story read as if a description of the feeling of melancholy.

Ensconced in the ancient house, the student is attracted by the sound of music to the garret of the old house. He reflects that he "heard Zann every night, and although he kept me awake, I was haunted by the weirdness of his music." The student pleads with Zann to let him into his room. The student wants to hear and see Zann play. Zann finally relents. In his dismal room, Zann appears always cast in shadow or despair. This is that "shadow of despair" of a melancholic for whom "there is no meaning aside from despair" (Kristeva, "On the Melancholic Imaginary" 5). The student describes Zann as a "small, lean, bent person, with shabby clothes, blue eyes, grotesque, satyr-like face, and nearly bald head." It is an image of a broken man with the mark of a satyr on him, but more from panic than sexuality. He seems emasculated. Zann is unable to speak, which is a characteristic of the form of depression that

5. "Dark" occurs frequently (eight times) in the story. "Blackness" and "darkness" appear several times as well. Such words are common when people suffering from depression try to describe their experience.

Kristeva explores. He has "nervous disorders" akin to the "nervous suffering" of the student. What is more he shows other characteristics of a melancholic: emaciation, keeping to himself in his garret room, and feelings of anxiety. Zann's frantic playing of the viol and his wild glances at the window seem a form of panic. Such disorders are a frequent complication of depressive illness (see Breier et al.). Some people suffering from depression experience sudden panic attacks. These panic attacks can be so terrifying and severe that some individuals feel they may die or must die to escape (see Hooley et al.).

Zann's melancholia is where linguistic meaning has collapsed, as Carolyn Culbertson might say, writing about Kristeva. Zann cannot speak. The manuscript he pens later in the story, explaining his anxiety and fear, is taken away by a wind. It becomes lost in the inexplicable darkness of the abyss outside the garret room window. He tries to interpret his own pain in that manuscript but fails. Zann has lost the capacity for meaningful communication except through his music. That music is his solace. It is his only protection, although temporary and fleeting, from the agony of melancholia. Kristeva suggests that music (and other art forms) can work to overcome (or sublimate) clinical depression. Kristeva argues that melody and rhythm secure "an uncertain but adequate hold over the Thing" (*Black Sun* 14), where the Thing is the lost object of melancholy or the expression of one's existential despair. Based on his clinical practice, Freud concluded that melancholia was like an "open wound" (163) continually inflicting pain on a sufferer. Stuck in a condition of suffering without being able to articulate it completely, the depressed person feels trapped by that lost Thing. In playing the viol, Zann strives to confront his loss. And he strives to communicate through his music. But the student acknowledges he knew "little of the art." The student does not understand Zann and fails to help him.

On his first visit to Zann's nearly barren room, the student listens to Zann play conventional music. Disappointed, he hums notes from the weird music he heard during his sleepless nights. Zann reaches out to the student's mouth to shush him. Later Zann embraces the student when he moves toward the lone window in the room to peer out at the city. The viol player's attempts at physical contact repulse the student at first. But when Zann gives him a friendly hand, the student relents and stays to listen. Zann appears to need to touch the student, but only at the very end does the student respond in kind. They seem a pair, with the student as an adoring admirer and Zann as the master wielding that bow over the viol. But later Zann distances the student. First he pays for a room on a lower floor of the house for the student and eventually banishes the student from the garret room. Not dissuaded by the rebuff, the student, so yearning to be near Zann, creeps up the rickety stairs to listen secretly at the locked door, as if a spurned lover.

The climactic scene occurs during a night when Zann's music screams with his anguish. As always, the student is listening next to the locked door. He thinks he hears a guttural howl from Zann. He bangs at the door. At last, a haggard Zann throws opens the door. He delights to see the student and clutches at his "coat as a child clutches at its mother's skirts." For a moment Zann perceives the student as his lost mother, as the primal lost object. Of course the student is not. And this precipitates an even more frenzied playing of the viol. The student describes Zann in a desperate panic. He plays like a mechanical thing while a storm assails the room. To Zann this storm appears as a living force from outside his window. Repeatedly he glances warily at the window. Lovecraft's story effectively depicts the experience of a melancholic, who is in the midst of a psychotic episode.

The window shatters. The candles go out and the room is plunged into a "savage and impenetrable darkness." The student feels the bow touch him. But when the student finally reaches out to return Zann's touch, he feels an "unbreathing face." The student is too late. Looking out the window, the student does not see the normality of bright lights of a city but the "blackness of space," as if he stares at the face of melancholia. He sees only "seething abysses" of collapsing language, "clouds and smoke" of sorrow and inexpressible despair, and "unimagined space alive" with dread. The student flees the room, the house, down the Rue d'Auseil, and runs back over the dark stone bridge spanning the foul smelling river.

The student's encounter with Erich Zann deepens his melancholia. For Zann becomes the figure of loss for the student—a loss he cannot rediscover, no matter how long he searches. But all is not lost. Kristeva sees art and writing as forms of release for those characterized by fragility. That is how she describes those caught in melancholia. They are trapped in an endless search for the unobtainable lost Thing. Lovecraft's story expresses melancholia, but it also represents a pathway to reconciling with depression, even if only temporarily. The student has searched carefully for the Rue d'Auseil. And he has made a story of his experience. At the end of the story, the student reflects that he is "not wholly sorry" at never finding the locale again. This suggests he may have reconciled with his loss. Kristeva argues that works of art are constructed to manage the affliction of depression. The artistic struggle is akin to "descending into hell" ("Dialogue with Julia Kristeva" 7). The hope is to transform sorrow, panic, and that terrible, scorching despair into images and ideas that lose their power to hurt by expressing them in an imaginary form. Early in the story the student crosses that foul, dark river,[6] as if going into hell. But manages to escape and tell the tale.

Lovecraft's story gives us a compelling narrative of the experience of melancholia, illustrating the vulnerability of individuals to its appalling hold, its damage, and its eclipsing power of darkness. Lovecraft describes vulnerability in the isolation and loneliness of the main characters. The figure of Zann represents extreme damage; he appears drained of life by melancholy. Dread engulfs both characters. Lovecraft's description of Zann in the final scene, through the eyes of the student, vividly symbolizes the paralyzing force of depression. In this story, Lovecraft's supernatural elements are metaphors for the anguish of melancholia. His story gives readers a visceral exposure to the lived experience of clinical depression. His descriptions of the Rue d'Auseil represent the perceptual disorientations of the student's depression. The ancient house filled with the aged and the damaged is a house of the dead and symbolizes the state of Zann's mind; that is, he feels hounded by death. And the unnatural, churning darkness outside Zann's window pictures memorably the dizzying emptiness and disturb-

6. The "dark river" is reminiscent of the River Acheron in Hades of Greek myth.

ing hollowness felt by individuals suffering from melancholia.

On the other hand, Kristeva's notion of melancholia helps us understand Lovecraft's "The Music of Erich Zann." Kristeva theorizes a form of depression or melancholia where a depressive person feels an existential loss, but is not able to articulate it completely. That is Zann. Zann's figure of loss is experienced as an overwhelming sense of dread expressed through a strange musical note and a visual black void. It is a space of immense darkness and emptiness, a void of no meaning. The student's initial depression may have arisen from the stress of his impoverishment and metaphysical studies, but his figure of loss becomes Zann. Melancholia commands him to search for his lost Thing. But there seems to be a release for him, because he has transformed his experience through artistic expression. Kristeva goes as far as to suggest there cannot "be an imagination that is not, manifestly or secretly, melancholic" ("On the Melancholic Imaginary" 5).

Overcoming his broken memory, the student shrugs off that paralyzing grip of the past and represents his experience of suffering creatively. By voicing his despair, by putting it into verbal form, he may be able to reconnect with the social world. His art prepares him to reengage in life, but this does not overcome his affliction. Miller, again following Kristeva, says melancholia is an individual disorder, but it also "involves a relation between the self and the world" (16). And this cannot be solved by medication alone. Nor can it be solved through art alone. In a testimonial fashion, Craig Greenman confirms this charged dynamic between depression and art, where art in any form is not complete reconciliation. Zann's music did not spare him. Struggle is continuous against the darkness of melancholia. Kristeva says it is an unceasing, losing struggle "until death strikes" imposing "its triumphant conclusion" ("The Melancholy of the Imaginary" 6).

Works Cited

Breier, Alan, Dennis S. Charney, and George R. Heninger. "Major Depression in Patients with Agoraphobia and Panic Disorder." *Archives of General Psychiatry* 41, No. 12 (December 1984): 1129–35.

Burleson, Donald R. *Lovecraft: Disturbing the Universe*. Lexington: University Press of Kentucky, 1990.

Conti, Lisa. "Down in the Dark." *Scientific American Mind* 19, No. 4 (August–September 2008): 12.

Culbertson, Carolyn. "The Omnipotent Word of Medical Diagnosis and the Silence of Depression: An Argument for Kristeva's Therapeutic Approach." *International Journal of Feminist Approaches to Bioethics* 9, No. 1 (2016): 1–26.

Freud, Sigmund. "Mourning and Melancholia." In *The Collected Papers, Volume 4*. Ed. Ernest Jones. London: Hogarth Press, 1950. 152–70.

Greenman, Craig. *Expression and Survival: An Aesthetic Approach to the Problem of Suicide*. Cambridge: Cambridge Scholars Publishing, 2008.

Haggerty, George E. *Queer Gothic*. Urbana: University of Illinois Press, 2006.

Harksen, Henrik. "Metaphysics in 'The Music of Erich Zann.'" *Lovecraft Studies* No. 45 (Spring 2005): 25–32.

Hooley, Jill, Susan M. Mineka, Matthew K. Nock, and James N. Butcher. *Abnormal Psychology*. 17th ed. New York: Pearson, 2016.

Joshi, S. T. *H. P. Lovecraft: A Life*. West Warwick, RI: Necronomicon Press, 1996.

Kristeva, Julia. *Black Sun: Depression and Melancholia*. Tr. Leon S. Roudiez. New York: Columbia University Press, 1989.

———. "Dialogue with Julia Kristeva." *Parallax* 4, No. 3 (1998): 5–16.

———. "On the Melancholic Imaginary." *New Formations* No. 3 (1987): 5–18.

———. *Powers of Horror: An Essay on Abjection*. New York: Columbia University Press, 1982.

Lévy, Maurice. *Lovecraft: A Study in the Fantastic*. Tr. S. T. Joshi. Detroit: Wayne State University Press, 1988.

Manchin, James. "Music Against Horror: H. P. Lovecraft and Schopenhauer's Aesthetics." *East-West Cultural Passage* 12, No. 1 (2012): 38–50.

Miller, Elaine P. *Head Cases: Julia Kristeva on Philosophy and Art in Depressed Times*. New York: Columbia University Press, 2014.

Price, Robert M. "Erich Zann and the Rue d'Auseil." *Lovecraft Studies* Nos. 22/23 (Fall 1990): 13–14.

Solomon, Andrew. *The Noon Day Demon: An Atlas of Depression.* 2001. New York: Scribner, 2015.

Styron, William. *Darkness Visible: A Memoir of Madness.* New York: Random House, 1990.

Tabas, Brad. "Dark Places: Ecology, Place, and the Metaphysics of Horror Fiction." *Miranda* 11, No. 10 (July 2015), miranda.revues.org/7012. Accessed 23 October 2017.

Wolpert, Lewis. *Malignant Sadness: The Anatomy of Depression.* New York: Free Press, 2000.

Briefly Noted

Numerous volumes of Lovecraft's letters are being prepared by S. T. Joshi and David E. Schultz, for publication in the coming months by Hippocampus Press. The most ambitious is an 1100-page volume, *Letters to Family and Family Friends,* containing Lovecraft's complete extant letters to his two aunts, Lillian D. Clark and Annie E. P. Gamwell, along with letters to his mother, Sarah Susan Lovecraft, and others. These letters offer unique glimpses into Lovecraft's daily life, especially during his New York years (1924–26), and his travels up and down the Eastern Seaboard. Other volumes in preparation are: *Letters to Wilfred B. Talman and Helen V. and Genevieve Sully; Letters to Donald Wandrei and Others* (incorporating the complete contents of the volume previously published as *Mysteries of Time and Spirit* [2002] and also including previously unavailable letters to Emil Petaja) along with the correspondence of Lovecraft and Howard Wandrei; *Letters to Rheinhart Kleiner and Others* (including letters to Arthur Harris, Winifred V. Jackson, Paul J. Campbell, and others); and *Letters to Alfred Galpin and Others* (including letters to Edward H. and E. Sherman Cole and John T. Dunn).

Feminine Powerlessness and Deference in *The Case of Charles Dexter Ward*

Cecelia Hopkins-Drewer

Critics have observed that there are very few female characters in the main body of Lovecraft's work. While it may be true that many of his narrators and protagonists are scholarly males, it is not true that there are no women. A close reading of *The Case of Charles Dexter Ward* reveals the presence of at least eight women. Significant women include: Eliza Tillinghast; Ann Tillinghast; Charles's mother; and Hannah. Some of these women are featured only briefly, but it can be observed that the woman all experience a degree of powerlessness in society and exhibit deference toward their male associates.

A pertinent question to ask concerns whether the author realized he was representing women as submissive, and furthermore, whether he perceived deference as part of their natural station in life. *The Case of Charles Dexter Ward* (*CF* 2.214–366) was written between January and March 1927 (Joshi and Schultz 31). The tale was designed to be a period piece, as part of the action was set in the seventeenth and eighteenth centuries, and was described by Lovecraft as "self-conscious antiquarianism" (Joshi 255). Hence we may deduce that Lovecraft intentionally represented an era when women were powerless in society, but may not have meant to imply that this was the ideal state of affairs.

Moreover in 1927, Lovecraft also worked on a revision of a tale by Zealia Bishop, detailing the emotional development of a character named Ella who suffered from excessive "suppression." Lovecraft suggested the title of "The Unchaining" as appropriate for the "bursting, liberation, or unshackling" of the woman's emotions. His advice to Bishop implied that emotional liberation was suitable material on which to hinge a plot, and demonstrated his awareness of some women's issues (*The Spirit of Revision* 33, 38–39).

The most fascinating woman in *The Case of Charles Dexter Ward* is Eliza Tillinghast. We are first alerted to her existence when Charles's genealogical research uncovers the fact that his "great-great-grandfather, Welcome Potter, had in 1785 married a certain 'Ann Tillinghast, daughter to Mrs. Eliza, daughter to Captain James Tillinghast' of whose paternity the family had preserved no trace" (*CF* 2.225). The mind immediately takes interest in the anomaly of the surname, because unless the mother married a cousin, a granddaughter is unlikely to share a surname with her maternal grandfather in a patrilineal society. The reader is not left to wonder long, because in the very same paragraph it is stated that a "legal change of name" was discovered: "in 1772 a Mrs. Eliza Curwen, widow of Joseph Curwen, resumed . . . her maiden name" (*CF* 2.225).

The reason for the change of name is that the husband's surname "became a publick Reproach" (*CF* 2.225). Eliza is described as a "loyall Wife" who would not believe evil of her husband until it had been proved "wholely past Doubting" (*CF* 2.225–26). This meticulous description carefully removes Eliza from association with her husband's sins, but also prevents any speculation regarding her faithfulness and moral character. Moreover, to encourage the fictional community to forget the incident, the pages of the record books were glued together and their numbers altered.

Charles begins an investigation into the mystery of Joseph Curwen and succeeds in reconstructing the past from a number of old letters and diaries. (For the purpose of our analysis, it is worth noting that while a number of diaries and letters are mentioned, none of them appear to belong to Eliza or her daughter Ann, so these women are never given a direct voice in the story.) Curwen is a fascinating character because of his unnatural longevity and bizarre interests, but these factors led to his being shunned by society, so he formed the plan to "contract an advantageous marriage" (*CF* 2.236).

Marriages designed to enhance social standing are not uncommon; however, it is unusual for a writer to describe the lady in such a utilitarian fashion as "a bridge" to connect the bridegroom with society. This image occurs in the Panther H. P. Lovecraft Omnibus 1 (165) and has been transcribed as literal "bride" in the *Collected Fiction* (*CF* 2.236). "Bride" reads in a smoother fashion, but the alternate transcription, even if it is a lucky error, conveys the meaning better. Curwen was not looking for a spouse; he was looking for a connector. Lovecraft here intends to leave the reader in no doubt that Eliza's experience was one of being 'used.' Moreover, Joseph Curwen was "aware of the horror and indignation" with which a romantic courtship would be received by any genteel woman and therefore looked for a way of exerting "pressure" on her parents (*CF* 2.236).

We are told that Eliza had to be beautiful, accomplished, and socially secure, because Curwen required these things in a bride. She was "gently" reared, attended a good school, and was also tutored by her mother in the arts of housekeeping. After her mother died in 1757 from smallpox, Eliza managed her father's house with the assistance of "one old black woman." Her attractiveness and amiability are underlined by the fact that at eighteen, she was already appropriately engaged to Ezra Weeden, second mate on the *Enterprise* (*CF* 2.237).

Once again Lovecraft underscores Eliza's voicelessness in society by refusing to represent her in her own words: "Her arguments with her father concerning the proposed Curwen marriage must have been painful indeed; *but of these we have no record*" (*CF* 2.237; my emphasis). As the author, Lovecraft could have allowed Eliza to write a surviving note to an aunt, a break-up letter to Weeden, or even a diary. The fact that he does none of those things emphasizes his assertion that Eliza had no say in the matter of her marriage.

The wedding was a society wedding, in the Baptist church (*CF* 2.237). After the wedding Curwen surprised the community by being a good husband, "displaying an extreme graciousness and consideration" (*CF* 2.238). Eliza lived in the new house in Olney Court and never visited the Pawtuxet farm where Joseph Curwen continued his more suspicious activities. Two years after the marriage, Eliza gave birth to a daughter who was christened at King's Church, according to the negotiated compromise between the parents' Congregational and Baptist backgrounds (*CF* 2.238–39).

Eliza's characterization must remain blameless and submissive, so Lovecraft employs the jilted Ezra Weeden as an instrument of justice and destruction. Intent on revenge, Ezra investigates Curwen until he has such evidence that the men in the community help him take Curwen down (*CF* 2.240–47). Eliza's father at first attempts to keep Eliza in ignorance of her husband's disgrace, but the severity of Captain Tillinghast's outrage results in his insisting his daughter and granddaughter change their name, burn Joseph Curwen's library, and erase the name off his tombstone (*CF* 2.263).

Eliza became known as Mrs. Tillinghast and lived with her father until she died (*CF* 2.264). From a feminist point of view, it is disappointing to discover that the name change was not an act of assertion on Eliza's part, but performed in deference to her father. From a romantic point of view, it is also disappointing that Eliza was not allowed to marry Ezra Weeden after gaining her freedom from the evil Curwen. Perhaps Ezra Weeden had married someone else by the time Eliza's remarriage would have been appropriate, or perhaps Eliza had developed a dislike of the institution of marriage.

While the story of Ann Tillinghast Potter is not spelled out explicitly, she remains significant, as she is Charles's great-great-grandmother (*CF* 2.239). Ann also provides Charles with his biological link to Joseph Curwen, and her marriage record is associated with the first clue that something sinister lurked "amongst his maternal ancestors" (*CF* 2.225).

Born "on the seventh of May, 1765," Ann was the only child of Joseph Curwen and Eliza Tillinghast. She was christened Ann Curwen by "the Reverend John Graves" (*CF* 2.238–39) and had her name changed to Ann Tillinghast by her mother, at the age of seven (*CF* 2.225). All we really know about Ann beyond that is she married Welcome Potter in 1785 (*CF* 2.225) and remained Episcopalian all her life (*CF* 2.229). Beyond that, Ann appears to have led a relatively 'normal' life, which in itself is an achievement because of the drama associated with her father's death.

The attack on the farm occurred on "April twelfth, 1771" (*CF* 2.254), about a month before Ann's sixth birthday. A child of this age is able to remember a parent and grieve their loss. The hostility of the community and attempts at the "obliteration" of her father's memory (*CF* 2.263), along with the subsequent name change, all represent potential threats to her self-conception. We presume Ann was brought up by her mother and grandfather at the residence in "Powers Lane" (*CF* 2.264), and that adopting her grandfather's respectable surname allowed her carers to rebuild her shattered sense of identity.

Charles's mother becomes a significant figure in the story after the ancestral research has been recounted and the portrait of Joseph Curwen discovered (*CF* 2.273–74). We are told that Mrs. Ward bore little "resemblance to her ancestor" although the similarity between Joseph Curwen and Charles Dexter Ward's physical appearances "was marvellous." Her memory allowed her to recall other relatives with similar features, but she "did not relish the discovery" of an ancestor of sinister reputation (*CF* 2.273–74).

A feminist reading might suggest that the discovery of a sinister ancestor on the maternal, rather than the paternal, side is also symbolic of the power imbalance between the genders. It may be a mere plot device because it is easier to lose track of maternal ancestors due to the patrilineal custom of changing the wife's surname from that of her parents to that of her husband's family. However, legal name changes and fathers who refuse to give their surnames to their offspring can occur upon the paternal side as well. Hence the choice to place the genealogical anomaly on the *maternal* side is still noteworthy.

The powerlessness of Charles's mother is underlined by her nomenclature. Joshi and Schultz (291) observe that she is "never named." This is a slight exaggeration, because she is referred to as "Mrs. Ward" (*CF* 2.273), which is a name—just not a first name! She is also referred to as "his mother," rendering her subservient to her relationship with Charles (*CF* 2.276), and in the collective as one of "his parents" (*CF* 2.277), part of "the Ward family" (*CF* 2.278) and one of "the Wards" (*CF* 2.283). The father, however, is clearly named as "Theodore Howland Ward" (*CF* 2.294).

Charles's mother's ineffectiveness is demonstrated in her inability to help her son. The father also experiences this powerlessness, but not to the same extent, as he is able to commission and command a few events. For example, when Mrs. Ward identified "something unwholesome" about the portrait, Mr. Ward, "a practical man of power and affairs," was still determined to purchase it for his son. The mother has to defer to the wishes of both her husband and son in this instance (*CF* 2.273–74). Both parents refuse to allow Charles to go to Europe at eighteen, but we get the impression the father's decision as "the senior Ward" held the most weight (*CF* 2.283).

However, a small inheritance "from his maternal grandfather" soon sets Charles free from both his parents' restrictions (*CF* 2.283). Once again, it is noteworthy that this inheritance comes from the maternal side. Not only are all the mysterious forces originating from the maternal side, but it is also more realistic that in a patriarchal society, a grandfather would withhold funds from a daughter to create an inheritance for a grandson.

Mrs. Ward is represented as a kind and caring mother who checks upon her son if his behavior indicates anything out of the ordinary, and is indulgent to a fault as she agrees to send his meals to his room (*CF* 2.276). She is perceptive and notices things, hearing motor engines in the night and, when going to the window, seeing men carrying a box (*CF* 2.228–29).

However, Mrs. Ward is powerless to influence her son's behavior and is reduced to "listening in despair outside her son's locked laboratory" (*CF* 2.292). Occasionally, fortified by the "mingled fear and blind courage of maternity" (*CF* 2.293), the mother attempts to enter the room and rescue her son. However, she faints and, over the months, listening to mutterings and murmuring from outside the laboratory door is all that she is able to do (*CF* 2.291–93): "Mrs. Ward had grown used to listening for sounds in the night, for the mystery of her son was fast driving all else from her mind" (*CF* 2.299). Her health is adversely affected by worry and she is sent to recuperate in Atlantic City by order of Dr. Willett (*CF* 2.301). Here her powerlessness is underlined by the fact that she is geographically removed from the situation and dependent on letters for any information (*CF* 2.304, 309, 311).

Mrs. Ward is allowed a kind of second-hand power through the agency of the men around her. When she moans, her husband responds with "protective instincts" (*CF* 2.294); and also by appeals to the emotions of her son: "All this must be stopped, or Mrs. Ward would be made ill and the keeping of servants become an impossibility" (*CF* 2.294). She is also able to overhear and memorize the "chanting" from within the room, and these chants are repeated by Dr. Willett in the underground chamber, resulting in vital clues (*CF* 2.291–92). Her other observations are used by Dr. Willett to solve the case, although it is too late to save Charles (*CF* 2.345–46).

The final significant woman in the tale is Hannah, "one of the present negro inhabitants" of the house in Olney Court (*CF* 2.271). Together with her husband Asa, Hannah plays a brief but key role in connecting Charles with one of the historic Curwen residences. The only personal details given are that she is "stout," "good," "old," and "black" (*CF* 2.271, 297); and moreover had "watched" Charles "grow up from birth" (*CF* 2.297). Hannah and her husband Asa are described as respectable members of the community: "much esteemed for the occasional washing, housecleaning, and furnace-tending services" (*CF* 2.271).

The couple "very courteously" show Charles around the house in Olney Court (*CF* 2.271), but there is no sense that Charles can take advantage of Hannah and Asa simply because they are black. The story stipulates they are "properly reimbursed for this invasion of their domestic hearth," when Charles decides to interfere with the walls (*CF* 2.273). Indeed, for some paragraphs their residency appears so stable that the reader gets the impression that Hannah and Asa are property-owning African American characters—which would have been progressive for the times! However, a "rodent-featured" landlord is located when Mr. Ward decides to purchase the portrait which has been built into the wall structure (*CF* 2.274).

Hannah and Asa therefore seem to hover somewhere in the no-man's land between the servant and contractor classes. Hannah "came to help with the spring cleaning" at the Ward house, which implies that she had some choice regarding the jobs she accepted (*CF* 2.297). The tone becomes patronizing as Hannah becomes a vehicle for gossip about Charles's "curious delvings in the cellar" and reports that he "was always very liberal to her." Furthermore, Hannah is "grieved" that Charles was "more worried than he used to be," placing her emotional tone somewhere between that of neighbor and old nurse (*CF* 2.297). It is clear, however, that Hannah is meant to be part of the community and intimately connected to the Ward family.

Additional women in *The Case of Charles Dexter Ward* include the unnamed wife of the Indian caretaker (*CF* 2.228), who together with her husband appear implicit in protecting the secrecy of the Curwen farm (*CF* 2.240). There are also an elderly French housekeeper responsible for the less sinister town house (*CF* 2.229) and the wives of Captain Whipple and Moses Brown, whose main concerns appear to be the health and activities of their husbands (*CF* 2.262). A mixture of feminine- and masculine-sounding names are included in the list of olden-day witches (*CF* 2.266–67, 319), indicating Lovecraft's perception of society as comprising a balance of male and female personages.

In conclusion, when I began reading Lovecraft's stories in search of female characters, I felt that I was searching for something very rare. However, I began to find female characters, cleverly woven into the fabric of the tales and slotted naturally beside their male connections. I suggest that the average reader is inclined to overlook these female characters due to a number of distractions, including the knowledge that the writer is male, the vehicle of a male narrator and/or protagonist, and general knowledge of the subservient place of women in society. However, exploring the experience of these female characters can make the stories much more complex and colorful.

Works Cited

Joshi, S. T. *A Dreamer and a Visionary: H. P. Lovecraft in His Time.* Liverpool: Liverpool University Press, 2001.

Joshi, S. T., and David E. Schultz. *An H. P. Lovecraft Encyclopedia.* Westport, CT: Greenwood Press, 2001.

Lovecraft, H. P. *The Case of Charles Dexter Ward.* In *At the Mountains of Madness and Other Novels of Terror.* (H. P. Lovecraft Omnibus 1.) St. Albans, UK Panther, 1985. 141–301.

———. *The Spirit of Revision: Lovecraft's Letters to Zealia Brown Reed Bishop.* Ed. Sean Branney and Andrew Leman. Glendale, CA: H. P. Lovecraft Historical Society, 2015.

Ravening for Delight: Unusual Descriptions in Lovecraft

Duncan Norris

It is an interesting, if somewhat galling, aspect of the literary criticism of H. P. Lovecraft that so much of it is criticism in the more popular understanding of the usage of the word. Few people would seriously attempt to deny the importance of Lovecraft's writings and his enormous and continuing influence in the horror, and indeed in the often-related science fiction, fantasy, and weird genres. Yet despite the obvious inconsistency it presents, there is a superabundance of articles and reviews, scholarly and popular, that basically posit, as baldly stated by early critic Edmund Wilson in 1945, that "Lovecraft was not a good writer" (Joshi 1018). Sadly, such a state of affairs regarding artists who rise above their peers is hardly a new circumstance. In the words of an antiquated saying concerning figures from antiquity. "Every poet has his Zoilus."[1] Such criticism is thus inevitably the price of success and may be taken with as many grains of salt as the reader chooses. Lovecraft himself offered many condemnations of various literary works in his private letters, and more publicly under the house name of the aforementioned Zoilus when offering criticism in the column "The Vivisector" in the amateur journal the *Wolverine* (Joshi 398–99).

More lamentably, this defamation of Lovecraft's writing began with the author himself, who habitually denigrated his literary works in his correspondence (*SL* 2.27, 3.192, 4.71, 5.338 ad nauseam). In this unfortunate tendency of authors to disparage and despair of their own creations, Lovecraft is in a large and exalted

1. Zoilus (died c. 320 B.C.E.) was a Greek writer and philosopher, an early and vociferous critic of Homer. His works do not survive, but multiple accounts of his death are offered, none of them pleasant.

literary company, stretching at least as far back as Virgil, who on his deathbed allegedly called for the *Aeneid* to be destroyed as not up to his self-imagined standard (*Oxford Classical Dictionary* 1603). Certainly, from a technical and aesthetic viewpoint, there is a valid argument to be made that Lovecraft's style breached the general conventions of modern (even for his day) writing, particularly in his penchant for lengthy sentences and extensive use of adverbs. Lovecraft himself, with a great deal of pride, openly admits as much concerning his lack of modernity in style (*SL* 3.96–97). That, in the hands of a unique and masterful writer such as Lovecraft was, it is highly effective in a manner generations of lesser adepts have failed to replicate, is perhaps the best argument against this perception of flawed writing style, while more tangible proof may be offered in the form of Lovecraft's publication by the prestigious Library of America in 2005.

However, scrutinizing all this much-turned critical earth is not the purpose of this monograph. Rather it is an examination of how Lovecraft's unusual, and even unique, language usage, particularly in his descriptors, adds an indefinable yet undeniably powerful element to his work. This overview of Lovecraft's descriptors is meant to be neither exhaustive nor definitive. After all, one person's unusual is another's cliché. Instead, it is by taking a selective sampling that this article seeks to highlight how, by the deft, studious, and creative manner in which Lovecraft crafted his stories he adds a distinctly powerful aspect to the effects he is trying to evoke in the stories he chooses to tell.

Before setting out to examine such language in Lovecraft's works, it is instructive to take a moment to look at examples of what it is not. While the few exemplars that follow are not in any way poor or inadequate writing, and in fact several are highly effective in their own right, it is important to differentiate them from the focus of this study. The small descriptive piece in *The Dream-Quest of Unknown Kadath* of Carter stopping "to watch a carnivorous fish catch a fishing bird" (*CF* 2.148) certainly adds to the surreal atmosphere of the tale, yet it is unusual not in its descriptors, but rather in what it describes. In a not unlike manner, "The Terrible Old Man" offers a description of the "wicked missiles" of small boys that is later harkened back to with the more murderous "cruel boot-heels" (*CF* 1. 141, 143) that terminate the burglars; but adding anthropomorphic traits to inanimate objects is a common, almost archetypal, poetical and literary device. Closer in usage, to the purpose of our examination, is the line from "The Strange House High in the Mist" that proffers that the "summer people do not believe that the same One has lived in the ancient house for hundreds of years, but cannot prove their heresy to any real Kingsporter" (*CF* 2.89). "Heresy" is used here for (subtle?) emphasis that the summer people are wrong. After all, heretics by definition hold incorrect beliefs. Yet the slightly comical air of the sentence robs it of the truly malevolent or weird. Such is not the case in other of Lovecraft's writings.

An early indication of this can be clearly observed in the short story "The Statement of Randolph Carter." This 1919 tale is basically a second transcription of a dream Lovecraft had, with details added to give it narrative coherence (*SL* 1.94–97). In describing the cemetery that is the locale for the story Lovecraft includes the line that it was "filled with a vague stench which my idle fancy associated absurdly with rotting stone" (*CF* 1.134). Superficially this is in fact an absurd notion, as the narrator literally notes. Thus by drawing our attention to the absurdity and acknowledging that in ordinary circumstances this would be absurd, the idea is once more rendered plausible contextually. This technique is frequently referred to as lampshading (the term possibly originating from Charlie Chaplin's ludicrous yet effective use of putting a lampshade on his head to escape the notice of a pursuer in *The Adventurer* [1917])—a technique that, while increasingly common in the pop-culturally saturated modern media, was used by no less a literary titan that Shakespeare, who has a character declare in *Twelfth Night* of the unfolding plot: "If this were play'd upon a stage now, I could condemn it as an improbable fiction" (3.4.140–41). Yet this lampshading is not the most important part of this particular sentence in "The Statement of Randolph Carter"; it is merely part of the set-up for the actual description that will allow the real ideas invoked to work.

Lovecraft uses the extremely visceral term "rotting" rather than the more neutral and scientific "decomposition," or even the less confronting "decay." Few people would not be instantly familiar with the foulness of odor emanating from something "gone rotten." But rotting stone is, by definition, an impossibility. Rot is a description that applies to the breakdown and decay of organic matter, and thus cannot be applicable to inorganic stone. Yet stone is certainly capable of breaking down and deterioration, a similar process to that which could be classified as rot in an organic substance. Thus this is an idea that is analogous enough that people reading of the stench of "rotting stone" can immediately have a mental image to go with that description, even though it is not something that allows them to have an actual or possible understanding of it. And the deeper current that flows under the idea, what is it about this place connected with "corpses that never decay" that yet causes even stone to rot, subtly reinforces and foreshadows the unspecified horrors to come. Hence with a single artfully positioned word Lovecraft takes the reader, almost without their awareness, from the realms of the knowable into the weird.

"The Hound," while a calculatingly overwritten piece and one dripping in baroque prose squeezed until it begins to purple, yet manages to employ a similar technique with some well-placed words. St. John and his companion in their underground fastness of horrors sometimes play compositions on "nauseous musical instruments, stringed, brass, and wood-wind . . . [and] produced dissonances of exquisite morbidity and cacodaemoniacal ghastliness" (*CF* 1.341). "Nauseous," and to a lesser degree "morbidity," here are the key words. While cacodaemoniacal ghastliness is a perfectly apt, if perhaps overwrought, phrase for evil music inspiring dread, "nauseous" means "feeling inclined to vomit," while "morbidity" refers to a diseased state as much as to a mental state inclined to excessive gloom, and in combination with "nauseous" invokes the former definition as much as the latter. Certainly, the desire for excitement and stimulation that drive the pair to such depraved activities doesn't seem to tally well with their being excessively gloomy when successful. Yet it is "nauseous" that is the true unusual descriptor. Musical instruments that incline someone to vomit don't make a great deal of sense unless the reader considers that perhaps they are made of distasteful substances. In the given context, this on initial reading does not seem at all unlikely. After all, the word "tibia" is derived directly from the Latin word for pipe, as in the musical instrument, not the connective hollow tubing (*OED*), for the obvious usage of the bone as the basis of the instrument. Yet it is harder to imagine, without excessive strain, stringed and most especially brass instruments as making someone inclined to vomit,[2] although the idea is foreshadowed by the use of the term "vomiting" more metaphorically in the preceding paragraph. However, literal dictionary definitions aside, in terms of creating atmosphere and a repulsion for the narrators' actions the term "nauseous" blends seamlessly into the literary and thesauric excesses that envelops the tale. Ultimately the reader does not think why the instruments might be inducing someone to physical sickness, merely that they do so. Extensive examination of Lovecraft's work certainly brings out such paradoxes, impossibilities, and contrasts between the literary functions of his word usages and their dictionary meanings, yet inside their stories as consumed by the casual, or even repeat, reader they are blended seamlessly into the fabric of the tale, potent yet artfully unostentatious.

Another excellent example of the unusual and carefully layered in description is with the simile "The narrow passage led infinitely down like some hideous haunted well" (*CF* 1.237) in "The Nameless City." Similes by their nature are generally designed to connect and conflate two different things, yet commonly use something more familiar to the reader in order to give elucidation or have a poetical, or occasionally humorous, effect. The usage of "well" here certainly fills this functions in the more traditional sense. The conventional image of the well is of a reasonably perpendicular shaft, which gives an immediate image and context to the nature of the narrow passage. Significantly, wells also have their important contents hidden, or at least located, at their bottom. Likewise, the term "hideous" conveys instantly that this is not an exciting or scientific exploration, reinforcing the preceding sentence that "It is only in the terrible phantasms of drugs or delirium that any other man can have had such a descent as mine" (*CF* 1.236–37). But the key descriptor is "haunted." Lovecraft here is evoking all the supernatural force associated with the word, but

2. For a notable exception to this, see the violin wielded by Dr. Dominique "Mo" O'Brien in Charles Stross's very Lovecraftian *Laundry* series of novels.

without ever giving it a larger explanation. The haunted well is not a particular well-known trope in horror, especially compared to the haunted house,[3] but the general concept of a haunted location is. Hauntings are of course since antiquity most commonly associated with the restless dead, frequently as a locale wherein their body lies or with which it is connected, such as the archetypal tale related by Pliny the Younger in his letter to Sura about the haunted house of Athenodorus Cananite in Athens, wherein the former owner had been chained and buried in the courtyard (*Letters* 83). In a related association, the death of someone in a well accidentally, or the nefarious dumping of a person or body therein, is a known danger and understood phenomenon, noted at least as far back as the biblical story of Joseph (Genesis 37:18–26). It is easy, without even a conscious attempt on the part of the reader, inside the context of a horror story to mentally conflate how one dark action creates the other to linger in an area. Yet simultaneously by failing to expound upon this point leaves the potential of the cause of such a haunting in our setting or its possible effects inchoate, and all the more fearful for the lack of definition. After setting up this idea of the narrow passage as a haunted well, without explanation, Lovecraft doubles down in the following sentences. First, he evokes the word "haunt" again in the character of the narrator as a "haunter of far, ancient, and forbidden places" (*CF* 1.237), the only times he will use these words in the entire story. Then Lovecraft resumes the descriptions as continuous stream, deliberately vague in tangible details, yet following on in the idea of the haunted:

> In the darkness there flashed before my mind fragments of my cherished treasury of daemoniac lore; sentences from Alhazred the mad Arab, paragraphs from the apocryphal nightmares of Damascius, and infamous lines from the delirious *Image du Monde* of Gauthier de Metz. I repeated queer extracts, and muttered of Afrasiab and the daemons that floated with him down the Oxus. (*CF* 1.237)

3. At least in HPL's time. The success of the *Ring* horror movie franchise has made the long-haired, demonic figure emerging from the well a pop-cultural icon.

These sentences give the appearance of explanation but in reality offer nothing tangible, forcing the reader to fill the patent gaps. This cascade of description follows a distinct pattern. It is naturally impossible to know of the narrator's potential store of daemoniac knowledge, and thus the reader's infinite imagination must therefore substitute. Equally impossible to know is the contents of Alhazred's fictional book, which is confirmed in later stories at the *Necronomicon.* It is certainly possible to have the information referred to in the books of Damascius and Gauthier de Metz, and the legends of Afrasiab in the *Shahnameh* (Book of Kings) and other sources. Yet these works are relatively obscure outside of specialist sources, and Lovecraft is evoking them no doubt in part for this obscurity. He then complicates this aspect by only vaguely assigning connections, which even a savant would have trouble attributing to specific sections of writing. Lovecraft is deliberately forcing the reader to mentally create constructs that such infamous works, by implication, must contain. That the *Image du Monde* is just a thirteenth-century encyclopedia complied largely from other authors' works and, while certainly filled with fantastic and Christian theological elements common to all books of its era, is hardly delirious is irrelevant. Likewise, the fact that Damascius was a Neoplatonist philosopher and final head of Athens's Platonic Academy, with his surviving works being on this topic and commentaries upon Plato's original writings, doesn't disrupt the impression of evil that the mention disingenuously proffers.

Then, switching away from that entirely designed to invoke the reader's own images which must inevitably lose some power eventually, Lovecraft, in mentioning Afrasiab and the Oxus, given the references to Dunsany and Moore that follow the abovementioned sentences, is subliminally evoking Poe's "The Premature Burial," in which they are also mentioned. This is thematically consistent and filled with oblique foreshadowing, given the dark descent into a claustrophobic underground environment soon to be revealed as a tomb-complex, and Poe would be a far more commonly known source to the average horror reader than the Persian epic of the *Shahnameh,* which is the origin this malign character. The exact Poe quotation referenced—"like the Demons in whose company Afrasiab made his voyage down the Oxus, they must sleep, or they will devour us—they must be suffered to slumber, or we perish" (969)—again hints at the main dangers that the story will unfold, with its malign entities for whom "that is not dead which can eternal lie, and with strange aeons even death may die" (*CF* 1.246). All this allusion is designed to evoke a fantastic and threatening atmosphere without giving substance to the specific threat. Yet it is all set in motion by having the narrator start his descent into the paradoxically unusual and familiar, yet undefined, horror of a "hideous haunted well." Like the *Necronomicon* quotation later arrogated to Cthulhu, Lovecraft was not above repurposing a fruitful idea from a lesser story into a greater one. This image of the haunted well was clearly one Lovecraft found evocative, as he would reuse it far more literally and extensively in "The Colour out of Space" and as the title and setting for stanza XI of *Fungi from Yuggoth*.

Yet not all Lovecraft's unusual descriptions are designed to be so subliminal or obtuse. Consider for example the manner in which he describes the unbroken windows of the church on Federal Hill in "The Haunter of the Dark": "Blake wondered how the obscurely painted panes could have survived so well, in view of the known habits of small boys the world over" (*CF* 3.456). It initially adds an almost folksy, gleeful charm to the scene and is a fine piece of writing just as such. But it has several deeper layers. It has a disarming quality, momentarily lessening the tension that has been building since Blake started his journey just for a brief instant before returning again to the dark fane of the watcher's interest, subtly stronger for the ephemeral light. It proffers the curious fact of the glass's intactness as a mystery, returning us to normal thought processes of what happens to glass in abandoned buildings, and at the same time hinting at darker forces at work that have prevented this from occurring. It is also a double foreshadowing, for the story begins to give further ideas why such glass may have survived intact other than the general anathema in which the building is held, as when viewing the windows from inside "Blake could scarcely decipher what they had represented, but from the little he could make out he did not like them" (*CF* 3.459), and then at the changes wrought after his visit when "every one of the tower's lancet windows was broken, and two of them had been darkened" (*CF* 3.469), warning of the appearance of the fearful creature of the title.

The same point that Lovecraft's use of unusual descriptions are more explicable yet remain tantalizingly underdescribed is well illustrated by another segment from the above paragraph. Looking at the church glass, Blake has the internal thought that "the few saints depicted bore expressions distinctly open to criticism" (*CF* 3.460). Christian religious art has many manifestations, and not infrequently quite sanguinary ones. Yet the iconic images of the faces of most saints, even in the more brutal depictions of their martyrdoms, tend almost universally toward the pathetic or the beatific. Readers must obviously decide for themselves what such criticism as Blake is mentally inclining to signifies, but it is more powerful for letting readers create such an image themselves yet while forcing them into a narrow range of negative interpretation only. Such forceful channelling of readers' contemplations and understandings into desired avenues to generate a specific type of thought but without a concrete explanation that would lessen the potential power of them is something Lovecraft was an old hand at. *The Dream-Quest of Unknown Kadath* states that the people abandoned the slopes of Ngranek, "since things were sometimes glimpsed in the darkness which no one could interpret favourably" (*CF* 2.125), while "The Cats of Ulthar" is basically this premise played over and again until it is enlarged to fill the entire short tale.

Yet these are not the only options utilized from Lovecraft's arsenal of literary techniques. By using paradoxical and even oxymoronic phrases he frequently creates a situation wherein the acutely impossible is presented as an understandable fact, yet without ever drawing attention to this innate impossibility. In "The Strange High House in the Mist" the owner of the titular dwelling speaks of the "pillared and weedy temple of Poseidonis [. . .] still glimpsed at midnight by lost ships, who know by its sight that they are lost" (*CF* 2.93). This is a classic Lovecraftian description that makes a perfectly outré sense even at it remains inexplicable. To sight a recognizable landmark at sea is to know where one is, yet by sighting Poseidonis such ships understand that they are lost. Such usage of the impossible description frequently propels Lovecraft's ideas of the truly weird. Arguably his most famous quotation, being itself an in-universe quote from the *Necronomicon*, "That is not dead which can eternal lie, / And with strange aeons even death may die," expresses just such a paradox, yet at the same time is rendered comprehensible in relation to both the inhabitants of the Nameless City and to Dread Cthulhu, to whom it relates in their specific tales. This paradox is even more clearly presented in the statement that "In his house at R'lyeh dead Cthulhu waits dreaming" (*CF* 2.34).

Yet for all their veneer of understandability in context, neither of these two statements makes any sense that can be understood rationally. Death, by definition, is a permanent state. Certainly the dead do not dream, yet this is precisely how humans were in communication with the dead master of R'lyeh. Attempting to unpack these statements in an analytical and consistent manner will not result in a "true understanding" of what they mean. Such unassimilable statements are more akin to the populist Western understanding of a Zen koan, in which it is not the answer that is the purpose, but contemplation of the question, the hunt for understanding, and a different mindset that is far more the objective. This type is paradox is ultimately rendered down to its essence as an oxymoron in descriptions of Azathoth, for while infinity by definition cannot have a midpoint any more than it has an end, it is precisely there wherein "bubbles and blasphemes at infinity's centre the mindless daemon-sultan Azathoth" (*CF* 2.210) in *The Dream-Quest of Unknown Kadath*. Lovecraft is very patently stating here that we are dealing with things that are far removed from our placid island of ignorance, and these very hints convey how unwise it is for us to voyage far. All this makes no logical sense and cannot be understood if processed logically, yet equally works a powerful storytelling alchemy to create a specific effect and distinct cognizance in the reader. The impossible becomes subliminally absorbed and accepted, and thus the weird atmosphere and intentionally ultramundane that Lovecraft strives for is more effective evoked.

Nor is the paradox in description limited to the more patently esoteric. In "The Dreams in the Witch House" Gilman "made a sketch of the singular angles described by the moss-grown rows of grey standing stones" (*CF* 3.234) on the island in the Miskatonic

River. Importantly, by the time of the introduction of this knowledge early in the tale the idea of angles and mathematics has already been twice established as important, and the island noted as a locale of significance. This further mention of angles seems superficially just a continuation of this theme, which indeed it also is. Yet the statement made makes little objective sense. Lovecraft understands the power of the word "singular," meaning "unexampled, unique (now rare) . . . remarkable from rarity, much beyond the average in degree . . . strangely behaved" (*OED*), and uses it with precision. He utilized it to great effect in the denouement of "The Cats of Ulthar," written twelve years earlier: "And when they had broken down the frail door they found only this: two cleanly picked human skeletons on the earthen floor, and a number of singular beetles crawling in the shadowy corners" (*CF* 1.154). Yet how are a series of angles, especially one in tangible form constrained by the necessities of physics and architectural necessity in a human-habitated and understood place, truly singular? The angles in R'lyeh are alien because the place is itself alien. An island is the Miskatonic River is not. Logically this use of "singular" makes little sense, unless the reader waters down the definition to the blandness of "extraordinary, unconventional, or unusual" and even then how are such angles unusual? Yet when Walter Gilman sees singular angles it adds credibility and the veneer of a plausibility to that which is occurring about him, subtly reinforcing the themes of the story without being something that could be logically described or cogently explained according to the generally accepted meanings of the words.

The absence of words also has a distinct power, of which the archetypical Lovecraftian example is in the title "The Whisperer in Darkness." The present author has heard this title mispronounced numerous times as "The Whisperer in *the* Darkness," and this is for a very obvious reason: such an addition adds logically, and with linguistic neatness, to the perceived intent of the title, which is to describe someone whispering in a place without light. The two titles are extremely similar in meaning, but it is in the subtle differences that the importance of the absent word becomes apparent. The Whisperer in *the* Darkness solely describes someone speaking in low volume in a place without light. The

Whisperer in Darkness does likewise, but could also be interpreted as the whisperer being without light, or being inside darkness as a tangible (or metaphorical) presence. It is a very slight differentiation, but it is of such slight differentiations that great, rather than the merely good, literature is found.

As the reader might rightfully question how much intent Lovecraft had in these minute changes and minuscule differences, it is worth proffering two examples to illustrate. In a 1923 letter to James F. Morton, Lovecraft rants repeatedly about the changes of single words in publications of his works (*SL* 1.217), and it is worth remembering that he personally edited by hand the copies of *Astounding Stories* that contained *At The Mountains of Madness* in order to reorder paragraphs and restore words that had been omitted or altered by the magazine's publisher and editor before he would show the story to his friends (Joshi 972). To Lovecraft there were no small issues as concerns his writings.

Yet perhaps the pinnacle of Lovecraft's use of the unusual descriptor occurs in his seminal masterpiece "The Call of Cthulhu." At first he carefully seeds a physical description of the Master of R'lyeh through much of the tale; then, when Cthulhu appears (it "lumbered slobberingly into sight and gropingly squeezed Its gelatinous green immensity through the black doorway" [*CF* 2.53]), rather than an intense extended external portrayal an emotional description of Its state is given. Great Cthulhu is "ravening for delight" (*CF* 2.53). Let us examine this absolutely unique phrase and see the power Lovecraft is able to pack into such a small trio of words. "Ravening" is an relatively infrequent word,[4] generally used in conjunction with wild animals, with various shades of meaning commonly explained as "extremely hungry and hunting for prey" (*Oxford Living Dictionary Online*) or "violently hunting for food" (*Cambridge Dictionary Online*). In addition to its meaning, it has the effective attribute of conveying menace in the word itself. Even someone unfamiliar with the word upon first reading would be unlikely to take it as a beneficent or even neutral term. So we understand that immediately upon awakening to freedom, without even taking a moment for anything else, Cthulhu is hungry

---

4. A Google search gives almost 558,000 results for "ravening," versus 7,750,000 for "Cthulhu" and 127,000,000 for "delight" (December 2017).

and wanting to rend living things to pieces and eat meat: after all, one does not violently hunt vegetables.

This is all very primal and animalistic. Indeed, the word "ravening" is commonly paired with wolves when used in literature or as an exemplar. Yet this is all being done with "delight." This word, denoting "high pleasure" (*OED*), is not something generally associated with animals. It is a very human emotion. Cthulhu is hunting humans to devour and deriving an ecstatic joy or satisfaction from the deed. Yet the connective word "for" adds curiously to this statement. It would be perhaps more common to explain that Cthulhu is "ravening in delight," which is to say it is extremely hungry, violently hunting and taking pleasure from the act. This is a very recognizable, and very human, description. But instead Cthulhu is "ravening for delight." It is violently hunting while driven by hunger but doing so for the pleasure it causes. This is a very unfamiliar perspective, a subtly odd bit of removal from the known to the unknowable meanings engendered by the word connecting the descriptive terms. Ravening in delight is explicable, ravening for delight is alien. And yet, after spending a paragraph examining these three words, what they mean is still elusive in creating a tangible image that is easily shared and understood. Ask any new or seasoned group of readers of Lovecraft what Cthulhu "ravening for delight" looks like, feels like, or explicitly means, and the questioner will not get a common consensus but a broad mixture of answers and understandings. It is a solid description, and the words are powerful and strongly evocative, but what they tangibly mean is as slippery as the ground Parker tries to flee from the actuality is.

Ultimately, perhaps the best way to describe Lovecraft is in his own words. Coming from the revision "Out of the Aeons," about another author of deep horrors in an uncaring yet malign cosmos, the comparison is disquietingly apt: reading Lovecraft truly does leave the reader "oddly disturbed by the oblique and insidious references," for the "savant had a poisonous way of suggesting more than he stated" (*CF* 4.419).

Works Cited

Chaplin, Charles (director). *The Adventurer.* Mutual Film Corporation, 1917.

The Concise Oxford Dictionary of Current English. 5th ed. Oxford: Oxford University Press, 1964.

Damascius. *Damascius' Problems and Solutions Regarding First Principles.* Tr. Sara Ahbel-Rappe. Oxford: Oxford University Press, 2010.

Ferdowsi. *The Shahnameh: The Persian Books of Kings.* Tr. Dick Davis. Washington, DC: Mage Publishers, 1997.

Gauthier de Metz. *L'Image du monde de maitre Gossouin.* Lausanne: Payot, 1913.

Joshi, S. T. *I Am Providence: The Life and Times of H. P. Lovecraft.* New York: Hippocampus Press, 2010.

The Oxford Classical Dictionary. 3rd ed. Ed. Simon Hornblower and Antony Spawforth. Oxford: Oxford University Press, 1996.

Poe, Edgar Allan. *Collected Works of Edgar Allan Poe: Tales and Sketches.* Ed. Thomas Ollive Mabbott. Cambridge, MA: Harvard University Press, 1978. 2 vols. (numbered consecutively).

Pliny the Younger. *Letters.* Tr. William Melmoth. London & New York: Heinemann/Macmillan, 1915.

Briefly Noted

Lovecraft and his work is exploding in various media outlets. Cadabra Records has been issuing numerous spoken-word LPs of Lovecraft's stories, all read by Andrew Leman of the H. P. Lovecraft Historical Society, and with liner notes by S. T. Joshi. The latest is a two-LP set of *The Call of Cthulhu.* The Lovecraftian novel *Lovecraft Country* (2016), by Matt Ruff, about an African American family in the 1950s and its involvement in Lovecraftian horrors, is being adapted into a miniseries for HBO by Jordan Peele, the director of the acclaimed film *Get Out.* S. T. Joshi and others are involved in a "biopic," *The Lovecrafts,* that they hope will do for Lovecraft what *The Whole Wide World* did for Robert E. Howard. The film focuses on the courtship and marriage of Lovecraft and Sonia H. Greene.

Where Lovecraft Lost His Telescope: His Kingston and the Towns around It

Robert H. Waugh

It is time to record the origins of my place in Lovecraft criticism, which was the Lovecraft Forum that I founded perforce thirty years ago through the efforts of a fan who appeared one day in the office of the English Department of SUNY New Paltz, saying to the Chair, "You need to have a Lovecraft Forum." "Why?" she asked mildly, and he answered that we must because Lovecraft had visited New Paltz in 1929. At this the Chair suggested that the fan should see Professor Waugh. I was only casually interested in Lovecraft at the time; but when the fan said he could provide me with his copies of *Lovecraft Studies* and *Crypt of Cthulhu* and bring such scholars as S. T. Joshi and Peter Cannon to the event, I acquiesced and have been running the Forum ever since. The few times I was gone students ran the Forum. The fan, whose name I have forgotten to my shame, has disappeared, on his way to Florida with his mother.

During the many years I lived in New Paltz and environs, I never took to heart the point of doing the Forum in that town. Later, when I moved seventeen miles north, preparing to retire to Port Ewen upon the Esopus Creek, I happened to read in Lovecraft's copious letter to Elizabeth Toldridge that besides the city Kingston he also visited the small towns of Hurley and New Paltz (*ET* 64–72), towns I am very familiar with and which Lovecraft visited at the same time as he visited Kingston. I had moved from one Lovecraft site to another; I could not escape him. So I gave up, and in this short essay I would like to outline what Kingston and those towns were like in the late 1920s when he visited them and to explore how he reacted to those towns.

Chartered in 1661, halfway up the Hudson River between

New Amsterdam and Albany, for several years Kingston grew until 1797, when it became the first capital of the new State of New York, its name acknowledging for some years its fealty to King George III. One can still see many of the old government buildings, reared in the solid rock and stone of the eighteenth century and in the ornamental brick that is now the signature of the city. It was his interest in architecture that led Lovecraft to put aside his telescope, searching out the details of the upper friezes; it was here, however, that someone stole his diary and telescope, which is now something of the true cross that we Lovecraftians still have to recover (Joshi, *I Am Providence* 731). In this city the Dutch Reformed Church and the Episcopalian Church vie for interest, but the Victorian style of the Episcopal church would not have excited Lovecraft's interest.

"Kingston itself interested me prodigiously," he wrote in a letter in May 29, 1929, "for it is a highly venerable & historic place full of reliques of the past" (*ET* 64). Let us consider this statement: "reliques of the past." Twice over he emphasizes that it is the past that he has come to admire. Thus it is "venerable," a place to be approached in adoration. Now adoration is difficult, no matter what its object may be, so we shall see that Lovecraft does adore as far as he can.

"Kingston" can then be many things to many people. Lovecraft is meticulous in describing the shape and history of the city, the history of Kingston proper and the history of Rondout and the Strand, which in Lovecraft's time had its own ferry across the Hudson to Rhinebeck. The vibrant scene of the railroad and the commercial trucking had led to the stagnant world of the Strand that Lovecraft knew. He, however, was quite fascinated by the society of the Strand, in his day "a somewhat picturesque slum" (*ET* 64). One may well think of the slums of Eastern Providence that attracted Charles Dexter Ward as a young man or "the queer dark courts on the precipitous hillside" where Professor Angell died upon being jostled by "a nautical-looking negro" (*CF* 2.22). These were slumming places that I believe sang to Lovecraft's secret sensibility.

Now things are very different along a Strand that has been quite renovated, as has the arcade in the center of the city where people slowly built the Stockade District. A great variety of pleasure boats dock at the Strand; the restaurants are excellent, thanks to the Culinary Institute across the Hudson, and the art galleries are interesting. The Strand has become gentrified. At least, that is how it seems at first; but when you walk to the west along the shore of the Esopus, things become a bit more sleazy. Consider, in comparison to this present, what Lovecraft thought of the area some eighty years ago: "Hilly Rondout on the river has become a sort of declassé section largely given over to foreigners, from whom Kingston proper is almost wholly free" (*ET* 66).

What shall we say, then, of the foreigners in the city of Kingston and the towns of Hurley and New Paltz? The building of the Delaware and Hudson Canal in the 1820s brought a great influx of Irish, especially to the work on what became known as Rosendale Cement (Evers 220–21). Rosendale is a town that came into existence between Kingston and New Paltz; but in his description of his trip to New Paltz Lovecraft has no word to spare on Rosendale; this is a shame, since he might have found the caverns of Rosendale of some interest. From 1905 to 1915 Italians arrived to work on the Ashokan Reservoir (Evers 388); later the work in the farms became important for Jamaican labor. Finally we must mention the State Teachers College that became one of the state universities with a strong emphasis in the last twenty years on a diverse student body. Clearly Lovecraft could not see what was in front of his nose when he said that Kingston and New Paltz were free of foreigners.

As I have suggested, Kingston provided Lovecraft with a wealth of architecture. Yes, there were the gambrel roofs in which he reveled. There were the stone houses of Hurley and New Paltz, and the ancient stone buildings in Kingston that survived the fire of the Revolution. Lovecraft is happy to speak for "a Dutch diplomat, visiting the place not long ago, [who] declared that as a whole [Hurley] is more typically & historically Dutch than anything now left in Holland!" (*ET* 68). He is happy to trip off his tongue "the railway station, P. O., public library, city hall, hospital, & Y M C A" (*ET* 66).

Lovecraft has considerably more interest in the street-car line, to which he devotes two long, complex sentences, and the motor coach service, to which he devotes two more spacious sentences;

these vehicles he believes must have "all the freshness, charm, & simplicity of a small village" (*ET* 66). It is easy to see what sorts of cities and villages Lovecraft preferred. It is possible, of course, that he appreciated the street-car lines, the motor coach, and the rail line because he traveled by them.

From Kingston Lovecraft visited Hurley for a day, a pleasant backwater of Kingston that had a number of old stone houses. To call Hurley a backwater today, however, is to forget the historical turmoil that the town suffered in its early life, for it and Kingston did become a part of the Indian Wars, which Lovecraft wisely took note of: "Severe Indian warfare harassed the town throughout its early history—incidents not unprovoked by the high-handed seizure of lands & arbitrary and cruel treatment of Indians by the Dutch settlers" (*ET* 65). In 1663 the Natives burned Hurley to the ground and carried off a number of women and children. Lovecraft, we see, pays attention not only to the architecture but to the history. It was the search for those captives that brought some of the French Huguenots to the valley they named New Paltz, which as Lovecraft put it brought him on his next "sub-pilgrimage" after visiting Hurley (*ET* 68).

New Paltz founded in 1687 by French Huguenots who had arrived in the New World via the Netherlands and stayed first in Hurley. They bought the land from the Natives lawfully, "a step which would have delighted Roger Williams," the Rhode-Islander within Lovecraft cannot help himself from remarking (*ET* 70). Once more they built the stone houses that properly fascinated Lovecraft and which lured him to the town, houses built in the seventeenth and eighteenth centuries that were still inhabited by the original families when he arrived. The main church was the Dutch Reformed Church, which had slowly superseded the French Huguenots. By Lovecraft's time there had been a great influx of Italian families, drawn by the cement works in the nearby town of Rosendale, a town with no architectural or historical interest for Lovecraft. Through the first half of the century many more Italians arrived to exploit the earth for the sake of vineyards and apple orchards. A Roman Catholic church had been built in the heart of New Paltz, not far from the State Teachers College, which he did notice. A small Episcopal church existed for the sake of the Anglican managers of the cement works. It was a very quiet town, on the verge of expressing its new tensions and of discovering the treasures it possessed in the old stone houses.

Did any of this material find its place in Lovecraft's fiction? Yes, in 1924 in "The Shunned House," but before he went to Kingston, Jacques Roulet, the horrible creature of that story, comes from a family of Huguenots who have settled in the neighborhood of the French Provence. More striking are Lovecraft's references to the local geography of Kingston in "The Man of Stone" and "The Diary of Alonzo Typer," but those stories have little to do with that geography. We cannot really say that these stories were affected by their geography.

I do wonder whether Lovecraft as he inspected the region was in any way influenced by Washington Irving, whom he certainly respected, though the light tone of Irving's work was certainly not the tone that Lovecraft preferred. At the beginning of "Rip Van Winkle" the narrator describes the Catskills as "fairy mountains," with "magical hues and shapes" (4). In the postscript to the story he adds that it is "a region full of fable," appearing often in the Native mythologies (19). With very little detail Knickerbocker refers to "the haunted regions of those mountains" (627) and their "enchanted regions" (629), but clearly those mountains do not belong to the mock-heroic style of that work. The mountains in both narratives are quickly dealt with; Lovecraft in his visit to New Paltz refers to "the quiet Dutch milieu so well exploited by Washington Irving" (*ET* 68), but for him as for Irving the Catskills and the Shawangunk hills are marginalized, and thus he speaks Irving's language when he says "the purple mountains loom mystically" (*ET* 67) and then turns once more to the details of Kingston, New Paltz, and Hurley. He writes in a manner fitting to "Rip Van Winkle" when he says of Hurley that "the place is delectably slow & sleepy, with true Catskill conservatism [. . .] tenanted by the same old families who built them" (*ET* 67).

When in Lovecraft's sub-pilgrimage he arrives at New Paltz, he reverts to the earlier language, "in the eternal shadow of the lordly & lovely Shawangunk Hills" (*ET* 68), innocent of the historical change by which the Shawangunks will become popular with moneyed rock climbers, training themselves for the Himalayas. It would not have been a change open to his sensibility. Instead, as he approaches New Paltz he rhapsodizes over "at least one old-fashioned *covered bridge*" (*ET* 69) that he sees—this, I dare say, is the bridge that is still in existence over the Wallkill, carefully preserved between Rosendale and Rifton.

New Paltz seems to have been everything he expected, very like Hurley but not slumbering. He especially appreciates the large stone house that is now the museum of the town: "under the immense sloping roof [. . .] a fine type of early colonial construction under Dutch influence, (though Frenchmen built it) & I examined it with the utmost thoroughness & interest" (*ET* 69), as I am sure he did. It is possible that at the end of this tour of Hurley and New Paltz he may have returned to the Strand by way of the bridge that had been built in 1922, but he never gave a clue that he had. Port Ewen, which had been founded in 1851 by the Pennsylvania Coal Company across from the Strand (www.nynjbotany.org/whudson/esopustown), never achieved a reputation of wonder or of true sleaze such as the Strand often did.

At the end of his stay in the upper Hudson valley Lovecraft turned his attention to the loss of French, which was the tongue of the French Huguenots, and Dutch: "Every effort was made to preserve the traditional piety & French ways of the forefathers, yet in the course of time the influence of the surrounding Dutch population could not help being felt [. . .] time took its revenge upon the once conquering Dutch language by pressing it to extinction as French had formerly been pressed—the latest conqueror being the all-engulfing English" (*ET* 70–71). This "engulfing" could not have been moral. It is upon this "pathos of the linguistic change" that Lovecraft concludes his meditation.

The physical evidence of this "engulfing" for Lovecraft can be seen in the fire that the British brought to Hurley; first it was a fire that the Natives brought, but now it was a war once more, "setting fire to all the edifices save those belonging to loyal subjects of our rightful sovereign" (*ET* 65). The sense of irony is alive here as Lovecraft suggests that "the political loyalty of the owner [was] the most probable" reason why the Van Steenbough house where the State Senate met was not burned (*ET* 65).

We should not be surprised that Lovecraft does miss some aspects of the city. Of great interest to him is the story of Aaron Burr, who in the Bogardus Tavern discovered the chalk drawings of a young boy upon a stable door and resolved to send the young man, John Vanderlyn, to Europe for artistic training (*ET* 66). We must keep in mind that this young man's first work of some strength some years later was the nude of Ariadne, a work that was not well received by his native city. This story, as Lovecraft tells it, is all about the perspicacity of Burr; but we have to bring to Lovecraft's account the more salient aspects of the Burr story, his duel with Alexander Hamilton in which Hamilton died and Burr's career was ruined. He was thereafter a man without a country, a fate that reminds us of Edward Everett Hale's poignant novella. The center of that work lies in the young man Philip Nolan's curse: "Damn the United States! I wish I may never hear of the United States again!" (Hale 23). As Lovecraftians we believe we have heard this story once before, not from the pen of Lovecraft but upon the lips of the Outsider. "I did not shriek, but all the fiendish ghouls that ride the night-wind shrieked for me, as in that same second there crashed down upon my mind a single and fleeting avalanche of soul-annihilating memory" (*CF* 1.271–72). This story is not a jest; it is deadly serious.

There is, however, another aspect of this city and its parasite towns that is ignored by Lovecraft, an aspect of the world that he either ignored or simply never heard of despite its powerful place in our world, at first after the Civil War and today in our multicultural world. This is the place of Sojourner Truth. Isabella was her slave name when she was born in 1797 in a rural cellar in Rifton; her house was sold for $100 in 1806 (nynjbotany.org/whudson/esopustown/), and she achieved her freedom with great difficulty in 1828 (Evers 186). During this time her only language was Low Dutch, i.e., Deutsch; shedding that language was her first step to freedom (Washington 18, 20). In time she became a powerful orator; but her freedom meant for her the freedom of all Americans, including the freedom of all women (Evers 186); thus she was more than an abolitionist before the Civil War. This demand for freedom in all its forms is one reason she remains a powerful figure for so many people. When a new library was built for New Paltz University, it was named in her honor, large photographs of her implacable, gnarly figure sitting above several of the staircases. She was illiterate, so we must learn that the letter is not the key to truth.

Lovecraft does not seem to be aware of this woman who looms above us like a fertile crack of doom. But despite this failure of imagination, two sculptures are now assumed by the two figures, the white man and the black woman, the conservative man and the progressive woman, the careful man and the outspoken woman. His statue stands firmly in place, the adult male in Providence, Rhode Island; and her statue stands as an adult in Northampton and as a young child in Port Ewen, just across the Esopus Creek from the Strand. He is gaunt, and she has been whipped. He of course does not mention her presence at all in his steps across the Rondout, for he did not believe in the freedom of the black existence; but as his own death marched upon him, the life of Sojourner Truth increased. The first plaque in her honor in Kingston was raised in 1883, before Lovecraft was born; the first in his honor was raised at the John Hay Library in 1990. We do imagine that neither would have appreciated the other, but I believe there is something of the child in both of them, and we are called upon to listen to the dark place in both.

Works Cited

Evers, Alf. *Kingston: City on the Hudson.* Woodstock, NY: Overlook Press, 2005.

Hale, Edward Everett. *The Man without a Country.* Boston: Little, Brown, 1915.

Irving, Washington. *Selected Writings of Washington Irving.* Ed. Saxe Commins. New York: Modern Library, 1945.

Joshi, S. T. *I Am Providence: The Life and Times of H. P. Lovecraft.* New York: Hippocampus Press, 2010. 2 vols. (numbered consecutively).

Lovecraft, H. P. *Letters to Elizabeth Toldridge and Anne Tillery Renshaw.* Ed. David E. Schultz and S. T. Joshi. New York: Hippocampus Press, 2014.

nynjbotany.org/whudson/esopustown/.

Washington, Margaret. *Sojourner Truth's America.* Urbana: University of Illinois Press, 2009.

Why Michel Houellebecq Is Wrong about Lovecraft's Racism

S. T. Joshi

The first published book by celebrated French novelist and poet Michel Houellebecq (b. 1958) was a little treatise entitled *H. P. Lovecaft: Contre le monde, contre la vie* (1991), translated into English in 2005 as *H. P. Lovecraft: Against the World, Against Life*. It has also been translated into Italian, German, Swedish, and Spanish. It is a very odd piece of work. Its basic thrust is that Lovecraft was "full of rage" (109), and that this rage—specifically manifested toward "the reality principle" (31), is what fuels the distinctive vision and ambiance in his fiction.

In all frankness, Houellebecq's conclusions are not based on sound research. Although it is evident that he read de Camp's biography (apparently in the French translation that appeared in 1988, when Houellebecq states that he wrote his treatise [see 240]), it is unclear whether he read any of Lovecraft's letters beyond those that appeared in the first (and only) volume of Francis Lacassin's translation of Lovecraft's letters (*Lettres* [1978]), containing letters only up to the year 1926. I assisted the translator of the English version of Houellebecq's treatise, Dorna Khazeni, and we were disconcerted to find that a number of his citations of passages from Lovecraft could not be located, including a strange passage (apparently from a Lovecraft story) about "certain ritual and particularly repugnant customs of the indigenous inhabitants of North Carolina" (75). The state of North Carolina is never mentioned in Lovecraft's fiction (including revisions). It would be unjust to suggest that Houellebecq simply invented these passages, since there seems no compelling reason for him to have done so; but at a minimum, his scholarship must be declared to be a tad careless.

Houellebecq heartily admires Lovecraft for what he believes to be Lovecraft's unique approach to literature; in particular, he declares that Lovecraft's work is "an antidote against *all forms* of realism" (29; my emphasis). Houellebecq elaborates on what he means by this remarkable assertion. Seizing upon Lovecraft's early lament that "Adulthood is hell" (*SL* 1.106), as if this view remained uniform throughout Lovecraft's life (as it clearly did not), Houellebecq states: "Lovecraft, for his part, knew he had nothing to do with this world. [. . .] The world sickened him and he saw no reason to believe that by *looking at things better* they might appear differently" (31).

But Houellebecq has confused *indifference* and *hatred*. The one does not imply the other, and Lovecraft himself rejected such a conflation. Houellebecq concludes his treatise by asserting that, for Lovecraft, "the world was evil, intrinsically evil, even by its very essence" (117). This makes Lovecraft sound like Thomas Ligotti, who really is a pessimist and misanthrope. Lovecraft explicitly denied that he was one:

> Contrary to what you may assume, I am *not a pessimist* but an *indifferentist*—that is, I don't make the mistake of thinking that the resultant of the natural forces surrounding and governing organic life will have any connexion with the wishes or tastes of any part of that organic life-processes. Pessimists are just as illogical as optimists; insomuch as both envisage the aims of mankind as unified, and as having a direct relationship (either of frustration or of fulfilment) to the inevitable flow of terrestrial motivation and events. That is—both schools retain in a vestigial way the primitive concept of a conscious teleology—of a cosmos which gives a damn one way or the other about the especial wants and ultimate welfare of mosquitoes, rats, lice, dogs, men, horses, pterodactyls, trees, fungi, dodos, or other forms of biological energy. (*SL* 3.39)

Nevertheless, Houellebecq clings to his view in defiance of all contrary evidence, because it serves as a vital basis for his view of Lovecraft's literary work. For Lovecraft, "hatred of life precedes all literature. He was to remain steadfast in this regard. The rejection of all forms of realism is a preliminary condition for entering his universe" (57). But what does Houellebecq really mean by "realism"? It soon becomes clear: "In his entire body of work, there is not a single allusion to two of the realities to which we generally ascribe great importance: sex and money. Truly not one reference" (57). Houellebecq must know this is preposterous nonsense. Bobby Derie has written an entire treatise on *Sex and the Cthulhu Mythos* (2014), with two substantial chapters, occupying 130 pages, on Lovecraft's own attitudes on sex and discussions or allusions to sex in his fiction. Here we can refer in passing to such things as the cosmic rape in "The Dunwich Horror," the obvious references to the Deep Ones' mating with humans in "The Shadow over Innsmouth," and the successive gender-swapping of Ephraim/Asenath Waite in "The Thing on the Doorstep." One can even cite *The Case of Charles Dexter Ward,* where the preternaturally aged Joseph Curwen probably committed marital rape on his unwilling wife, Eliza Tillinghast, in order to produce offspring—Ann Tillinghast, who became the direct ancestor of Charles Dexter Ward. Allusions to money are less frequent and less significant in Lovecraft's stories, but this one from "The Shadow over Innsmouth" should suffice: "I had no car, but was travelling by train, trolley, and motor-coach, always seeking the cheapest possible route" (*CF* 3.160).

Let us be charitable to Houellebecq's exaggerations. Even if we grant that his references to "sex and money" are meant to allude more broadly to the social realism that dominated European fiction up to and beyond Lovecraft's day, two significant caveats need to be made. First, much the same analysis could be made of many of Lovecraft's predecessors in weird fiction, from Poe to Bierce to Machen to Dunsany to Blackwood; in this regard, Lovecraft's avoidance of "sex and money" is only a more extreme instance of a tendency that long dominated a genre that had very different foci. Some of these writers had a few more female characters than Lovecraft did, and some (notably Poe and Machen) did refer covertly to sex, usually of an aberrant sort (as in the suggestion of brother-sister incest in "The Fall of the House of Usher" or the sexual depravities of Helen Vaughan in "The Great God Pan"). But Lovecraft is not a notable outlier in this regard. It is significant that Houellebecq cites the work of Richard Matheson as a sharp contrast to Lovecraft (51–52). It was, indeed, precisely the contention of Matheson and other writers of his generation that Lovecraft and his cohorts in *Weird Tales* had ignored the "realism" of daily life and sought to return weird fiction to that level.

Well and good. But this brings me to my second caveat: there are other types of realism than merely the mundane realism of portraying ordinary human beings going about their daily affairs. When Houellebecq repeatedly states that Lovecraft rejected "all forms" of realism, he is plainly contradicting Lovecraft himself. Although Houellebecq reveals some familiarity with Lovecraft's commonplace book, he is apparently ignorant of the essay "Notes on Writing Weird Fiction" (1933), where Lovecraft states unequivocally:

> In writing a weird story I always try very carefully to achieve the right mood and atmosphere, and place the emphasis where it belongs. One cannot, except in immature pulp charlatan–fiction, present an account of impossible, improbable, or inconceivable phenomena as a commonplace narrative of objective acts and conventional emotions. Inconceivable events and conditions have a special handicap to overcome, and this can be accomplished only through the maintenance of a *careful realism* [my emphasis] in every phase of the story *except* [Lovecraft's emphasis] that touching on the one given marvel. (*CF* 2.177)

The realism Lovecraft is here referring to may or may not be realism of character portrayal; but in his own work he certainly emphasizes meticulous realism of setting and landscape, to say nothing of realism in regard to the facts of science. Houellebecq even admires the "oneiric precision" (74) of the description of the Old Ones in *At the Mountains of Madness*, but fails to acknowledge that this is a "realism" just as compelling and just as vital to Lovecraft's purpose as the "utterly banal settings (supermarkets, gas stations . . .)" (51) found in Matheson's work.

But if Houellebecq is far off the mark in this aspect of his analysis of Lovecraft, he goes even further astray in regard to the most controverted aspect of Lovecraft's life and work—his racism. Because Houellebecq is convinced that the essence of Lovecraft's work is "Absolute hatred of the world in general, aggravated by an aversion to the modern world in particular" (57), and believes that Lovecraft himself is "misanthropic and slightly sinister" (99)—a view we have already seen to be largely false—he focuses on racism as some sort of secret key to understanding the totality of Lovecraft's literary work. He maintains that Lovecraft's difficult two years in New York—where, unlike in Providence, he was forced to rub shoulders with people of all different races in a bootless quest to secure income—were a kind of crucible that led him to his great burst of creativity when he returned to Providence for the final decade of his life.

Houellebecq trots out the now-familiar passages from Lovecraft's letters on this topic, notably the discussion of the "Italo-Semitico-Mongoloid" (*SL* 1.333–34) denizens of the Lower East Side (although this passage relates to Lovecraft's first trip to New York in April 1922). This passage is now, in Houellebecq's view, to be regarded as an all-purpose hermeneutic for the interpretation of the "great texts" of Lovecraft's later years: "His descriptions of the nightmare entities that populate the Cthulhu cycle spring directly from this hallucinatory vision" (107). What is the proof of this remarkable assertion? Houellebecq offers . . . "The Horror at Red Hook" (1925). Well, yes—but, if I may lapse into common parlance, what else have ya got? How do the foreign-born people of the Lower East Side bear any relation to the entities depicted in Lovecraft's later work—whether it be the crustacean fungi from Yuggoth in "The Whisperer in Darkness," or the barrel-shaped Old Ones in *At the Mountains of Madness,* or the Great Race in "The Shadow out of Time," or even the nebulous entities (assuming there is more than one) that come down in the meteorite in "The Colour out of Space" and corrupt both the landscape and the human denizens of the Gardner farmhouse? Any parallels are, as I have asserted elsewhere (see "Charles Baxter on Lovecraft" 120–21), rather opaque. And this is apparently why Houellebecq simply doesn't even discuss the matter; he doesn't even cite the Deep Ones of "The Shadow over Innsmouth," which of all the "great texts" of Lovecraft's last decade of writing could be plausibly assumed to be founded on racist presuppositions (in this case, the dangers of miscegenation).

Houellebecq does claim that the various cultists who worship the Great Old Ones are "almost always half-breeds, mulattos, of mixed blood, among the basest of species" (109). Even this description is not accurate in its details and seems largely derived from the portrayal of the Cthulhu cultists in "The Call of Cthulhu." The sinister Mr. Noyes in "The Whisperer in Darkness," who is clearly allied with the fungi from Yuggoth, is unimpeachably Caucasian and well-bred. Otherwise, however, Houellebecq simply *asserts* the ubiquity of the racial motif in Lovecraft's fiction without making any attempt to establish it with compelling evidence—or evidence of any sort.

It may be helpful to contrast Houellebecq's discussion of this topic—and especially of the effect of Lovecraft's two years in New York upon the rest of his life and work—with the comments of someone who *actually knew Lovecraft* and could speak much more authoritatively on the matter. In his celebrated memoir, *In Memoriam: Howard Phillips Lovecraft* (1941), W. Paul Cook speaks eloquently of how Lovecraft became a very different human being after New York:

> But Lovecraft never became thoroughly humanized, he never became the man we love to recall, until his New York experience. To the very end of his days he hated New York with a consuming passion. I mean the city itself, not the many good friends he had there. But it took the privations, trials and testing fires of New York to bring his best to the surface. And it took personal contact with those cultured, clever, sophisticated New York amateurs and semi-amateurs to make him look out and not in, to broaden him so that he could cultivate an artistic tolerance, if not entirely altering his viewpoint.

This sounds a lot more like the Lovecraft that we see in the letters of his last decade of life—and, more pertinently, in his literary work of that period.

Houellebecq's characterization of Lovecraft's racism is part and parcel of his view that Lovecraft was an "obsolete reactionary" (115)—but again, he must know that this is false. Even de Camp's biography makes plain Lovecraft's late conversion to moderate (non-Marxist) socialism, and his later letters are full of condemnations of his own earlier conservatism in the political and economic sphere. But this fact would constitute a serious qualification of the conclusions Houellebecq has already arrived at, and therefore he simply ignores it. Here as in other facets of his book, it becomes clear that Houellebecq has evolved a specific view of Lovecraft, derived from early readings (he first read Lovecraft in French translation at the age of sixteen) and augmented by highly selective absorption of other texts, and he has by accident or design dispensed with evidence that would contradict that view.

It is, on the face of it, implausible to think that a young French enthusiast who may or may not have read much of Lovecraft's work in English, who does not claim to be a literary scholar, and who clearly has his own agenda in portraying Lovecraft as he did (for which see Spaulding), could have come up with a magic formula for understanding Lovecraft's work—that it is all based on "racial hatred"—that has eluded the hundreds of other critics, in English and in other languages, who have assessed the Providence writer's work. Houellebecq is not shy about his purported breakthrough. In his preface to the 1999 French edition of his book he declares that he experienced two surprises when first reading Lovecraft—one was his "absolute materialism," and the "other great cause of my surprise was his obsessive racism; never in the reading of his descriptions of nightmare creatures could I have divined that their source was to be found in *real* human beings" (24). Here again he simply asserts the point, apparently believing that it has been proven in the body of his treatise; but it hasn't. Elsewhere he remarks, without the least trace of irony, that "[t]he role of this racial hatred in Lovecraft's body of work has often been underestimated" (108). Just so! But this circumstance does not incline Houellebecq to raise doubts about his own conclusions.

Houellebecq's views in his rather sophomoric treatise have had a lamentably wide influence on other critics who have harped on the same theme. China Miéville has maintained that the "depth and viciousness of Lovecraft's racism is [*sic*] known to me . . . It goes further, in my opinion, than 'merely' being a racist—I follow Michel Houellebecq . . . in thinking that Lovecraft's oeuvre, his work itself, is inspired by and deeply structured with race hatred" (quoted in Joshi, *Lovecraft and Weird Fiction* 83–84). Needless to say, Miéville himself provides no evidence for this assertion, believing that Houellebecq has done the job for him; but he hasn't. Charles Baxter, in his extremely hostile review of Leslie S.

Klinger's *The Annotated H. P. Lovecraft* (*New York Review of Books*, 18 December 2014), claims that Lovecraft was a "pathological racist" (see Joshi, "Charles Baxter on Lovecraft" 109) and goes on to maintain that racism was central to Lovecraft's literary work; he does not specifically cite Houellebecq as a source for this view, nor does he argue for his view with anything approaching convincing evidence.

There is some amusement in noting that Houellebecq himself stated, in his 1999 preface, that "it seems to me that I wrote this book as a sort of first novel. A novel with a single character (H. P. Lovecraft himself)—a novel that was constrained in that all the facts it conveyed and all the texts it cited had to be exact, but a sort of novel nonetheless" (23). We have seen that Houellebecq's citation of Lovecraft's texts is far from "exact," but otherwise he is sadly accurate in stating that his work really is a kind of novel. It should be emphasized that his view of Lovecraft is on the whole a positive one, and he has great admiration for Lovecraft as a prose stylist and as one who contributed something genuinely new to the literature of the world; even his discussion of Lovecraft's racism is largely free of the rancor and bitter hostility that we have seen in a number of other commentators on this subject. But even so, the sad fact is that Michel Houellebecq has promulgated a scurrilous falsehood—based on inadequate evidence and a jaundiced view of what he wants Lovecraft's work to represent—that has infected the work of critics and scholars far more hostile to Lovecraft than he is.

Works Cited

Houellebecq, Michel. *H. P. Lovecraft: Against the World, Against Life*. Tr. Dorna Khazeni. San Francisco: Believer Books, 2005.

Joshi, S. T. "Charles Baxter on Lovecraft." *Lovecraft Annual* No. 9 (2015): 106–23.

———. *Lovecraft and Weird Fiction: Selected Blog Posts, 2009–2017*. Seattle: Sarnath Press, 2017.

Spaulding, Todd. "Lovecraft and Houellebecq: Two Against the World." *Lovecraft Annual* No. 9 (2015): 182–213.

"Whaddya Make Them Eyes at Me For?": Lovecraft and Book Publishers

David E. Schultz

H. P. Lovecraft had six brushes with book publishers in his lifetime. As is all too well known, all came to naught. Three other, more nebulous discussions with book publishers were similarly fruitless.

Popular Fiction Publishing Co. Farnsworth Wright, editor of *Weird Tales* magazine, had suggested in 1926 the possibility of publishing a book of Lovecraft's work. To that end, Lovecraft prepared a list of the stories he'd include in such a book, to be called *The Outsider and Other Stories.*[1] But the poor sales of the Popular Fiction Publishing Co.'s first attempt at book publication, *The Moon Terror* (1927), which contained "The Moon Terror" by A. G. Birch, "Ooze" by Anthony M. Rud, "Penelope" by Vincent Starrett, and "An Adventure in the Fourth Dimension" by Farnsworth Wright, made Wright wary of undertaking another such venture. Of course, the failure of that book had much to do with its lackluster content. (Lovecraft panned Starrett's story when it first appeared.) Lovecraft was a popular author among *Weird Tales* readers, and Wright placed much value on reader response in regard to what he published. In that light, it seems a book by Lovecraft would have been a sure thing, but Wright was reluctant to take the risk.

In suggesting stories for such a book, Lovecraft felt that the

1. The stories to be included, per a written list in HPL's papers, were "The Music of Erich Zann," "The Outsider," "The Temple," "Dagon," "Facts concerning the Late Arthur Jermyn and His Family," "The Rats in the Walls," "The Tomb," "The Statement of Randolph Carter," "The Picture in the House," "The Unnamable," "The Festival," and "The Terrible Old Man." This list differs somewhat from the stories he suggested in his letter to Wright of 22 December 1927 (13–16).

content should be driven somewhat by reader preference, although he railed against such practice when it came to rejection of his best stories by Farnsworth Wright, who always feared reader reaction to stories that might be *too* weird.

As late as November 1928, Wright noncommittally expressed vague interest in doing such a book (*DS* 166), to be the second *Weird Tales* book (the third being a collection of H. Warner Munn's Werewolf of Ponkert tales). Wright dangled the project before Lovecraft for another year, but Lovecraft finally wrote a correspondent "I'm almost glad Wright seems to have given up the book idea" (*ES* 215). The onset of the Great Depression may have influenced Wright's decision. And so the matter was dropped.

Simon & Schuster. Lovecraft himself never approached a book publisher. The mountain had to come to Mohammed. In 1930, Clifton Fadiman (1904–1999) of Simon & Schuster wrote Lovecraft asking if he had a book to offer for consideration, because Edward J. O'Brien, editor of *The Best Short Stories of 1928 and the Yearbook of the American Short Story* (1928), which contained a three-star notice of Lovecraft's "The Colour out of Space" (and Lovecraft's capsule autobiography), mentioned Lovecraft's "name [. . .] as that of a most promising & interesting writer."[2] Since 1925, Fadiman had been a reader at Simon & Schuster, where he worked for ten years, leaving as its chief editor. He manned the *New Yorker's* book review section from 1933 to 1943, became a judge for the Book of the Month Club in 1944, and on radio and television became a recognized personage in the publishing industry. Fadiman said "he would give careful attention to anything I did submit. I replied that I had nothing of novel length, but would like very much to get a short story collection published—to which, however, he responded that they do not consider short story collections" (*ES* 340).

Lovecraft didn't entirely dismiss the publisher's proposition. He wrote to Clark Ashton Smith, "During the coming summer I may write quite a number of things—perhaps even a weird *novel;*

2. HPL to Lillian D. Clark, 20–21 May 1930 (ms., JHL), where see Fadiman's entire letter.

[Lovecraft's emphasis] since I have had a note from the firm of Simon & Schuster (who got hold of me through the O'Brien anthology) saying that there is a demand for such a thing" (217–18). Lovecraft had *The Case of Charles Dexter Ward* on hand in manuscript, but he never typed it. Despite Fadiman's interest, and because Lovecraft could not bear to type this "lengthy" piece (only as compared to his other stories), he replied that he had no novels to offer. Fadiman wrote again early in 1931 to remind Lovecraft that Simon & Schuster was still willing to consider a novel. About this development, Lovecraft wrote: "With this receptive attitude on their part, I shall certainly send them anything of the kind I may ever grind out" (*ES* 341). At that very time, Lovecraft was grinding out his third novel, *At the Mountains of Madness,* but he did not offer it, or anything else, to Fadiman. When August Derleth sought a publisher for *The Outsider and Others,* the typescript for the book was submitted to Fadiman for review. Fadiman encountered Lovecraft's work once again, when he also wrote the preface to Basil Davenport's anthology, *Famous Monster Tales* (1967), which contained "The Outsider."

G. P. Putnam's Sons. A few months later, Winfield Shiras (1900–1985) of G. P. Putnam's Sons approached Lovecraft, having seen his work in *Weird Tales.* Shiras was a graduate of Yale, where he was chairman of the *Yale Record* and editor of the *Yale Literary Magazine.* He was grandson of George Shiras, a former justice of the Supreme Court of the United States, and of whom he wrote the biography *Justice George Shiras, Jr., of Pittsburgh* (1953). Lovecraft selected thirty-eight stories as worth sending them, but submitted only thirty that he had on hand. He then "recalled all loans & finally sent Putnam's various MSS. which were not on hand for the first shipment [. . .] The shipments now include every publishable thing of mine (counting out the new long story) except 'Hypnos' & 'Erich Zann', of which I have no duplicates" (*DS* 310). The publisher sat on the manuscripts for four months, only to return them, in battered condition, according to Lovecraft. As in the case of *Weird Tales* (and later with Alfred A. Knopf), Shiras seemed mildly interested but wanted a guarantee of sales, as seen in August Derleth's assessment of the matter: "The Putnam letter hedges. What the man seems not to realize is that 5,000 copies of a collection of Lovecraft tales could be sold to W. T. readers alone, people who have read all the tales before" (*ES* 358). Derleth's guess at sales is wildly optimistic. When he published *The Outsider and Others* in 1939, Arkham House sold only 1,268 copies and the book did not go out of print until 1944. What Putnam's had told Lovecraft was that "one of their bases for rejection [was] that of an over-explanatory element in many of my tales" (*Letters to Elizabeth Toldridge* 192).

Vanguard. In early March 1932, at the suggestion of Arthur Leeds (another one of Lovecraft's writer friends now in the book business), Vanguard (formerly Macy-Masius) approached Lovecraft with the usual request. Macy-Masius had published Lovecraft's "The Horror at Red Hook" in *Not at Night!* (1928) and several books by M. P. Shiel. Lovecraft was reluctant to send his manuscripts (which were ill-handled by Putnam's) and instead sent an "explanatory letter" (*OFF* 27) to Percy Elias, "the editor or sub-editor or something or other of the Vanguard Press,"[3] who replied in the manner Lovecraft expected. "What they really want is a novel, but they've asked to see some of my short stories nevertheless" (*OFF* 28). Once again, Lovecraft demurred at sending a novel, even the typed *At the Mountains of Madness.* Whereas he previously had inundated publishers with stacks of stories, in this case he sent only "The Dunwich Horror," "The Call of Cthulhu," "The Rats in the Walls," and "Pickman's Model," saying that his best material (including "The Colour out of Space" and "The Music of Erich Zann") was on loan to others. Lovecraft had written: "I wouldn't have let Leeds mention me to the Vanguard if I had known of his intention" (*ES* 469), but that intention is not known, since the inquiry seemed to be like all the others—publishers were looking for novels, not collections of short fiction.

Alfred A. Knopf. Regarding rejections of Lovecraft's work by publishers, we have little evidence other than his testimony. There is one exception. Although the assessment of his work by a publisher, in the publisher's words, is meager, it does give some insight into what publisher wanted and what they thought of Lovecraft's work.

On 1 August 1933, at the suggestion of Samuel Loveman, Allan

3. HPL to Wilfred B. Talman, 22 March [1932] (ms., JHL).

G. Ullman of Alfred A. Knopf wrote Lovecraft requesting manuscripts of his work to evaluate for publication. Ullman (1908–1982) was bookseller (not an editor) at Knopf from 1931 to 1934. He was a 1929 graduate of the Wharton School of the University of Pennsylvania and a book advertising salesman for *The Times* from 1935 until 1947, when he became promotion director of Random House, Inc. His later career involved promotion and publicity at Random House (1946–53); assistant vice president of Book-of-the-Month Club (1953–64); Director of Publications, *New York Times* (1964–75). Ullman wrote several thrillers based on screenplays. These were *Sorry, Wrong Number* (1948), based on a radio serialization by Lucille Fletcher; *Naked Spur* (1955), based on a screenplay by Rolfe Bloom; and *Night Man* (1958), a novelization of a screenplay by Lucille Fletcher. He also wrote *The Plaid Peacock* (1965), a children's book, under the pseudonym Sandy Alan.

Loveman, a close friend of Lovecraft, also sold books, albeit used books, at Dauber & Pine in New York City. It is unknown how Loveman and Ullman knew each other, but suffice it to say that both were in the book trade, and Loveman was ever a staunch promoter of Lovecraft and his work. Ullman had already read Lovecraft's "The Dreams in the Witch House," which had just appeared in the July 1933 issue of *Weird Tales*. If Ullman had not picked up the magazine himself, Loveman probably lent it to him.

Lovecraft replied to Ullman on 3 August, sending "a few tales for examination at your leisure." Lovecraft described them as his best work, and to bolster that opinion described any accolades they may have received. The stories were "The Picture in the House," "The Music of Erich Zann," "The Rats in the Walls," "The Strange High House in the Mist," "Pickman's Model," "The Colour out of Space," and "The Dunwich Horror." As an aside, Lovecraft mentioned that "Loveman has always encouraged my fictional experiments most generously—so that in a sense he is responsible for the existence of most of them."[4]

Ullman informed Loveman that he wished to see more of Lovecraft's stories—what Loveman described as "everything [Lovecraft] or others have thought good in the past." Lovecraft provided another eighteen stories on 16 August, again providing

4. HPL to Allan G. Ullman, 3 August 1933 (ms., JHL).

Farnsworth Wright

Clifton Fadiman

Louis Kronenberger

June Barrows Mussey

explanation as to why he was sending those particular tales, but typically more derogatory than supportive, with such comments as "not a favourite of mine," "not so bad," and "nothing remarkable" and almost warning Ullman against reading them, saying "I don't envy you the task of wading through all these MSS." They were "The Tomb," "Dagon," "The Statement of Randolph Carter," "The Temple," "Facts concerning the Late Arthur Jermyn and His Family," "The Cats of Ulthar," "The Outsider," "The Moon-Bog," "The Lurking Fear," "The Festival," "The Unnamable," "The Shunned House," "In the Vault," "The Horror at Red Hook," "The Call of Cthulhu," "Cool Air," "The Silver Key," and "The Whisperer in Darkness." Loveman, who owned the draft of "The Shunned House," advised Ullman that he should be sure to read that story. Lovecraft withheld "long MSS.—115 & 72 pp—written in 1931," even though he had been asked to send everything he thought good. The stories were *At the Mountains of Madness* and "The Shadow over Innsmouth," both previously unpublished.

Ullman, through Loveman, had requested "a special story 'more gruesome than anything I have ever done'," [5] apparently suggesting that if Lovecraft did not have such a thing, he might consider writing one. Lovecraft responded: "I dare say I could evolve one if the venture advanced enough to demand it!" [6]

Ullman passed along the stories to two readers for evaluation. Cary Abbott (1890–1948) was a graduate of Yale University (1911), where he was editor if the *Yale Banner and Pot Pourri* and managing editor of *Yale Literary Magazine*. He held banking positions from 1911 to 1927. In 1927 he became a secretary at Knopf to a classmate from Yale, serving until 1929, when he became an agent for the publisher in the Midwest, serving at that position from 1929 to 1930. He joined the editorial staff there in 1930. Louis Kronenberger (1904–1980) attended (but did not graduate from) the University of Cincinnati (1921–24). In 1924 he joined the *New York Times*. He became an editor at Boni & Liveright in 1926, and at Alfred A. Knopf in 1933. He published a novel, *The Grand Manner*, in 1929 and became a drama critic for *Time* in 1938, where he worked until 1961. He also wrote numerous biog-

5. HPL to Allan G. Ullman, 16 August 1933 (ms., JHL).

6. Ibid.

raphies, including *Oscar Wilde* (1976).

Ullman selected only eight stories from Lovecraft's stack of twenty-five to assign to the readers. It is unknown which stories he provided, but he described them as best of the lot. It is unknown whether he read the stories himself, selected them based on Lovecraft's evaluations of them, or selected them based on Loveman's advice. Knopf's manuscript record states that the stories were received on 21 August, meaning that Ullman or someone else had held the stories some time before they were entered into Knopf's administrative system with the serial number 64T. Under the heading "Title" the manuscripts are merely identified as "Short Stories." The stories were immediately placed with Abbott for review.

Readers submitted their evaluation of a manuscript on a printed form. As can be seen, evaluations were intended to evaluate the potential salability of manuscripts, although the publisher was willing to take a risk on worthy books.

IMPORTANT: Please answer these questions fully and if you have further remarks to make put them on the other side of this page.

READERS' REPORT

[N.B. The individual reviewers' assessments follow this generic form.]

NOTE TO MSS. READERS

We aim to publish primarily:

1. Those books that are so good as to leave absolutely no doubt in the reader's mind of their being worth publishing. Such a manuscript happens along but rarely.

2. Foreign books that are of a great interest as such even when their intrinsic merits are not so obvious.

3. Those serious books that are pioneers in their fields. Such books must not be judged so severely as:

4. Other serious books that are well written and authoritative and of a timely nature or permanent interest.

5. Occasionally a book for its popular appeal pure and simple. This, recognizing that our own tastes if followed exclusively would rule out a great many harmless enough books of the sort that offer real pleasure to masses of readers and are legitimate gambles for the publisher.

A. Does this mss. fall into any of the above classes? If so, which?

If not, stop where you are unless you desire cordially to recommend its publication.

B. If you recommend us to publish the book give your chief reason in a single sentence.

C. Make any suggestion that you think would improve the mss.

D. Would you expect this mss., if published, to have (1) a modest, (2) a considerable, (3) a great sale?

(1) 2000 (2) 5000 (3) 10,000 and upwards.

E. Is there anything in the book that would make it liable to prosecution by the Society for the Suppression of Vice? If so, please designate such pages.

F. If you recommend rejection, do you nevertheless feel the author worth encouraging for the future?

G. Is this a book you would yourself want to buy, own and read, if you saw it announced by another publisher? Say very briefly why.

Neither reviewer made any comments in the spaces given for items A through G. Their brief assessments are given below.

Author Lovecraft, H P. *Date Submitted* 8/21/33 *Date of Report* 8/25/33
Title SHORT STORIES *Reader* C. Abbot
Submitted by author *Instructions for Return* none

H. Synopsis. A collection of horror stories by a well-known writer in this type of tale. As a rule he gives a very good performance in this slow, dignified, rather old-fashioned style which accelerates to a wild tempo toward the climaxes.

I don't know of any recent books of this sort, and there must be a market for these, particularly as they have such realistic backgrounds. I think they are better than the Wandrei book read some months ago.[7] /over./

Mr. Ullman who has read correspondence with Mr. Lovecraft, has a number of others as well, but he selected these as the best.

CA

---

7. Donald Wandrei, another writer friend and correspondent of HPL, had submitted his novel *Dead Titans, Waken!*, later published as *The Web of Easter Island* (1948). At least three other publishers rejected the novel.

Author H P. Lovecraft *Date Submitted* — *Date of Report* 9/7/33
Title Eight horror stories *Reader* Kronenberger
Submitted by author *Instructions for Return* —

H. Synopsis. Quite good in an old-fashioned way, though perhaps too much alike, and too much given to atmosphere and not enough to action. In their own way, however, they are effective.

Lots of people undoubtedly like this kind of thing: the whole question is, are they book-buyers or pulp readers? Since the whole matter is a purely commercial one, I think we should make some kind of check-up in bookstores, finding out whether there is a call for horror stories of popular grade. Simply to publish these in hope of a sale would be pointless.

The reviews are surprisingly favorable. Both reviewers characterized Lovecraft's style as "old-fashioned," calling the stories "quite good," "effective," and a "good performance." They suggest that the publisher seemed to be open to publication; and so Knopf sought expert advice in the matter. Lovecraft learned that "Knopf approached W T [. . .] & asked whether Farnsworth Wright could manage to dispose of 1000 copies through the magazine. When Wright said he couldn't be sure, the proposition fell through" (*Letters to F. Lee Baldwin* 266). Lovecraft was not asked to revise his work for further consideration. And so the manuscript was officially rejected on 26 September. Not long thereafter, Lovecraft could report to Clark Ashton Smith:

> [. . .] the enclosed note from Knopf's (which please return) marks the amply expected bursting of the latest book bubble. I knew damn well the whole business was a farce like the Putnam & Vanguard fiascos—yet when Ullman requested the MSS. I hated to leave any stone unturned. Well—my only loss is the postage one way . . . . . . though I feel tempted to address these publishing birds in the words of the proletarian folk-ballad of 15 or so years ago—"Whaddya wanna make them eyes at me for, ef they don' mean wot they say?" (*DS* 447)[8]

8. HPL quotes from the song "What Do You Want to Make Those Eyes at Me For (If They Don't Mean What They Say!)" (1916), words and music by Joe

Smith, who himself had a collection of his poetry rejected by Knopf, was indignant at the rejection He wrote: "Knopf should remove the Borzoi from his imprint, and substitute either a Golden Calf or a jackass with brazen posteriors" (*DS* 456). The following summer, Lovecraft dubbed one of R. H. Barlow's cats "Alfred A. Knopf."

Loring & Mussey. In February 1935, August Derleth urged his publisher, the short-lived (1933–1936) Loring & Mussey (operating in the same building as Dauber & Pine, where Loveman worked) to make an overture to Lovecraft. The publishing company was run by Percy Albert Loring (b. 1897) and June Barrows Mussey (a.k.a. Henry Hay; 1910–1985). After working at the Boston Public Library, Loring learned bookselling with Charles E. Lauriat Co., and later he joined Marshall Jones Co. and the Medici Society of America. Loring had left A. & C. Boni to found his publishing company in 1934. In 1936 the company became Barrows Mussey, Inc. (Loring having left to become a sales representative for Viking) and failed not long thereafter. Mussey was the anonymous translator of *Mein Kampf: The First Complete and Unexpurgated Edition Published in the English Language* (1939) and author of books about magic and sleight-of-hand.

Lovecraft downplayed the request when mentioning it to others, saying he merely sent "a few yarns." Derleth was well aware of how Lovecraft had been crushed by previous rejections and so he asked the publisher to notify *him*, not Lovecraft, in the case of rejection. But the publisher did not heed Derleth's request and discussed the matter directly with Lovecraft, who reported to a correspondent, "things don't look any too well for those MSS. at Loring & Mussey's. Mussey is indecisive; his wife (who is in the business) doesn't like the stories & wants to turn them down; & Loring hasn't read them. I think I shall shortly request the return of the MSS., since I need them for lending" (*OFF* 273).[9] The publisher manhandled, and lost, some of Lovecraft's submitted material, and of course rejected his work. The experience caused Lovecraft to write Derleth: "This

---

McCarthy, Howard Johnson, and Jimmie Monaco.

9. Dagmar Mussey (1926?–2012), whom Barrows married in Germany following World War II, was his second wife, and so is not the reader in question. His first wife was Jane (Alley) Mussey (1916–2000).

about finishes me with writing. No more submissions to publishers" (*ES* 703). The effect was quite the opposite of what Derleth had hoped to accomplish, but ultimately, such was not the case. Buoyed by the acceptance of both *At the Mountains of Madness* and "The Shadow out of Time" by *Astounding Stories*, Lovecraft promptly wrote "The Haunter of the Dark" in November, and about a year later he accepted, though perhaps dragging his feet, an invitation to submit material once again to a book publisher.

William Morrow. Lovecraft's ebullience was short-lived. In early October 1936, when he was in poor health and probably suspicious that he was not long for this world, his friend, the writer and editor Wilfred Blanch Talman, who was attempting to become a literary agent, offered to facilitate submittal of Lovecraft's work to William Morrow & Company. Talman had intended to become an author's agent and thought Lovecraft could be a key client, along with his former associates from the *Times*.

Later in the month, Talman reported that the publisher (the specific contact there is not known) expressed admiration for Lovecraft's stories, but for much the same reasons that other pro-

Publisher	Recommended by	Editor/Reviewer	Date Proposed	Date Terminated
Popular Fiction Publishing Co.	Farnsworth Wright	Farnsworth Wright	mid-July 1927	September 1929
Simon & Schuster	—	Clifton Fadiman	May 1930	February 1931
G. P. Putnam's Sons	—	Winfield Shiras	April 1931	July 1931
Vanguard	Arthur Leeds	Percy Elias	12 March 1932	April? 1932
Alfred A. Knopf	Samuel Loveman	Allan G. Ullman, Cary Abbott, Louis Kronenberger	1 August 1933	26 September 1933
Loring & Mussey	August Derleth	Percy A. Loring June Barrows Mussey	February 1935	July 1935
William Morrow	Wilfred B. Talman	?	October 1936	November 1936
Philip Allan & Co.	Julius Schwartz	?	c. August 1936	Early 1937

spective publishers, turned them down, hoping instead to see a novel. Lovecraft's regard of the matter must have puzzled Talman, who felt he was doing Lovecraft a great favor. Lovecraft recognized the favor and did not wish to seem ungrateful. And so, even though he probably had no intention of undertaking a new work for Morrow's consideration, he replied to Talman in an extremely evasive manner. He did not want to commit to any sort of schedule or agreement, because his usual practice was to write when he felt moved to do so. Talman did not realize that Lovecraft was a dying man, and so Lovecraft's somewhat frantic but laborious response must have been baffling. The tone of Lovecraft's letters to Talman sounds as though Lovecraft, beset by many difficulties in his last months, to say nothing of his failing health, was on the verge of a nervous breakdown similar to those he suffered throughout his life.[10]

Philip Allan & Co. Julius Schwartz was simultaneously attempting to find British publishers for some of Lovecraft's work, having successfully sold *At the Mountains of Madness* to *Astounding Stories.* It is not known what stories had been provided to Schwartz[11] and Talman, although Lovecraft told Willis Conover (31 January 1937) that one of the stories with Schwartz was "The Colour out of Space." Schwartz intended to approach Philip Allan & Co. of London, which had published Edmond Hamilton's collection *The Horror on the Asteroid and Other Tales of Planetary Horror* (1936) as part of its "Creeps Library" series, which included the anthologies *Creeps: A Collection of Uneasy Tales* (*LL* 223) and *Shudders: A Collection of Uneasy Tales* (*LL* 873), which Lovecraft owned. Clearly nothing came of Schwartz's attempts.

Houghton Mifflin. In late January 1937, Derleth sent Lovecraft "application blanks for a HM fellowship, which I urge you to try for at least—mayhap a study of the supernatural in literature—show them your ms. and suggest revision, lengthening, and bring-

---

10. The Morrow affair is discussed at length in *SL* 5.338–40, 343–48.

11. HPL had intended to send Schwartz "The Thing on the Doorstep" and "The Haunter of the Dark" but was surprised (or so he said) that *Weird Tales* accepted the stories.

ing up to date, additional research, etc.—might interest them sufficiently to merit their attention. Paul Brooks of Houghton Mifflin suggested that I send these out to persons whom I thought to literary promise" (*ES* 765). Brooks (1909–1998), environmentalist, writer, and editor, was editor-in-chief at Houghton Mifflin for twenty-five years and editor for both Rachel Carson and Roger Tory Peterson. Lovecraft, as usual, demurred, though this time undoubtedly because of his highly weakened state. He wrote:

> Regarding the Houghton-Mifflin fellowship blank—extreme thanks for the compliment of sending it! Actually, I don't believe it would be wise for me to make any promises or assume any obligations in my present state of uncertain health and depleted energies (I've had to sidetrack a speculative proposition of Talman's for lack of strength to do one single thing more than I'm doing)—for nothing is more ignominious than biting off more than one can chew. (*ES* 767)

By now Lovecraft was acutely aware that his health was failing.

Within a month Lovecraft was dead, and his only book, *The Shadow over Innsmouth* (1936), a shoddy if well-intentioned book containing a single story, was a rather poor literary legacy. With the single greatest impediment to Lovecraft having a book published—Lovecraft himself—no longer in the way, August Derleth now sought to have a collection of Lovecraft's work printed. He himself ran into the usual excuses from publishers—these being companies he worked with himself. They were not interested in collections of stories but wanted novels instead. In light of such lack of interest, he published a book of Lovecraft's work himself, with the assistance of R. H. Barlow and Donald Wandrei.

Lovecraft's reaction to rejections from book publishers seems disingenuous. He is quick to notify correspondents "in each case I submitted it only at the publisher's request" (*Letters to Robert Bloch and Others* 192). He seems to feel that if he made the inquiry to the publisher (as when he submitted stories to *Weird Tales*), he could understand getting a rejection—as he often did. But since the publishers had specifically asked to see his work—had wooed him, as he suggests to Clark Ashton Smith—they should follow through and not merely tease. After all, *they* asked. Even so, Lovecraft still submitted material to publishers when asked, always with some slim hope that there would be an acceptance.

Works Cited

Alfred A. Knopf, Inc. records, Manuscripts and Archives Division, The New York Public Library. MssCol 47. Readers' reports on fiction by H. P. Lovecraft, b. 21 f. 10.

Lovecraft, H. P.. *Letters to F. Lee Baldwin, Duane W. Rimel, and Nils Frome.* Ed. David E. Schultz and S. T. Joshi. New York: Hippocampus Press, 2016.

———. "Letters to Farnsworth Wright." Ed. S. T. Joshi and David E. Schultz. *Lovecraft Annual* No. 8 (2014): 5–59.

———. *Letters to Elizabeth Toldridge and Anne Tillery Renshaw.* Ed. David E. Schultz and S. T. Joshi. New York: Hippocampus Press, 2014.

———. *Letters to Robert Bloch and Others.* Ed. David E. Schultz and S. T. Joshi. New York: Hippocampus Press, 2015.

———. O *Fortunate Floridian: H. P. Lovecraft's Letters to R. H. Barlow.* Ed. S. T. Joshi and David E. Schultz. Tampa, FL: University of Tampa Press, 2007. [Abbreviated in the text as *OFF.*]

———, and August Derleth. *Essential Solitude: The Letters of H. P. Lovecraft and August Derleth.* Ed. David E. Schultz and S. T. Joshi. New York: Hippocampus Press, 2008. [Abbreviated in the text as *ES.*]

———, and Clark Ashton Smith. *Dawnward Spire, Lonely Hill: The Letters of H. P. Lovecraft and Clark Ashton Smith.* Ed. David E. Schultz and S. T. Joshi. New York: Hippocampus Press, 2017. [Abbreviated in the text as *DS.*]

Thanks to Derrick Hussey for bringing my attention to the Knopf records, to Jordan Douglas Smith for obtaining copies of them, and to Kenneth W. Faig, Jr., and Christopher O'Brien for their usual insightful comments.

Two Centenaries: H. P. Lovecraft and Elsa Gidlow

Kenneth W. Faig, Jr.

In my first message in the *Fossil* for October 2014, I commented on the centenaries of the beginning of World War I in August 1914 and of the founding of the Providence Amateur Press Club on October 30, 1914.

Nearly four years have now turned on the calendar, and we will not mark the centenary of the end of World War I until November 9, 2018. However, the arrival of July 2017 provides occasion to celebrate the centenaries of the commencement of two notable presidencies of amateur journalism organizations: the election of H. P. Lovecraft (1890–1937) to the presidency of the so-called Hoffman–Daas faction of the United Amateur Press Association in Chicago, Illinois, and the election of Elsie Alice Gidlow (1898–1986) (later known as Elsa Gidlow) to the presidency of the so-called Erford–Noel faction of the same association in Montreal, Canada, at about the same time. Verna McGeoch was elected as official editor of Lovecraft's faction and dutifully produced six bimonthly numbers of the *United Amateur* during her term, while Gidlow's official editor, Chester O. Hoisington, managed only one number of the rival official organ.

Lovecraft had been recruited for the Hoffman–Daas faction of the UAPA in April 1914 by Edward F. Daas (1879–1962) himself, as a result of his participation in a long-running "war" over the romantic fiction of Fred Jackson in the letter column of the *Argosy*. He was appointed chair of the Department of Public Criticism by President Dora Hepner as early as October 1914 and continued in that office through 1919, with the exception of his presidential term in 1917–18, when the work was taken over by his friend and fellow poet Rheinhart Kleiner. Edward H. Cole (1892–1966) of Somerville, Mass., early on connected Lovecraft with the Providence Amateur Press Club, founded by evening high school alumni and alumnae in Providence at the end of October 1914. Irishman John T. Dunn (1889–1983) was probably the central figure in the club; Lovecraft eventually broke with him because of his refusal to register for the draft and his resulting imprisonment. Lovecraft became known for intellectual controversies with Charles D. Isaacson, Elsa Gidlow, F. Graeme Davis, and others in the columns of his own amateur journal, the *Conservative*, of which he published thirteen numbers between 1915 and 1923. Lovecraft was advanced to First Vice President of his association as early as its Rocky Mount (North Carolina) convention in July 1915. Curiously, however, he was never to attend any of the conventions of his faction of the UAPA. Perhaps his mother's fragile health and her unfavorable opinion of the hobby inhibited his attendance.

Perhaps the most notable event of Lovecraft's 1917–18 UAPA presidency was his decision to join the NAPA in early November 1917. NAPA stalwart F. Graeme Davis had been railing against the UAPA in the editorials in his *Lingerer* in 1917. However, when he became NAPA's Official Editor in July 1917, Davis agreed to forego attacks on the UAPA if Lovecraft would do the same regarding the NAPA. UAPA hard-liners like Edward F. Daas were furious with Lovecraft for joining the NAPA, but the president maintained that his action would help to promote inter-association cooperation and to dampen feuding and raiding for members. Lovecraft was succeeded by three friendly UAPA presidents: his friend Rheinhart Kleiner (1918–19), Mary Faye Durr (1919–20), and his protégé Alfred M. Galpin (1920–21). He served as official editor in Galpin's administration and carried over to the same position under the succeeding president Ida C. Haughton (1921–22). Lovecraft and Haughton, however, had a rocky relationship. She wanted him to broaden the appeal of the *United Amateur* and to open its columns to contributors other than his own circle of literary friends. In addition, she infuriated him by accusing him of mishandling the Official Organ Fund. In a stinging rebuke, the members of the UAPA voted Lovecraft and his faction out of office in the succeeding administration of Howard Conover (1922–23).

When his old opponent William B. Dowdell resigned the presidency of the NAPA at the end of November 1922, Lovecraft's friend James F. Morton, as a member of the NAPA's board of executive judges, recruited Lovecraft to assume the NAPA presidency. Edward H. Cole wanted Lovecraft to stand for a full term as NAPA president in 1923–24, but Lovecraft declined the honor. His future wife, Sonia H. Greene, was elected UAPA president in July 1923, and Lovecraft served as Official Editor. They were returned to the same offices for the 1924–25, after Lovecraft had married Greene on March 3, 1924. But the United of which they assumed the helm in 1923–25 was a pale shadow of the lively association of 1915. Alma Sanger, the former treasurer in the Howard Conover administration (1922–23), refused to turn over the funds in the treasury. As a result, Mr. and Mrs. Lovecraft were able to produce only a few thin issues of the *United Amateur*. For the 1925–26 term, Lovecraft's friend Edgar J. Davis was elected President, and his recruit Victor F. Bacon Official Editor, but activity virtually ceased. No officers were ever elected for the 1926–27 year, and the so-called Hoffman-Daas United perished. The only United left in the field was the one presided over by Roy Erford and Clyde Noel from Seattle. After having lived in New York City since his marriage, Lovecraft moved back to Providence in April 1926. He did not involve himself again actively in amateur affairs until he attended Boston's NAPA convention in 1930. He did yeoman's service on the NAPA's board of critics in 1931–35, serving as chair in 1933–35, and was elected an executive judge in 1935–36 in honor of his service. (He had previously served in that role in 1923–24—a traditional role for the retiring president.) He died, aged only forty-six, of cancer on March 15, 1937. Of course, his professional writings, beginning in *Weird Tales* in 1923, eventually secured his fame. His *Tales*, selected by Peter Straub, were published as a volume in the prestigious Library of America in 2005.

Lovecraft's rival president, Elsa Gidlow, became famous in her own right. She became active in the rival United association about the same time as Lovecraft. At age nineteen, she served as in-house editor for a company paper, *Factory Facts*. By 1917, she had gathered around herself a literary circle including students at

McGill University in Montreal. They began to publish a spirit-duplicated paper, initially titled *Coal from Hades*, but eventually retitled *Les Mouches Fantastiques* (*The Fantastic Flies*). Gidlow and her associate Roswell George Mills (1896–1966) also published work in W. Paul Cook's *Vagrant*. Aesthetically, Gidlow was an advocate of free verse. Philosophically, she and her circle attacked traditional religious values and advocated a materialistic, hedonistic outlook on life, including advocacy of same-sex love.

Gidlow had published her poem "Two Lovers" and Mills his poem "Once" in Cook's *Vagrant* for June 1918. Writing to his friend Rheinhart Kleiner on May 5, 1918, Lovecraft commented:

> Cook's latest *Vagrant* is assuredly a marvel. The literary standard is this time even higher than before, I think. The esthetic Elsa Gidlow's outburst could undoubtedly be a great deal worse, as free verse is reckoned. Of the "two lovers that woo her unceasingly," I would advise her to choose oblivion. That is the best way for all *vers-libristes*. Her colleague, Rossy George, tangles himself all up in some words & phrases, in which a trace of metre is observable. His spasms, however, are less definite in thought (if, indeed, there be any definiteness in imagistical chaos!) & less meritorious altogether. (*Letters to Rheinhart Kleiner* 137)

Lovecraft's protégé Alfred Galpin wrote a parody of Gidlow's poem entitled "Two Loves"; eventually, Lovecraft published Galpin's poem, as by "Consul Hasting," in the *Conservative* for July 1918. In the same number, Lovecraft commented:

> It seems to The Conservative that Miss Gidlow and Mr. Mills, instead of being divinely endowed seers in sole possession of all Life's truths, are a pair of rather youthful persons suffering from a sadly distorted philosophical perspective. Instead of seeing Life in its entirety, they see but one tiny phase, which they mistake for the whole. What worlds of beauty—pure Uranian beauty—are utterly denied them on account of their bondage to the lower regions of the senses! It is almost pitiful to hear superficial allusions to "Truth" from the lips of those whose eyes are sealed to the intellectual Absolute: who know not the upper altitudes of pure thought, in which empirical forms and material aspects are as nothing. (*CE* 1.204)

Gidlow published her signature essay "Life for Life's Sake" in Horace L. Lawson's *Wolverine* for October 1919. She wrote of her life-centered philosophy:

> The usual accusation of materialism need not be advanced to meet Life for Life's sake for it is too absurd. If logic and scientific truth are materialism, we need more materialism, for it is healthy and strong and selfish, and antagonistic to the sentimental idealism that the weak-willed, weak-charactered, weak-minded lean to, and that is the cause, or one of the causes, as well as the effect of their weakness. (33)

In the same month, Mills had published his lesbian play *Tea Flowers,* dedicated to "Sappho" (Gidlow's nickname among her associates), in Cook's *Vagrant.* Earlier the same year, F. Graeme Davis had published an extended defense of *Les Mouches Fantastiques* in his *Lingerer.* "Life for Life's Sake" drew several rebuttals, including Lovecraft's "Life for Humanity's Sake," eventually published in John Milton Heins's *American Amateur* for September 1920.

Davis had risen to the NAPA presidency for the 1918–19 term, but he skipped NAPA's July 1919 Newark convention to spend a month with Gidlow and her circle in Montreal. Davis fell in love with Mills, whom he hoped to make his permanent partner. However, Gidlow's Montreal ménage was not to endure much longer. In March 1920, Gidlow and Mills issued a final, typeset number of *Les Mouches Fantastiques.* They were planning to relocate to New York City and perhaps intended the typeset number of *Les Mouches* as a calling card for American amateurs. Gidlow finally broke away to New York in April 1920, and Mills followed her there a few months later. He subsequently broke Davis's heart by taking Khagendrenath Ghose as his lover.

Young John Milton Heins, son of Charles W. Heins, cultivated the friendship of Gidlow and Mills. Young Heins met Gidlow, Edna Hyde ("Vondy"), and Hyde's fiancé Philip B. McDonald for a May Day outing in Central Park on May 1, 1920. Heins and his father both visited Gidlow in her apartment on 34th Street on September 25, 1920. Later, Gidlow and Mills both attended the famous gathering at the Heins home in Ridgefield, New Jersey, on October 17, 1920. This gathering was made famous by Edna Hyde's alleged rude treatment of her hosts, which young John Milton Heins publicized in his magazine, the *American Amateur*, where he was also publishing the works of Gidlow and Mills. Heins had published a scathing article by Gidlow, entitled "The Literary Decadence of E. G.," in his number dated July 1920. She declared:

> That is what is wrong with amateur journalism—it is futile. None of its members appear to have anything to say, yet they write unceasingly. I have read all amateur journals that have appeared during the past six years and I can truly say that I have not found in those journals, in all that time, as many as six original ideas, or six artistic expressions of any sort of ideas. (35)

She wrote scathingly of amateurdom's poets:

> All amateurdom is pervaded by an atmosphere of middle age, mustiness, fossilism. Every pseudo-poet writing in AJ imitates or plagiarizes Poe, Shelley, Keats, Wordsworth or Pope, and some bend their muse to lengthy pastorals. The favorite subjects of the prose writers are mysticism, politics or theosophy, evidently culled and rehashed from Sunday afternoon forums and newspapers.
>
> If these were the first fluttering attempts of younglings, one could be tolerant, trustful of development, but this is not so. Most of these offenders are middle-aged, settled and hopeless and they will ride their wooden "hobby" at a dull, satisfied joy-trot till it or they shall crumble.
>
> There is Mr. Goodenough with his rhymed very-moral maxims; Mr. Lovecraft with his morbid imitations of artists he seems not even able to understand; Mr. Ward Phillips who admires Poe wisely and far too well, since he mimics him so laboriously, and a host of others, male and female, who apart from having no new word to speak, cannot write three consecutive rhymed verses in even metre, although they raise their voices continuously and wildly against "modern" poetry and that in their opinion heretical expression of a perverted intellect, *vers libre*. (36)

Pearl K. Merritt, James F. Morton, and Lovecraft all replied to Gidlow's essay in the pages of the *American Amateur*. Lovecraft's response in "Life for Humanity's Sake" was fairly measured:

> Miss Gidlow has discovered the fact that there is no vast su-

> pernatural intelligence governing the cosmos—a thing Democritus could have told her several centuries B.C.—and is amazingly disturbed thereat. Without stopping to consider the possibility of acquiescence in a purposeless, mechanical universe, she at once strives to invent a substitute for the mythology she has cast aside; and preaches as a new and surprising discovery the ancient selfish hedonism whose folly was manifest before the death of its founder Aristippus. (*CE* 5.45)

Perhaps he revealed his real feelings toward Gidlow more clearly in his comments in "Lucubrations Lovecraftian" in the *United Cooperative* for April 1921:

> In the July *American Amateur*, the precocious Miss Elsie (alias Elsa) A. Gidlow of *Les Mouches* fame refers with admirable courtesy to "Mr. Lovecraft with his morbid imitations of artists he seems not even able to understand." Perhaps Mistress Elsie-Elsa would prefer that the amateurs follow her own example, and perpetrate morbid imitations of morbid artists whom nobody outside the asylum is able to understand. (*CE* 1.284)

Lovecraft made his hatred of Mills even clearer in his letter to Rheinhart Kleiner dated May 21, 1920:

> As to day-dreams & Rossie George—I am afraid that the wildest of his flights is rather tame compared with what I have seen in other universes whilst asleep. He can't even get off this one poor planet, or rise much above the animal instincts here. Carcass-worshippers like Rossie & Elsie make me so infernally sick & tired that I lack patience with them. This reminds me—I never shewed you that putrid fellow's letter, which he wrote me last summer. I promised to do so, & will enclose it herewith. My personal comment is twofold: (a) Nobody home. (b) Throw it in the garbage pail behind the house & cover well with chloride of lime. Kindly return this bit of mental & moral aberration for preservation as a horrible example in my private museum of mental pathology. (*Letters to Rheinhart Kleiner* 190)

Mills's letter to Lovecraft does not appear to survive among Lovecraft's papers as preserved in the Lovecraft Collection at Brown University.

Gidlow and Lovecraft were both residents of New York City in 1924–26, but there is no evidence that they ever met. For part of this time, Gidlow worked as a cataloguer for the antiquarian bookseller W. A. Gough. While she resided in New York, Will Ransom of Chicago published Gidlow's first collection of poetry, *On a Grey Thread* (1923), often described as the first volume of explicitly lesbian poetry published in the United States. In 1926, the same year Lovecraft returned to Providence, Gidlow migrated to the San Francisco Bay Area, where she spent the rest of her life. She published a further poetry collection, *Sapphic Songs* (1976), and her autobiography, *Elsa: I Come with My Songs* (1986). On February 9, 1937, she wrote to Edwin Hadley Smith of her involvement in the amateur journalism hobby:

> I have pleasant memories of amateur days and some friendships grew out of them. Some of us had fun editing and publishing. I imagine the members did not realize what a child I was when they were corresponding—about 15 or 16 when invited to join the association. Since 1921 I have been a professional writer, editor, or journalist of one sort or another. (Faig, "Il Duce's Sons" 20–21)

Gidlow numbered Kenneth Rexroth and Alan Watts among her friends in San Francisco. She devoted much time to her artists' community at Druid Heights. In old age, she traveled to Japan and China and was admired as a spokesperson for women's rights. She had two long-term lovers, Violet W. L. Henry-Anderson, who died in 1935, and Isabel Grenfell Quallo.

As for the other players, Roswell George Mills spent much time in Europe in the 1920s, but eventually returned to the New York area. He was working as a reporter for the *Brooklyn Eagle* and resided with his widowed mother when he registered for the draft in 1942. Eventually, he retired to Miami, Florida, where he died in 1966. F. Graeme Davis, who had been ordained as an Episcopal priest in 1910, was deposed from the priesthood in 1925. He subsequently became a Liberal Catholic priest, then an Old Catholic bishop in Chicago. He attended NAPA's 1934 Chicago convention in full bishop's regalia and published one last amateur journal, *Letters from the Lingerer*, in 1937, the year before his death.

I don't know how many amateur journalists of today will find much to remark in the lives or the work of Lovecraft and Gidlow. For me, they remain two of the most interesting figures who ever participated in our hobby.

Works Cited

Faig, Kenneth W., Jr. "Lavender Ajays of the Red Scare Period: 1917–1920." *Fossil* No. 329 (July 2006): 5–17.

———. "Were Il Duce's Sons Amateur Journalists?" *Fossil* No. 345 (July 2010): 18–22.

Gidlow, Elsie A. "Life for Life's Sake." *Wolverine* No. 5 (October 1919); rpt. in *Fossil* No. 329 (July 2006): 33.

———. "The Literary Decadence of E. G." *American Amateur* 1, No. 5 (July 1920); rpt. *Fossil* No. 329 (July 2006): 35–36.

Lovecraft, H. P. *Letters to Rheinhart Kleiner*. Ed. S. T. Joshi and David E. Schultz. New York: Hippocampus Press, 2005.

Portions of this essay originally appeared in Graeme Phillips's journal *Cyäegha* (whole no. 7) for Autumn 2012 under the title "Gidlow versus Lovecraft." A revised edition appeared as "President's Message: Centenaries Once More," *Fossil* No. 329 (July 2017): 5–8.

2001: A Lovecraftian Odyssey

Michael D. Miller

The remarkable cultural endurance of Stanley Kubrick's *2001: A Space Odyssey* and the literary works of H. P. Lovecraft resonate today perhaps more than ever before. The longevity of these works may be attributed to their unprecedented visions of our future, to imagining contact with alien races beyond human intelligence, or subjective epiphany through terrifying confrontations with the unknown. What becomes evident (when examined in unison) as the quality giving these works a lasting impact beyond their time and ours is cosmicism. The cosmic as an element in speculative fiction is one of Lovecraft's greatest contributions to the field, and his last works (certainly "The Shadow out of Time") even project his vision beyond the future of human existence. Spanning millennia after the year 2001 C.E., Lovecraft imagines events such as these: in 2518, the Australian physicist Nevil Kingston-Brown, who exchanged minds with one of the Great Race of Yith, dies; in the year 16,000, the wizard Nug-Soth exchanges minds with a Yithian; the year 50,000,000, when a new race of beetle-like insects arises possessed by the Great Race of Yith; and even further, a billion years or more in the future, the last inhabitants of Earth, a species of arachnids, live within the interior of the dying world. That great expanse of time is one component of cosmicism, as is interstellar mind-exchange, and these are the same aspects that give *2001: A Space Odyssey* a life beyond the first year of the twenty-first century.

A more direct explanation of this can be found in Richard L. Tierney's remark, "Lovecraft turned the whole universe into a haunted house, so to speak, linking the findings of modern science to the flavor of Gothic horror. In so doing, he created a type of 'creepy' story that 20th Century man could continue to believe in even after the traditional trappings of cemeteries, crumbling castles, haunted mansions, etc., began to acquire the flavor of clichés" ("The Derleth Mythos"). In short, man was no longer alone or the center of the universe. I propose that Kubrick's film is in many ways a visual journey through Lovecraftian cosmicism. As the film moves through four distinct symphonic movements, we will move in a like manner: 1) aliens intercede in human evolution; 2) centuries of advancement allow mankind to unearth a type of ancient object/hidden lore—a Monolith—similar to a Lovecraftian tome with consequences; 3) acquiring the knowledge to travel to a "gate" (while defeating an avatar of "machinism"); and 4) shifting beyond space and time to return as nothing less than the embodiment of "the old (or perhaps new) ones."

I will not be discussing the novel by Arthur C. Clarke, director Stanley Kubrick, the making of *2001*, or its criticisms; however, it is worth noting that Clarke has acknowledged the difficulty of trying to describe superior civilizations or "attempting the impossible." In his memoir, *The Lost Worlds of 2001*, Clarke explains, "Stanley Kubrick and I had to describe—*and to show on screen*—the activities and environments, and perhaps the physical nature, of creatures millions of years ahead of man. This was, by definition, impossible" (188). Lovecraft's work is driven by the eventual confrontation with something that is almost indescribable, or beyond words, yet he possessed the talent to take us as close to the unknown as possible through the narrative style he developed and honed to achieve these ends. We experience the final development of Lovecraft's vision with his alien civilization, the Great Race of Yith, an overwhelming success at describing "the impossible." As for *2001*, Clarke concludes by alluding to Kubrick's remark that "if anything could be written he could film it [. . .] if given unlimited time and budget" (189). Film productions being what they are, Kubrick subverts the dilemma and gives us the Star-Gate sequence (or "the ultimate trip"), which we will see is a visual equivalent to a Lovecraft encounter with cosmic horror. As a starting point, no story after 1936 dealing with alien influence or space-time continuum confrontations exists free of Lovecraft's direct or indirect influence. Even Clarke admits this to some extent, as S. T. Joshi pointed out in his discussion in "Cthulhu's Empire: H. P. Lovecraft's

Influence on His Contemporaries and Successors," when referring readers to Clarke's autobiography, *Astounding Days* (1990), where he speaks enthusiastically of how much he enjoyed *At the Mountains of Madness* and "The Shadow out of Time" when they appeared in *Astounding* in 1936 (34). Even a cursory reading of Clarke's "The Sentinel" (1948) could be summarized as *At the Mountains of Madness* set on the moon. Clarke's short story was used as the initial plot-germ for *2001: A Space Odyssey*.

My own recent experience brushing up with the cosmic in *2001* came from preparing with anticipation a screening of the film for a "Film as Literature" course I was teaching at the same time I was rereading R. L. Tierney's essay, "Lovecraft and the Cosmic Quality in Fiction." Most scholars know that Lovecraft felt those with the cosmic quality were "rarer than hen's teeth" and those of us with that quality may find it hard to explain to the non-cosmic among us. A viewing of *2001* is also mired in the same vacuum, often met with the criticism that it lacks human emotion. Fortunately, Tierney clears this matter up quickly. First he divides fiction into three categories: (1) human centered, (2) human evolution centered, and (3) cosmic centered (194). This division provides the answer for those who dismiss works like *2001* for not conforming to (1) or (2) above. Tierney's description of (3) is of importance, for it clearly applies to Kubrick's film: "the subject attempts to ease the reader away from preconceived notions entirely and leave him with the awed feeling that he really knows nothing about the cosmos at all—*but is about to know*. Its limitation is that it can never really describe, only suggest" (194). This I would argue is also the experience of watching *2001: A Space Odyssey*.

To test this further one need only start with the opening of the film. Silence and blackness the shape of a letterbox . . . a rectangle . . . the Monolith looks at us . . . or we gaze into it . . . Then we are aurally confronted with music (Ligeti's "Atmospheres") while pondering or anticipating this black screen, or alien lifeform, or the abyss of the cosmos itself. This is the first contact with the cosmic and preparation for the odyssey to follow. This type of cosmic experience is described in detail by Lovecraft and quoted in a letter to Clark Ashton Smith that closes Tierney's essay. "As for me, I think I have the actual cosmic feeling very strongly . . .

the lure of unplumbed space, the terror of the encroaching outer void, & the struggle of the ego to transcend the known & established order of time, space, matter, force, geometry, & natural law in general" (194). With that as context, it shouldn't surprise anyone that in discussions following the screening of the film, one student responded with paraphrasing Lovecraft's famous insight: "The oldest and strongest emotion of mankind is fear, and the oldest and strongest kind of fear is fear of the unknown."

1. At the Dawn of Madness

The use of "distancing devices" by connecting them to the evolving plot of a story is a staple in most weird fiction, and Lovecraft pioneered its use with his erudite knowledge of the past. When used effectively as enhancements for the mood of a story, ancient temples in Syria or forgotten monolithic stones in the decadent countryside expand the sense of narrative depth approaching the cosmic. Lovecraft's signature move to connect these distancing devices to an eons-older outside world in *At the Mountains of Madness* (with the revelation that mankind is nothing but an experiment of a far older alien race) is one of the greatest instances of terrifying cosmicism. Dyer narrates what he and Danforth have pieced together: "[T]he builders of the city were wise and old, and had left certain traces . . . in rocks laid down before the true life of earth had existed at all. They were the makers and enslavers of that life . . . the Great Old Ones that had filtered down from the stars when earth was young . . . It is of course impossible for me to relate in proper order the stages by which we picked up what we know of that monstrous chapter in pre-human life" (*CF* 3.91–93). Yet by 1968, more than thirty years after the story's publication, this idea may have no longer been usable as such a revelation.

Kubrick's film starts with the interstellar involvement with a distancing device right away. A black Monolith appears and transmits its influence before mankind had evolved from its ape ancestors. It is worth mentioning that *in the film,* this influence may not necessarily be the assumed good intention of providing primitive man with a nudge to use technology. Contact with this Monolith gives a group of somewhat peaceful primitives a lesson in how to hunt better with use of weapons, but this development signals much more significance. With effective use of the cosmic, the film moves into the future via the famous match-cut, placing us in the atmosphere with an orbital satellite. But a study of the matter reveals it is a nuclear-armed satellite capable of massive obliteration of life. In this sense, the alien hand in human civilization evolves from learning to kill a single enemy to engineering mass extinction. In this light the initiation at the dawn of man is quite terrifying, and certainly in the realm of a Lovecraftian use of cosmicism.

While Lovecraft the writer makes all this work through his literary style and sense of narrative, the film must find a substitute for language; and the combination of visual imagery with powerful music is how *2001* crafts its cosmic mood. Only a few seconds into Ligeti's chilling *Requiem for Soprano, Mezzo Soprano, Two Mixed Choirs and Orchestra* combined with the overbearing Monolith in sync with the planets in alignment (an image you might say substitutes for the phrase "the stars are right") produces a true cosmic experience. The music itself is cosmic in the sense that it challenges and transcends known, accepted forms of music. A pioneering work of *micropolyphony,* Ligeti's composition overlaps, molds, and reshapes vocal musical lines until sounding unintelligible. I think Lovecraft would have found this satisfying, as it also seems to fulfill certain descriptions in "The Music of Erich Zann." "I often heard sounds which filled me with an indefinable dread—the dread of vague wonder and brooding mystery. It was not that the sounds were hideous, for they were not; but that they held vibrations suggesting nothing on this globe of earth" (*CF* 1.286). The key concepts of "dread" and "vague wonder" continue throughout the film.

2. *Cosmic Waltz*

There could be a lot of conjecture on whether this movement of the film evokes the cosmic and if Lovecraft would have embraced such long-extended musical sequences. It certainly seems to be going away from anything resembling Poe's "unity of effect" (but Lovecraft would abandon this as well with his longer works, dwelling in the "musicality" of his description for the sake of sustaining mood). Writer/critics like Harlan Ellison have even pointed these weaknesses out: "So now we go from the ape hurling the bone-weapon into the air, to the space-shuttle spinning down through the void to dock (at unbearable length) at the space station. They take half the two hours and x minutes of the film to let you in on the big deal surprise of another monolith being discovered on the Lunar surface" (69). But the way to truly understand this cosmic waltz is that cosmicism has two sides, horror *and* wonder. Wonder is certainly something the cosmic can embrace, "an unsettling experience that makes one aware there might be more to the perceived object than meets the eye" (Pedersen 26). Or in simpler terms, waltzing to wonderment. Only speculation can address how Lovecraft might have responded to the role music plays in the film. As S. T. Joshi has discovered in the essay "Further Notes on Lovecraft and Music," Lovecraft "was so thorough a student of the eighteenth century that it is a tragedy that he did not expand his appreciation to the domain of music" (25). This would be a hard task for the music Kubrick selected. For the most part recordings were not yet mass-marketed during Lovecraft's lifetime. *The Blue Danube* was before Lovecraft's time and Johann Strauss II had been dead since 1899. *Also Sprach Zarathustra* and Richard Strauss were of his time, but this song was not recorded until 1936. The remaining composers, Gyorgy Ligeti and Aram Khatchaturian wrote their musical selections long after Lovecraft's time. We have only Joshi's scholarship for further insight: "Lovecraft seemed more attuned to vocal music than to instrumental—although of Wagner's he singles out the 'Ride of the Valkyries,' and Alfred Galpin records that Lovecraft was strongly affected by Chopin's instrumental work" (25).

Yet this movement does have one element Lovecraft surely would have respected: the "fascistic socialism" on display in the future. Much of the imagery and structuring of society in the movement recall Lovecraft's letters with Robert E. Howard. Without going into specific detail in the film (although a viewing of the briefing scene on Clavius would suffice), it seems that this society (with its orbiting nuclear weapons) has carried out many of the ideas of Lovecraft's letter from 7 November, 1932:

> A strong organization of fascists, led by university economists and students of history and with official administrative posts filled

> with members of the old executive class (duly chastened by the proletarian menace and willing enough to work for any responsible government, plutocratic or not), would then have a very good chance to sweep into power—backed by the militant and enthusiastic youths of the intelligible middle class. It would, of course, have to be military in character . . . But once the ideology was established, its possibilities for effective and harmonious civil functioning would be enormous. (*Means to Freedom* 472)

Most future speculative fiction does feature societies in various states of Lovecraft's "fascistic socialism," including the use of government cover-up. *2001* hides the discovery of the Moon-Monolith from all but the highest-level administrators just as they hide the true nature of the Jupiter mission from the crew of the *Discovery*. Lovecraft had already established such cover-ups in the U.S. government's bombing of Devil Reef in "The Shadow over Innsmouth" (and to a lesser extent in the cover-up of events in "The Colour out of Space").

3. *Heuristically Dissociated Algorithmic Knowledge*

While this movement of the film may seem the least cosmic and more of an action sequence (hence its place as a favorite for many fans), we are still surrounded by reminders of isolation and insignificance—the sounds of breathing, the tight confines of the *Discovery*, the vulnerability of space walks, and the unflinching stillness of the black void filling most of the scene frames. We are still at the mercy of space. The importance of this movement in a Lovecraftian sense is that most of his tales involve a direct confrontation with something life-threatening—not to defeat it and save the day (as occurs in "The Dunwich Horror" or the work of many Lovecraft imitators), but in order to escape and tell the tale or, in rare occasions, to merge into a new life form. These sequences are similar to classical narratives where the protagonist must survive a journey to the underworld to continue a quest. When such an odyssey is of the cosmic quality, the underworld is a confrontation with the embodiment of a meaningless and uncaring universe.

HAL serves in many ways like an "outer god" similar to confrontations with Yog-Sothoth or Nyarlathotep. They need to be "shut down" or prevented from crossing the gate or, in HAL's view, from taking over the mission. As such a test is the one "not-so-cosmic" element in this type of fiction; the movement champions humanity as victor over what I'll call "machinism." Lovecraft and others of his time had no love of "machine-like" existence. Lovecraft even included this in the history of the Old Ones, who found a mechanized state dissatisfying. His own view was, "The future of civilisation of mechanical standardisation of life *and thought* [my emphasis] is a monstrous and artificial thing which can never find embodiment either in art or religion" (quoted in Joshi, "Alien Civilisations" 129). So within this movement, it is Lovecraftian to defeat HAL, even if part of the victory requires physical action—having to blow the airlock when HAL refuses to open the pod bay doors. This moment of action is almost like a Howardian response that surfaces as it rarely does in Lovecraft during his exchanges with Howard: "I am not blind to the need of preserving a certain amount of the old physical stamina as a supplement to the newer qualities" (*Means to Freedom* 422). Without the action of reverting to violence, HAL—the Heuristic Algorithm—survives and makes the journey through the star-gate. Interestingly, correlation of dissociated knowledge spells the end of many protagonists, but the process is reversed with HAL where the correlation is essentially undone to his memory circuits (think of the red eye as Yog-Sothoth or Nyarlathotep sent back into the gate). Humanity wins but for a second, then the cosmic element of the film is back with a vengeance.

4. *The Colour out of the Star-Gate*

From this point onward there are no words in the film; it is simply image and music, the cadence of the cosmic. This is established once again by a flying Monolith, planets in alignment, and the "Erich Zann–like" sounds of Ligeti's *Requiem.* There is something about color, and the visual color trip that Bowman (and the audience) go through, that merges both wonder and terror. Watching the facial expressions of Bowman as he traverses the space-time continuum shows us this as a maddening horrific event. He shakes and trembles, going through physically what we as watchers cannot, while the color spectrum light show locks us into the cosmic unknown.

Lovecraft existed in a world of black and white, at least when considering the films, photography, and print media of the time. There is even some recorded research done from studies on children that grew up watching only black-and-white movies where they describe dreaming in black and white, something none of us now can imagine. It is in the color that wonder is brought back into the odyssey along with the dread of the unknown. Lovecraft was very keen on using color to evoke the dimensional magnitude of cosmic events. In "The Colour out of Space" we get all the horror and wonder of the Star-Gate:

> It was a scene from a vision of Fuseli, and over the rest reigned that riot of luminous amorphousness, that alien and undimensioned rainbow of cryptic poison . . . seething, feeling, lapping, reaching, scintillating, straining, and malignly bubbling in its cosmic and unrecognizable chromaticism . . . a bombarding cloudburst of such coloured and fantastic fragments as our universe must needs disown. (*CF* 2.396)

If it can be written, it can be filmed. Director John Landis once remarked at a fortieth anniversary screening of the film: "Prepare to have your minds blown." To which he could have added: by the unknowable.

Bowman's journey ends not so pleasantly as we find him still in shock inside the pod, experiencing the same epiphany as the narrator of "The Colour out of Space," when he divulges that "It was just a colour out of space . . . from realms whose mere existence stuns the brain and numbs us with the black extra-cosmic gulfs it throws open before our frenzied eyes" (*CF* 2.399). This is probably all the more true considering we swim in the imposed image of Bowman's eye for a good portion of the sequence.

This sequence or "ultimate trip" is permanently seared into the brain of the viewer for reasons beyond color: the music and dissolving images, sometimes inversed, create (as close as we can get in cinema) a time-warp voyage. This visual equivalent with Lovecraft prose is also found in "The Challenge from Beyond," when George Campbell is thrust into a similar trip courtesy of an Eltdown Shard:

> As the mist-blurred light of the sapphire suns grew more and more intense, the outlines of the globe ahead wavered and dissolved into chaos. Its pallor and its motion and its music all

> blended themselves with the engulfing mist—bleaching it to a pale steel-colour and setting it undulantly in motion. And the sapphire suns, too, melted imperceptibly into greying infinity of shapeless pulsation. (*CF* 4.508)

It is historically noted that *2001* gave us visions of earth and space before we were able to photograph them from orbit, but Lovecraft was able to imagine the physical aspect of such travel long before: "The sense of forward, outward motion grew intolerably, incredibly, cosmically swift. Every standard of speed known to earth seemed dwarfed, and Campbell knew that such a flight in physical reality would mean instant death to a human being . . . the quasi-visual impression of meteor-like hurtling almost unhinged his mind" (*CF* 4.508). Campbell and Bowman have gone through similar events, and each emerges in another time and place.

5. *In Lovecraft's Louis XIV Room*

Let's indulge this: H. P. Lovecraft would have been delighted to end up in the eighteenth century. For many neo-classicists and historians of Western civilization, the Enlightenment was the highest level man had ever risen to, so it seems a pleasant irony that it would also be the perfect prison for observation and evaluation by a higher life form. Subject to endless interpretations, this sequence has only a few simple plot points that serve as the climax to the odyssey: Bowman as a prisoner, who ages to the point of natural death, then continues to exist by merging into a higher form. Although similar to the prisoner/observation state in "The Challenge from Beyond," Lovecraft's magnum opus "The Shadow out of Time" has another incarnation of the prisoner as a kind of observation or experiment. "Meanwhile the displaced mind, thrown back into the displacer's age and body, would be carefully guarded. It would be kept from harming the body it occupied, and would be drained of all its knowledge by trained questioners" (*CF* 3.387); or, "When the captive mind's amazement and resentment had worn off, it was permitted to study its new environment and experience a wonder and wisdom approximating that of its displacer" (*CF* 3.387); or even "Now and then certain captives were permitted to meet other captive minds seized from the future" (*CF* 3.388).

The visual end of this climatic sequence is surprisingly simple:

a meal. Is it the last meal? Civilization, and one Lovecraft might have preferred, is cultivated, and even the consumption of food has an elegant aesthetic to it. But what of our captive astronaut Bowman? He reaches for the flute of wine and fumbles with the glass, dropping it from the table, where it smashes on the floor. Broken glass = too clumsy—not good enough for the universe. Movement beyond the enlightenment of the eighteenth century is shattered glass, and alien involvement follows—perhaps to correct its original mistake. . . . Philosophically this echoes the themes of *At the Mountains of Madness* and "The Shadow out of Time" while reaffirming man's insignificant placement in the working of the cosmos as seen through the presence of advanced alien life. Or, if that is going too far, as the Monolith does have *some* interest in human life, we are not so insignificant or different but still our destiny is determined by a higher form—we are only and always will be violent apes no matter our level of technology. Looking at "The Shadow out of Time" directly, even the best of mankind is not possible without outside cosmic influence. "From the accomplishments of this race [i.e., the Great Race] arose all legends of *prophets*, including those in human mythology" (*CF* 3.386). All this was advanced by Lovecraft long before *2001*, "The Sentinel," or the History Channel fad *Ancient Aliens.*

2001: A Space Odyssey crosses the threshold of cosmic wonder, that interstellar point where fear of the unknown and wonderment draw us into the blackness of the Monolith. This experience, to some, may be a nightmare beyond the laws of reality, but to others is a dream of what lies beyond our limited perceptions. As Jan B. W. Pederson surmises in the essay "On Lovecraft's Lifelong Relationship with Wonder," when analyzing Les Edwards's 2010 drawing of Celephaïs, "Further aesthetic appreciations would have us wonder about where [and when] the 'unknown' actually is . . . because it is difficult to locate in any particular time and place" (24–25). This may account for why this scene and its subjective effect on the viewer is one of the most analyzed for interpretation. Another aspect of penetrating this border of fear and wonder is echoed in Pederson's essay when discussing the protagonist Robert Olmstead of "The Shadow over Innsmouth" and the narrator of "The Nameless City." The one action that substantiates a possible cross-over can only be the acceptance of a new reality by "cast[ing] aside his fear of change and transformation in favor of seeking wonder" (32). Bowman's last act, independent of the true (and unknown) motives of the Monolith, seems to be the act of willing transformation or a step forward that is only possible when fear and wonder merge into acceptance.

At this point it must be briefly pointed out that this merger could be one of horror or wonder. As the intention of the Monoliths cannot be fully known, we don't know (in the film) if it is indeed Bowman reaching out to the alien shape to merge willingly and become a higher life form, or if the black vertical rectangle of infinity is actually drawing Bowman into itself. One could propose that Bowman has sacrificed himself to the Monolith so that he (we) can advance to the higher incarnation of the Star-Child. But it is also quite possible (in the film) that this alien Monolith is what is transformed by absorbing the human captive, allowing it to become that Star-Child and return to Earth for a purpose altogether unknown. In this sense the cosmic dread is still all too real, and human life remains at the whim of higher forces in the cosmos, just as it was at the dawn of humanity.

This thematic revelation is quite clear and more ominous in both *At the Mountains of Madness* and "The Shadow out of Time," yet the intentions of alien abductors for merging or transformation in this instance (and the Jupiter Monolith can be viewed as a captor in a certain sense—that Bowman, as he is, will not return from this) is perhaps closer to "The Whisperer in Darkness." The letters of Henry Akeley have a great "before and after" effect on readers once they discover through protagonist Albert N. Wilmarth that an alien abduction/transformation has occurred. While Akeley's mission may be more private concerning the protection of his immediate surroundings, Bowman's situation in *2001* is essentially carrying out the mission parameters. Both of these characters end up more or less as prisoners of a superior alien civilization. Akeley's first letter to Wilmarth relays some interesting remarks and questions not completely unrelated to the Jupiter mission in *2001:*

> *The things come from another planet, being able to live in interstellar space and fly through it* . . . They will not hurt us if we let them alone, but no one can say what will happen if we get too

> curious about them . . . They could easily conquer the earth, but have not tried to so far because they have not needed to . . . They like to take away men of learning once in a while, to keep informed of the state of things in the human world. (*CF* 2.477–78)

These statements could apply to any interplanetary or quasi–science fiction story, and in *2001* they embody the concerns of the mission, including the possibility that these Monoliths are enemies that would reflect the fascistic socialism war state to which humans have evolved in the film. We also have no idea (in the film) what message the Moon-Monolith signaled after it was excavated from its lunar burial mound, but it may have been similar to the recordings made by Akeley—of the sharp intense *buzzing*. Another point for consideration if we go in this direction is that "The Whisperer in Darkness" also features a "black stone" the aliens are seeking to reclaim (while destroying the phonograph records) from Akeley. As noted, these black stones, often covered in strange hieroglyphs, are used quite frequently in cosmic fiction as a talisman for the impossible, a device for transferring alien knowledge, not unlike the Monoliths in *2001*. In Akeley's third letter (dated September 6) we get a chilling revelation that borders on Bowman's own odyssey in completing the mission and passing into the gate: *"They want to take me off alive,* away outside the galaxy *and possibly beyond the last curved rim of space"* (*CF* 2.496). Unlike Akeley, Bowman does this willingly. Then in the mysterious fifth letter from Akeley revealing his change of heart toward the alien species:

> The alien beings desire to know mankind more fully . . . With such an exchange of knowledge all perils will pass . . . The very idea of any attempt to *enslave* or *degrade* mankind is ridiculous. The Outer Ones have naturally chosen me as their primary interpreter on earth . . . In place of terror I have been given a rich boon of knowledge and intellectual adventure which few other mortals have ever shared. (*CF* 2.502)

Of course, we can't trust this any more than we can trust the Bowman/Monolith in the new Star-Child incarnation. The only truth we can ever know is a cosmic one similar to a sentence written near the closing of Akeley's letter (and one that is pure Lovecraft): "The space-time globule which we recognise as the totality of all cosmic entity is only an atom in the genuine infinity which is theirs" (*CF* 2.503). Surely this is the message inherent in the final image of earth juxtaposed in equal size to the imposing image of the Star-Child.

To touch the (or a) Monolith, to merge with an alien form, is the true climactic moment of the film experience where the transformation theme featured throughout the movements of the narrative has been achieved. Not only does it go beyond revelations that protagonists like Olmstead experience as epiphany in yearning to visit "marvel-shadowed Innsmouth," we follow him to "Cyclopean and many columned Y'ha-nthlei," in Bowman's journey through the Stargate, yet the film takes us even further—we return from the transformation itself. Bowman (or the Monolith) arriving as a Star-Child looking over the Earth is in many ways a prophetic fulfillment akin to the return of the "Great Old Ones," as the stars are finally right. From the onset, beginning with Lovecraftian origins of human life and continuing throughout the myth-cycle, the confrontation with this realization is always present. Kubrick had originally conceived the Star-Child showing up to destroy Earth's orbiting nuclear satellites, hinting at a benevolent encounter with advanced life; *the film* implies that we don't know what the arrival portends, and it could mean apocalyptic disaster for life on Earth. It is beyond comprehension.

The whole odyssey then is a journey of painful cosmic alienation, nothing short of Lovecraftian cosmicism. I can imagine Lovecraft perhaps criticizing certain aesthetic choices of the film's storytelling elements, but certainly in this visual poetic quest for transcendence it delivers two elements Lovecraft defined as mandatory for the weird (and cosmic):

> A certain atmosphere of breathless and unexplainable dread of outer unknown forces must be present; and there must be a hint . . . of that most terrible conception of the human brain—a malign or particular suspension or defeat of those fixed laws of Nature which are our only safeguard against the assaults of chaos and the daemons of unplumbed space. (*CE* 2.84)

Lovecraft also "emphasized the importance of evoking a sense of 'outsideness' and 'cosmic dread' in science fiction stories" (Dziemianowicz 194) in his essay "Some Notes on Interplanetary Fiction." S. T. Joshi classified (quasi) science fiction as part of the weird tradition in his thorough study *The Weird Tale.* Whatever supernatural illusion there may be is revealed as a kind of ignorance of natural law (7), in this case revealed through communication with the Monoliths. Thus, *2001: A Space Odyssey*—through the Monoliths as the embodiments of the unknown—is a true Lovecraftian journey of cosmic horror and wonderment.

Works Cited

Clarke, Arthur C. *The Lost Worlds of 2001.* New York: Signet, 1972.

Dziemianowicz, Stefan. Review of H. P. Lovecraft's *Letters to C. L. Moore and Others. Lovecraft Annual* No. 11 (2017): 190–98.

Ellison, Harlan. *Harlan Ellison's Watching.* Los Angeles: Underwood-Miller, 1989.

Joshi, S. T. "Cthulhu's Empire: Lovecraft's Influence on His Successors and Contemporaries." In *Pulp Fiction of the 1920s and 1930s,* ed. Gary Hoppenstand. Ipswich, MA: Salem Press, 2013. 19–35.

———. "Further Notes on Lovecraft and Music." In *Lovecraft and a World in Transition: Collected Essays on H. P. Lovecraft.* New York: Hippocampus Press, 2014. 22–26.

———. "Lovecraft's Alien Civilizations: A Political Interpretation." In *Lovecraft and a World in Transition.* 122–43.

———. *The Weird Tale.* 1990. Berkeley Heights, NJ: Wildside Press, 2003.

Lovecraft, H. P., and Robert E. Howard. *A Means to Freedom: The Letters of H. P. Lovecraft and Robert E. Howard.* Ed. S. T. Joshi, David E. Schultz, and Rusty Burke. New York: Hippocampus Press, 2017. 2 vols.

Pederson, Jan B. W. "On Lovecraft's Lifelong Relationship with Wonder." *Lovecraft Annual* No. 11 (2017): 24–32.

Tierney, Richard L. "Lovecraft and the Cosmic Quality in Fiction." In *H. P. Lovecraft: Four Decades of Criticism,* ed. S. T. Joshi. Athens: Ohio University Press, 1980. 191–95.

———. "The Derleth Mythos." *Nightscapes,* 9 Aug. 2004. www.epberglund.com/RGttCM/nightscapes/NS04/hplnf3.htm.

That Fool Olson

Bobby Derie

In the 1930s, a circle of weird pulp writers developed an interwoven correspondence, with prominent members including Robert E. Howard, H. P. Lovecraft, Clark Ashton Smith, August Derleth, E. Hoffmann Price, and Henry S. Whitehead. The exact correspondence varied according to the tastes of each, but they all participated in answering letters, circulating stories, lending books, artwork, and other materials, and of course sharing the latest news and leads regarding their mutual field of endeavor. One of the most intriguing sidelights of this mutual correspondence involved a particularly deranged fan, mentioned by Clark Ashton Smith in a letter to August Derleth dated 15 May 1932:

> No word from Bates about my various stories. He sent me yesterday, however, a terrific communication from one G. P. Olsen of Sheldon, Iowa, which had been addressed to me in care of *S.T.* I've had letters from madmen before, but this one really took the gilt-edged angel-cake. Twelve single-spaced pages, much of it phrased with a lucidity almost equal to that of Gertrude Stein or Hegel. Among other things, as well as I could make it out, the fellow seemed to be desirous of correcting certain erroneous ideas about demons and vampires which he had discovered in "The Nameless Offspring." Also, he wanted to point out the errors of Abdul Alhazred! Some of the stuff about vampires was really weird: "You never thought of a Vampire in your life but he appeared like an Emperor or an Archangel." Then he exhorts me to refrain from putting vampires in a bad light, since, by virtue of a little blood-sucking, they really confer immortality on those they have chosen! Later, apropos of godknowswhat, he told me that "you must realize it will never be stood for if you act in any other way than that befitting a Spanish Don." The letter is the damdest

> mixture of paranoia, delusions of grandeur and mystic delirium that ever went through the U.S. mails. The fellow writes of Ammon-Ra and Ahriman—a regular hash of Oriental mysticism—in the language of an illiterate Swede. He ends with something to the effect that his letter is the most momentous intellectual promulgation of the age. I'm not in the habit of ignoring letters; but there's nothing else to be done in this case. (*CAS* 177)

"The Nameless Offspring" was published in the June 1932 issue of *Strange Tales of Mystery and Terror* (which often hit stands a month prior to the cover date), which was edited by Harry Bates. The mention of Alhazred refers to Smith's "The Return of the Sorcerer" (*Strange Tales*, September 1931, the premiere issue), so Olson (or Olsen, as Clark Ashton Smith wrote his name) must have been reading *Strange Tales* from the start. The mention of vampires is odd, as neither of Smith's stories features an actual vampire—"The Return of the Sorcerer" involves another form of undeath, and "The Nameless Offspring" a ghoul—but this appears to have been a characteristic obsession of Olson, as detailed by Robert E. Howard to Tevis Clyde smith in May 1932:

> I've gotten some more letters from that fool Olson, in Iowa. I could endure his lunacy, but his illiteracy gets on my nerves. This time he's frothing at the mouth on account of my "Horror from the Mound". He lashed himself into a perfect frenzy because I said a vampire was really dead. He says that there is no death in the first place, and that Christ was a vampire. Also that a vampire is in "reallity" an idealist, with an earth-gravity of 50 per cent. Whatever the hell that means. He says that I ought to be ashamed "tweesting" the facts around and "making the allmighty God look like the dirtiest devil from Hell." He also says that he is going to "proove" the Medical Society is a pack of fools shortly. He alleges to "proove" his "prooves" by Einstein, Genghis Khan, Napoleon, and other great scientists and philosophers. He seems to have the mysteries of life at his finger tips. Well, what the Hell. (*CL* 2.342–43)

"The Horror from the Mound" appeared in the May 1932 issue of *Weird Tales*. Howard had, ironically, first submitted it to *Strange Tales*, but it was rejected; he wouldn't have a story in *Strange Tales* until June 1932. So it is reasonable that Olson was a regular reader of *Weird Tales* as well as *Strange Tales;* Howard had previously addressed the subject of vampires in "The Moon of Skulls" (*Weird Tales,* June–July 1930) and "Hills of the Dead" (*Weird Tales,* August 1930), and Olson had apparently previously written to Howard about the latter tale (*CL* 2.354, *MF* 1.292). Howard's story was, as described by Jeffrey Shanks and Mark Finn, probably derived from Bram Stoker by way of Universal Pictures and Bela Lugosi (8–9). The vampire de Valdez would be familiar to contemporary readers, a suave nobleman vampire along the lines of Count Dracula; Olson's ideas of vampires, by contrast, are very atypical even by the pulp standards of 1932, not in keeping with traditional Eastern European folklore as used by Stoker in *Dracula* (1897) or Montague Summers in *The Vampire: His Kith and Kin* (1928), or even the more occult notions of the vampire promoted by Helena P. Blavatsky in *Isis Unveiled* (1877).

Olson's comments on gravity recall one of his few fan-letters that has been published, in the November 1932 issue of *Amazing Stories:*

> *Editor,* AMAZING STORIES:
>
> We observe in the August AMAZING STORIES an article under the heading "Discussions" having reference to the nature of "Gravity" as "pushing" the atoms together.
>
> For the information of every one concerned allow us to broadcast the statements made relative to "Gravity" by the "Gravity-Control," a new school of universal mechanics recently organizing.
>
> The "Gravity-Control" proves that the temperature in space using Newton's law of radiation on the figures supplied by Professor Picard, would be minus 780 degrees Fahrenheit (below zero) 40 miles away from the earth and using the same system even a few hundred miles from the earth the temperature would drop several thousand degrees below zero. At about 750 below zero Fahrenheit matter is proved to shrink out of existence, resulting in a vacuum as great as the displacement of matter, it being the case that the "space" holds a condition as if it were filled with solid stone, then stopping the vibration of the atoms because of there being nothing to agitate them. The bottomless cold sets in and the "matter" shrinks away and in its place is the vacuum which is then a greater force of static electricity or sectional hungers. The "Gravity-Control" proves further that this "Space Gravity," because of its furious cold, drove the atom, these later traveling under stark fear, to seek the various planetary centers in the uni-

> verse existent and that the space is lying out there with threatening overpower to hold the planets down in form and order, while the natural mechanisms of the space are operating the elements to bring intellect out of the "matter."
>
> The "Chapter A" of the "Gravity-Control's" "General Universe" deals with this at some length and the remaining chapters of the "Gravity-Control's" "Alphabetically Vibratory Universe" explains the balance so as to connect the beings themselves up with the universe. The "Gravity-Control" is prepared to prove its every statement, using every scientist on earth to prove it and all the philosophers and all the facts that every one knows. "The Gravity-Control" does not merely "believe" it to be so, it proves and shows how men came to live, what they live from and why, and precisely how "gravity" is made and why.
>
> G. P. Olson,
>
> Sheldon, Iowa.
>
> (This letter we publish and leave it to tell its own story as there is not detail enough given to bring out anything like an adequate criticism. —EDITOR.)

"Discussions" was the letter-column section of *Amazing Stories*, and the letter Olson was responding too was presumably Cecil Hollmann's comment on "Worlds Adrift" by Stephen G. Hale (*Amazing Stories*, May 1932). No trace has yet been discovered of "Gravity-Control" in Olson's context, or the *General Universe* text he appears to cite. Whatever Olson's immediate sources, his fan letters appear to be a personal combination of occult metaphysics . . . and physics, as Howard recounts in a later letter to Clyde Smith:

> More gems from Olson: "The A-Rama is Einstein A-Space, the B-Rama is brain or Brama, the C-Rama is Solar Plexus or Pain and in it's cappacity of being organic Pain it is Visshnue the creator and the D-Rama is that thing we know as Drama, which is the four-armed ballance of Shiva the destroyer, being the basical gender in nature and being in effect also sex, since sex and ellementairy nature is the same thing actually, as soon as I explain it——" "The chief thing Jesus tried to impress was that want is in itself all-might and that by means of training the mind for greater wants and the body to hold greater hungers, if anything hapens to the consciousness, the atoms hold the hunger and do not break in decay, accordingly as the stomack eats up the filler and the blood thins down, the person comes up with high hungers and if he is a

> fool he is then a vampire." "Accordingly, no vampire, however vampirally ignorant he may be, can possibly be as vampirical as yourself and all the people of the earth, since not knowing this, you account not at all the strict code that is Mrs. Cornelius Van-derBilt or Mrs. Astor or that of any Duke or Duchess of the world—Why do you suppose that a Duke considers that he may withouth regrets pierce with his sword a man that refuses to pay him respect—A man that refuses to stop and utterly postpone the filling of his hungers the instance the Duke appears in the vicinity?" He also sends me a damnable chain letter and tells me I dare not refuse to continue the chain. Like hell I don't. I might excuse his insanity, but writers of chain-letters are a blight and a stumbling block on the road of progress. (*CL* 2.350–51)

This rant at least contains a few more recognizable elements: "Brama" (Brahma), "Visshnue" (Vishnu), and Shiva are deities in the Hindu religion and form a divine trinity; the forehead and solar plexus are typically associated with chakras in tantric yoga, and so suggest Olson was tapping into Hindu or Theosophical materials. The reference to Einstein's "A-Space" is vague, but appears to be an interpretation of Einstein notation with regards to his theory of General Relativity—although I've yet to find a source that uses the exact nomenclature, Einstein notation does involve the use of vectors. Howard apparently communicated something of Olson to Lovecraft, who replied on 7 May:

> As for this Olson—I haven't ever been honoured by his direct attention, but I have seen some of the letters with which he has been pestering poor Whitehead during the last few months. It appears that he is quite a notorious nuisance among 'scientifiction' writers, especially those contributing to the Clayton magazines. He is—in the opinion of Bates, Whitehead (who has had some experience as a psychiatrist) and myself—a genuine maniac; though we don't know whether or not he is under actual restraint. He may be a relatively harmless case living with his family—though none the less wholly demented in certain directions. He has been giving Whitehead long and frantic lectures on "vectors", and "A, B, and C-space". It seems there is something especially sinister and menacing about C-space—so that it will bring about the end of the world very shortly unless all living sages get busy

> and call in the aid of the "Vectors". Olson also has some startling and unique biological theories. According to him, the blood is not the life but the death. It is our blood which makes us die—and therefore, since food makes blood, the one simple way to become immortal is to discontinue the use of food! Poor devil—I suppose he is an ignorant, weak-brained fellow who saturated himself with odds and ends of popular occult and scientific lore either before or after the crucial thread of sanity snapped. As Whitehead says, there is nothing to do but ignore the letters of a case like that. (*MF* 1.287)

Whitehead had published stories in both *Strange Tales of Mystery and Terror* and *Weird Tales* in the months leading up to May 1932, none of which involve vampires per se, although "Cassius" (*Strange Tales,* November 1931) and "Seven Turns in a Hangman's Rope" (*Adventure,* 15 July 1932) come close. Other writers to whom Olson made a nuisance of himself included August Derleth (*CAS* 289), whose vampire story "Those Who Seek" appeared in *Weird Tales* (January 1932), and Hugh B. Cave, whose vampire tale "The Brotherhood of Blood" was the cover story of *Weird Tales* (May 1932). Cave, in a letter to Carl Jacobi dated 29 April 1932, gives us the longest sustained glimpse at Olson:

> When I first received Olson's letter, I tried hard to analyze it. However, I was stumped for the simple but damnable reason that the man knew more than I did. True, I did check on some of his references, and found him to be basically correct; but it was impossible to find more than one twentieth of those names, etc., in my reference books.
>
> First I formed this opinion: The man was a recluse, living on some dilapidated farm in Iowa. He had become interested in WEIRD TALES and thus studied similar material, going deep into philosophy, metaphysics, and spiritism. BUT he did not have the fundamental education—the a-b-c's—so necessary for a complete understanding of such advanced subjects. And, as a consequence, these studies had unbalanced him.
>
> Later letters from him, however, rather knocked this alalysis to a cocked hat. I believe now that he is a Swede (note his constant references to the Swedish language) He also speaks a mongrel French and Spanish. He is fairly consistent in his arguments,

throughout this whole series of letters; yet the arguments are in themselves the most amazing things imaginable.

Furthermore, you'll notice his constant request (almost a command) that I send copies of his letters to "trusted" men. Also the comments that he has written to Edison, Senator Brookheart, etc. AND RECEIVED ANSWERS.

Now then, perhaps I am making a grave mistake in sending his letters on to you; yet I'm so intensely interested in them myself that I can't resist sharing them. More than that, I'll admit, is my desire to have your opinion on them—and the opinions of your friends whom you mention. I'm stuck with an almighty sensation of helplessness and gross ignorance whenever I look through these letters. I wish I knew more about the things he brings up.

Now then, in conclusion, I suggest (if you want this man to write to you) that you drop him a SHORT note, mentioning that I have sent you copies of his letters, and you would like to hear from him. After that, you need not write him. Nut or not, he is completely enslaved by his theories, and he will welcome the opportunity to write you. When he first wrote to me, the letter so interested me (the same letter I sent on to you before) that I answered as follows: "Dear Sir: Your interesting letter is here and I thank you for it. If you care to write further, I shall be glad to give your letters my careful consideration." That's all. After that one, I got at least a dozen before I wrote again. Then I wrote this way: "I find your letters consistently interesting. As you suggest, I am having copies sent to reliable men who will also be interested." You'll note that I was speaking no lie, and it was merely a ruse to make him keep on writing. I HAVE shown the letters to two reliable men—to my brother and to you.

Now then, I mentioned these letters to Wright and he replied that the man was a nut—had written to all the authors in the magazines he reads. "Paul Ernst got so sick of reading his insane letters that he asked us to drop them in the waste-basket instead of forwarding them."

Ernst many be right, and yet, after reading some of Mr. Ernst's work I'm inclined to think that a study of this "nut's" letters would do Ernst a hell of a lot of good in the way of getting new material, at least. There is material galore in these letters, Carl. They are choked with it. Titles for stories, themes for expansion, descriptions, basic ideas for horror, names which suggest fantasies—everything you could wish. Even more than that, perhaps, is the "padding" material—stuff which can be included in your horror stories to give them an air of authenticity and realism.

Now then, back to Olson. I believe he is a Swede, as I've already said. I don't take his spelling to be a sign of ignorance—rather to be a sign of his unfamiliarity with our language. He knows the root words and knows their origin, which is fundamentally more than a mere knowledge of English. He has, I believe, studied enormously.

So I'm sending, with this letter, all the stuff he has written. Take your time reading it, Carl. Don't wade in, or you will tire of it in half an hour. Look it over at your leisure. Take a month or two. TYPE OUT ANYTHING THAT MAY BE MATERIAL FOR YOUR WRITING—and I warn you, you will find plenty. If you feel like making a carbon copy of your notes, for this Cave guy's benefit, I'll appreciate it. Later, when you return these letters, I'm going through them myself, and I'm going to make a list of story titles, ideas, references, descriptions, etc. etc. (everything that has any story appeal)—*and I'll make a carbon for you, too.* It will be both interesting and instructive, and valuable, for each of us to have both lists.

This is only a suggestion. Don't do it unless it appeals. In any event, don't let it slow up your regular work, old man. And, I repeat emphatically, there is absolutely no need to rush through this stuff. I am going up to Maine, fishing, about June 5th, and if I have the stuff (or some of it) then, I may go through it up there. But even that is non-essential and I probably wouldn't even get to it. So figure on keeping these letters at least a couple of months. And you are at liberty, of course, to show them to anyone you like. And if you want to drop Olson a line, in order to get him to write to YOU, that's entirely up to you.

You mention passing this on to Derleth. Judging from the man's letters, I should guess that he has already written to Derleth. Also to Francis Flagg. Flagg, I should say, has been quick to realize the genuine story material beneath all this rambling talk, and has encouraged Olson to continue to write. Derleth might have done the same. You'll note that the man now says (in his last letter) that he is writing to Whitehead. He comments on "The Great Circle."

Finally, the most sensible thing to do is probably to make a

> large haw-haw about all these letters and to heave them into the waste basket. If I were not writing stories for a living, I'd probably do just that. Paul Ernst did so, you see. But the fact remains that these letters mean money—they have ideas. And I intend to keep Olson writing them, even though they at times become boring. Where it will all end I am not sure; but meanwhile I'm curious. My girl is positively afraid of them; and certain statements in these letters would seem to bear her out rather grimly. But what the hell. Stuff like this makes life worth living.
>
> The signature at the end, which you commented on, seems to be Phillips—which may be the man's middle name.
>
> And that's that, Carl. If you don't want to wade through the mess, just shoot 'em back and I wouldn't blame you a nickel's worth. But frankly speaking, I believe this man's letters will go a long way to making us top-notchers with WEIRD TALES, if we go through them carefully and weed out the story material therein. (29 April 1932; cf. Parente 18–19)

While Cave does not quote Olson's letters, there are some interesting details to chew over. "Senator Brookhart" would be Smith Wildman Brookhart, a Republican senator from Iowa (Parente 19). Pulp writer Paul Ernst's work includes the reanimated corpse story "The Tree of Life" (*Weird Tales,* September 1930) and the vampire story "The Duel of the Sorcerers" (*Strange Tales,* March 1932); Francis Flagg (Henry George Weiss) had a scientific vampire story in "The Heads of Apex" (*Astounding Stories,* October 1931)—Flagg was also another of Lovecraft's correspondents. However intense the initial deluge of correspondence Olson sent to Cave, it apparently dropped off just as quickly:

> You've got me all screwy on those nut letters. So much so that I've decided to ignore the writer of them entirely and simply use the letters for what they may or may not be worth. If I were you I wouldn't put too much time on them—merely weed out the few significant things, such as title suggestions, plot ideas, references, etc. Perhaps I shouldn't say "few." They—the letters—were full of such things, as I remember them. Oddly enough I had only one more letter after sending the bunch to you. And since then, nothing. (Cave, 2 June 1932; cf. Parente 19)

While Cave may have wished to coax more material out of Olson, Robert E. Howard was disinclined to humor him, as the Texan wrote to Lovecraft in a letter dated 24 May 1932:

> Poor Olson—what you say of him clinches my conclusion that he is completely insane. I first heard from him a long time ago when he wrote commenting on my "Hills of the Dead"; favorably, by the way. "The Horror from the Mound" seems to have enraged him. He hasn't pulled any "C-Space" or "vectors" on me, though he has had considerable to say about "Ramas" A,B,C, etc.. Neither has he given me the secret of immortality, though he has hinted darkly at it. I've never answered any of his letters, though the impulse has been strong to reply with a missive that would make his ravings sound like the prosaic theorizings of a professor fossilized in conventions. But it would be a poor thing to make game of the unfortunate soul. (*CL* 2.354, *MF* 1.292)

Howard also passed along an abbreviated version of Lovecraft's record of Olson's rantings to Clyde Smith (*CL* 2.369). More interesting, perhaps, is the telephone game as writers passed along news of Olson. When Clark Ashton Smith heard from him, he mentioned it to Lovecraft, and Lovecraft duly passed the news on to Howard in a letter dated 8 June 1932:

> As for the cracked and ubiquitous Olson—Clark Ashton Smith has been hearing from him now. He is fairly frothing at the mouth over what he considers Smith's disrespectful treatment of vampires—who, he argues, are the saviours of the world because they take away the blood which forms the death of us all! Obviously, the poor fellow's epistles admit of no reply. All one can do is to let him keep on writing—which doubtless relieves his agitated and disordered emotions. (*MF* 1.307)

Olson continued to be a point of discussion for Lovecraft and Clark Ashton Smith. In a June 1932 letter, Lovecraft wrote:

> That Iowa nut is a well-known pest of weird & scientifiction writers, & has written some wildly chaotic stuff to Whitehead & Howard. He censures them because they do not invoke "the Vortices" & "C-space" against some peril which is about to destroy our degenerate world. Oh, yes—vampires are noble beings, because

> they help us to get rid of blood—the great poison that drags us down & withholds us from immortality. Christ, he wrote Howard, was a vampire—the greatest of them all. Another thing—we might be immortal if we would abstain from *eating*. Food makes blood, & blood is death. Olson was very eloquent on that point with Whitehead—& I hope it consoled H S for the strict diet he was on then! You seem to have won the longest of all letters from this cracked genius (he's never written me). I wonder how he manages to retain his liberty so long in a cold, materialistic, & uncomprehending world! (*DS* 372–73)

Olson's odd assertion "food makes blood" may owe something to the writings of Hereward Carrington, author of *Death Deferred* (1922), which emphasizes the transformation of food into blood and the beneficial effects of fasting. Lovecraft apparently came to Olson's attention after "The Dreams in the Witch House" was published in the July 1932 *Weird Tales* and received his own letter—much like Smith's, Howard's, and Whitehead's in content, though apparently too offering the "secret of immortality" which Howard said he had hinted at. Lovecraft forwarded the letter to Smith, adding:

> I've seen several of Olson's inspired epistles—here's one he wrote to me. (Please return) Pretty interesting stuff, if one knows what it's about. . . . Hugo the Rat or Efjay Akkamin ought to take it & make a scientifictional masterpiece out of it! Being short of cash, I passed up the opportunity to receive a personal call from Savant Olson—though his offer to come & enlighten me for 25 bucks was truly unselfish . . . . since his round trip from South Dakota would have been away beyond that even on the cheapest 'bus! The true missionary spirit. And to think, I didn't even send the 2 fish for Dr. Conner's "Reflection"! Well—it's not every guy who passes up a chance for "all might & the control of the universe." Fancy! I might, with Olson's aid, have shoved the planets at my will & turned back the hand of time to Ubbo-Sathla itself! (*DS* 477)

"Hugo the Rat" refers to science fiction pulp editor Hugo Gernsback, so called for his non-payment to his writers, including Clark Ashton Smith; and "Efjay Akkamin" is Forrest J Ackermann, a science fiction fan who became embroiled in a conflict with Lovecraft and Smith in the letters columns of the *Fantasy Fan.* The reference to "South Dakota" suggests Olson may have left Iowa in the early 1930s. "Reflection" by Dr. Conner has not been identified. Smith replied on 4 December 1933:

> The Olsen letter, which I return, is most illuminating. Someone, I forget whom, has fathered a book on the sort of cosmogony at which O. is apparently driving. Of course, if you accept the idea that the earth's surface is really the *inside* of a sphere surrounding the negligible remainder of the cosmos, then the space-conceptions implied in your Witchhouse story are most egregiously fallacious. The letter is really a marvel of lucidity compared to the 10 or twelve page monograph on the nobility of ghouls, vampires et al which I received from Olsen in correction of my "Nameless Offspring" and the errors of Abdul Alhazred. It would seem that the bats in Olsen's belfry—or the spirochetae in his spinal column—are less gyrationally active than of yore. However, it is plain that he has not relinquished his position of mentor-in-chief to the *Weird Tales* contributors! His offer to instruct you in person for 25 paltry pazoors is truly magnanimous not to say magnific. (*CAS* 242–43, *DS* 492–93)

The "Hollow Earth" theory has been around in one form or another for centuries, and by the early twentieth century was the domain of cranks, occultists, and fiction writers—he might possibly have been thinking of Marshall Gardner's *A Journey to the Earth's Interior* (1913; rev. 1920). "Spirochetae" is a reference to syphilis, with Smith implying that Olson was suffering from advanced stages of the disease, which can cause delusions and hallucinations; obviously, the Californian never knew that Lovecraft's father had died of neurosyphilis (and it is unknown if Lovecraft himself was aware of the exact nature of his father's terminal illness). Lovecraft in turn echoed:

> Yes—Olsen is certainly less picturesque than he used to be. His early harangues to Whitehead on "C-space" & "the vortexes", & his discourses to Conan the Cimmerian on Christ as a Vampire, exhibit a pyrotechnical ebullience scarcely paralleled in this recent emanation. I recall how he told Canevin that abstinence from food would give one immortality. Blood is death; food makes

> blood; therefore, no food, no death! How simple—yet the world is too dense & callous to accept this great truth & win eternal life! Your Olseniana would seem to be of the really vigorous & colourful sort. I wonder if anybody has ever *answered* one of the fellow's epistles! (*DS* 504)

Smith repeated his assertion that Olson suffered from syphilis in a letter to August Derleth dated 13 April 1937:

> As for me, I'll never forget the letters from that paretic Swede, Olsen; one of which letters corrected at great length certain mistaken notions of Abdul Alhazred. But I remember also that you had some experience with Olsen and his patents of infernal and grandiose nobility! (*CAS* 289)

From that point on, Olson apparently became a familiar enough touchstone to be mentioned in passing in Lovecraft's letters (*Letters to Robert Bloch and Others* 256), but was rarely mentioned. One final reference by *Weird Tales* regular Carl Jacobi's secondhand encounter with Olson:

> In the early days of Weird Tales a compulsive letter writer began to pester some writers whose work appeared in that magazine. A lot of those letters were directed to me. Hugh B. Cave, Clark Ashton Smith, Robert E. Howard and August Derleth were also singled out for his correspondence. This writer was apparently an educated man who had read widely in the fields of psychology, philosophy, and primitive beliefs. But somewhere along the line he had cracked. He would begin with complimentary comments on the receiver's story. Then he would expound some learned treatise. And then the continuity of his letter would fall away, and his madness would become evident.
>
> I still remember what *Weird Tales* editor, Farnsworth Write said about him. "Excuse the mixed metaphor," he wrote me, "but that bird is a complete nut. But we can't stop him from writing." Hugh Cave said he was keeping the fellow's letters on file. Their very "strangeness," he said, made them possible sources for fantasy story ideas. But August Derleth grew tired of this madhouse correspondence and finally wrote the man that his address was changed and that in the future all mail addressed to him—Derleth—should be sent to Rome in care of the Vatican. (Jacobi 96)

This last comment echoes a letter from Derleth to Smith dated 20 May 1932, where Derleth claimed he wrote a letter to Olson "and couldn't resist having a little fun with him" (*DS* 506n9). Other than these fragments, we know very little about this individual; no Olson or Olsen with those initials is listed on the 1930 US census for Sheldon, Iowa. There is currently no evidence of letters from Olsen before 1930 or after 1933, at least in the published correspondence of Howard, Lovecraft, Smith, & co. Probably there's some truth to Lovecraft's assessment that Olson "saturated himself with odds and ends of popular occult and scientific lore"—what with the disparate homebrewed mix of vampirology, Christian apocrypha, Einsteinian physics, Theosophy or Hindu religion, and Hollow Earth Theory—Olson certainly qualifies as one of the weirdest correspondents in a weird circle.

Works Cited

Cave, Hugh B. Letters to Carl Jacobi, 29 April 1932 and 2 June 1932. Carl Jacobi Manuscript Collection. Bowling Green University Popular Culture Library, Ohio. Scans of Cave's letters to Jacobi provided by Bowling Green University's Popular Cultural Library. Permission to quote them here provided by the Hugh B. Cave Irrevocable Trust.

Howard, Robert E. *Collected Letters of Robert E. Howard.* Edited by Rob Roehm. n.p.: Robert E. Howard Foundation Press, 2007–08. 3 vols. [Abbreviated in the text as *CL.*]

Jacobi, Carl (1983). "Some Correspondence." *Etchings & Odysseys* #2 (1983): 96.

Lovecraft, H. P. *Letters to Robert Bloch and Others.* Edited by David E. Schultz and S. T. Joshi. New York: Hippocampus Press, 2015.

———, and Robert E. Howard. *A Means to Freedom: The Letters of H. P. Lovecraft and Robert E. Howard.* Edited by S. T. Joshi, David E. Schultz, Rusty Burke. New York: Hippocampus Press, 2009. 2 vols. [Abbreviated in the text as *MF.*]

———, and Clark Ashton Smith. *Dawnward Spire, Lonely Hill: The Letters of H. P. Lovecraft and Clark Ashton Smith.* Edited by S. T. Joshi and David E. Schultz. New York: Hippocampus Press, 2017. [Abbreviated in the text as *DS.*]

Parente, Audrey. *Pulp Man's Odyssey: The Hugh B. Cave Story.* Mercer Island, WA: Starmont House, 1988.

Shanks, Jeffrey, and Mark Finn. "Vaqueros and Vampires in the Pulps: Robert E. Howard and the Dawn of the Undead West." In *Undead in the West II: They Just Keep Coming,* ed. Cynthia J. Miller and A. Bowdoin Van Riper. Lanham, MD: Scarecrow Press, 2013. 3–25.

Smith, Clark Ashton. *Selected Letters of Clark Ashton Smith.* Edited by David E. Schultz and Scott Connors. Sauk City, WI: Arkham House, 2003. [Abbreviated in the text as *CAS.*]

Briefly Noted

A new annotated edition of some of Lovecraft's stories has been published by McFarland, edited by Leverett Butts, a professor of American literature at the Gainesville campus of the University of North Georgia. Entitled *Selected Works, Critical Perspectives and Interviews on His Influence,* the volume includes the stories "History of the 'Necronomicon,'" "The Call of Cthulhu," "The Color out of Space," "The Dunwich Horror," "The Whisperer in Darkness," and "The Shadow over Innsmouth"; the poems "Waste Paper" and *Fungi from Yuggoth;* and the essay "Supernatural Horror in Literature." In addition, it includes critical essays by S. T. Joshi, Robert M. Price, Shannon N. Gilstrap, Tracy Bealer, Joseph Mulford, and Jim Moon, along with "reflections" on Lovecraft by Brad Strickland, Richard Monaco, and T. E. D. Klein, and interviews of Cherie Priest, Caitlín R. Kiernan, and Richard Monaco.

A Placid Island: H. P. Lovecraft's "Ibid"

Francesco Borri

The story "Ibid" was originally published in 1938, after H. P. Lovecraft's death, in the amateur journal *O-Wash-Ta-Nong*. Information on its existence goes back to the late 1927, when Maurice W. Moe (1882–1940), a longtime friend of Lovecraft, wrote him on 17 December 1927: "a girl cobbled me up a pretty fair theme on 'Friendship' evidently with Bartlett close at hand, and during the course of it she slipped me this: 'As Ibid remarks in his *Lives of the Poets*'" (Lovecraft, *Letters to Maurice W. Moe and Others* 17). Moe was probably referring to John Bartlett's popular *Familiar Quotations* (originally published in 1855 and reissued ever since), while the anonymous girl would have mistaken the author of the *Lives* because of the quotation system of Bartlett's entries. Lovecraft seized the opportunity for a humorous development of this slip-up. Answering Moe, he included a fictional life of the Roman rhetor called Ibid. The story is an impressive testimony of Lovecraft's talent. In the composition, indeed, the odd sentence of Moe is cunningly boosted to the greatest extent and much of the narrative structure appears to be determined by it. As a clear statement of intent, the girl's few words become the opening quotation of the short story.

"Ibid" (*CF* 2.410–16) is among the shortest and most peculiar of Lovecraft's fictions, being one of the very few dominated by a light-hearted content and style meant to amuse its intended single

---

The writing of the research behind this article was financed thanks to the Austrian Research Council through the FWF Project 29004. I would like to express deep gratitude to S. T. Joshi and David E. Schultz for generously providing me with information and ideas that greatly improved my article in many ways. I would also like to thank Katharina von Winckler for help and support.

reader (Joshi, *I Am Providence* 254, 382). The themes and tropes characteristic of Lovecraft's oeuvre do not figure into the story, which recalls the amusing "Old Bugs," written around 1919.

It is perhaps due to its strange nature that the story has not gathered much attention. The purpose of this essay is therefore twofold. First, looking at the excellent work that has been done for the annotated volumes of Lovecraft's fiction and essays, my remarks are meant to offer some background and explanation to the story. Second, these pages are intended to draw near to the fiction's meaning and its place in Lovecraft's broader output.

I.

"Ibid"'s plot is well known. It is a mock-scholarly essay, narrating the shame, glory, and eventual afterlife of a character with the unusual name Ibid (itself the nickname of a much longer one), from the fifth century C.E. up to Lovecraft's days in the early twentieth. Ibid was a gentleman native of Italy, perhaps Rome or Ravenna, who lived a long life among the ruins of the Roman Empire dying at the age of 102. After his death, Ibid became the protagonist of an exciting afterlife, with his skull reaching twentieth-century Milwaukee: his misadventures are staged in the shadow of the era's great men, including emperors, popes, and oddly named American adventurers, as well as the important political and cultural happenings of the age, such as the rise and fall of the barbarian kingdoms, Cromwell's wars in England, and the colonization of New England.

Our hero was born in 481, when Odoacer was ruling Italy (476–93) in the aftermath of the empire's fall of 476. Ibid was a Roman, stemming from the noblest clan of the Anicii (Cameron, "Anician Myths"), even if his Romanness was somewhat "mongrelized" by the unsettled times he was living in. As a boy, Ibid studied in Athens and eventually returned to Italy to become a courtier of King Theodoric (r. 493–526), who had succeeded Odoacer; we may suppose that he must have served under his successors, Amalasuntha (r. 526–34) and Theodahad (r. 534–36), although Lovecraft does not mention these rulers in his narrative. We are in the years when war broke out between the empire and the Goths ruling Italy. It was a long and extended conflict that lasted more the two decades, saw the crushing of countless armies with innumerable victims among the military and the civilian, and witnessed the final breakdown of the Roman structures and (to simplify a bit) the outbreak of the Middle Ages in Italy (Jacobsen). This is also the historical moment that L. Sprague de Camp chose to stage his novel *Lest Darkness Fall*, probably written in 1939 and published in 1941.

Once the usurper Witiges (r. 536–40) rose to power, Ibid fell out of grace, and was briefly imprisoned. Eventually released by the conquering Romans and having shortly joined their armies, he repaired to Constantinople, where he prospered and finally died in 587, under emperor Maurice (r. 582–602), a ruler who greatly admired the venerable Ibid. While Ibid was in Constantinople, the Lombards, a barbarian population like the Goths, had conquered Italy. Led by king Alboin, they had left Pannonia, which was the Central European frontier of the Roman world (between present-day Hungary and Slovenia), and entered Italy in 568. Lovecraft maintained that it was in this time that Ibid's remains were shipped to Italy in order to be buried in Classe, the ancient harbor of Ravenna, at the time one of the capitals of the peninsula. Shortly thereafter, his mortal remains were exhumed by an anonymous Lombard duke of Spoleto who had conquered the Roman town (we know him to be a Faraoald [Gasparri 73]). The Lombard duke carved a bowl out of Ibid's skull, which he eventually gave to Authari, a successor of King Alboin (r. 584–90). The bowl was handed down from king to king until 774, when the Franks conquered Italy. "It was from this vessel, indeed, that pope Leo administered the royal unction which made of the hero-nomad a Holy Roman Emperor." Through the actions of Alcuin of York (735?–804), a courtier of Charlemagne, the vessel was transported to England, where William the Conqueror eventually found it in the unidentified abbey where Alcuin's kinsfolk had placed it. Relocated to Ireland by a "devout papist" in 1539, Ibid's remains were spared by the "rough soldiers" of Oliver Cromwell (1599–1658), when in 1650 they destroyed Ballyclough Abbey.

Captured by the private soldier Read-'em-and-Weep Hopkins,

the skull of the now St. Ibid, "or rather Brother Ibid's, for he [Read-'em-and-Weep] abhorred all that was Popish," was given by him to his son Zerubbabel, who was traveling to New England in 1661, and eventually landed in Salem. The skull went from hand to hand until it was lost in the caves under Lake Michigan. It was only in Lovecraft's day following an earthquake, Ibid's skull re-emerged in Milwaukee. "For there, full in the rifted roadway, lay bleached and tranquil in bland, saintly, and consular pomp the dome-like skull of Ibid!"

II.

The story is clearly an extended pun (in the preface of the Italian edition, Giuseppe Lippi defined it a "scherzo": Lovecraft, *Tutti i racconti* 187). Lovecraft's narrator is a scholar of some sort; I would argue a historian, who is writing a brief biography of the hero Ibid. The narrator has broad knowledge of the past, stronger on the early medieval centuries and the most recent ones of American history, with a deep gap in the between. The two historical periods are treated with striking differences, an outstanding and enigmatic feature of the story.

In the first half, Lovecraft ridicules scholarly debate of minutiae (Joshi and Schultz 123), using the occasion to impress the reader with his own knowledge of a rather obscure time of history (more so then than now). Since the story is a jest, this precondition is the most amusing element of the fiction. The protagonist's name, provided in Moe's letter, echoes the scholarly usage of *ibid.* (which Lovecraft, following Moe, referred in the highly unusual form without the final period). As universally known, *ibid.* is a reference to a source already cited above in a text; it is an abbreviation of the Latin adverb *ibidem,* which means "in the very same place." Therefore, the narrative implies that wherever we meet an *ibid.* browsing the endless footnotes of a scholarly work, we actually find a citation of this great lost author Ibid (he would be the most quoted author in history!). Not only that: the work that covered Ibid with immortal glory was *Op. Cit.*, his masterpiece "wherein all the significant undercurrents of Graeco-Roman expression were crystallised once for all." Like the name of its author, *op. cit.* (without the capital letters) is again a scholarly abbreviation; in this case for *opus citatum*, which is a reference to a previously cited work. As with Ibid's name, in Lovecraft's story all citations of *op. cit.* in academic publications should be read as references to Ibid's work. Ibid had allegedly a fellow author referred to by the even more enigmatic name Cf. (this time with a period), who was the author of certain *Lives of the Poets* (*Vitae Poetarum?*), but often mistakenly attributed to Ibid (as Moe's girl said). Cf. is again a name following an academic abbreviation (*cf.*) meaning *confer* and used to refer the reader to further literature. Lovecraft clearly aimed to create a pantheon of writers and works named after scholarly references.

Lovecraft depicts Ibid as one of the leading intellectuals of his age. The rhetor's life allegedly was recorded by Procopius of Cesarea (500?–554?) and Jordanes (fl. 550), two of the most important sixth-century historians living in Constantinople under the aegis of emperor Justinian (r. 527–65) and recording their master's policy made of wide-ranging diplomacy and titanic military campaigns. Their narratives dealt with the major figures of the fifth and sixth centuries, such as Attila the Hun (r. 434–53), Pope Virgil (537–55), and the Roman generals Aetius (390?–454) and Belisarius (500?–565). Since, Jordanes concluded his narrative around 540 and Procopius with the year 551, Ibid's death in 587 must have been recorded by other historians (there would have been few candidates for the occurrence), but Lovecraft does not state which did so. It is also possible that it was an inaccuracy (in the narrative there are few of them). As we shall see, however, blunders become revelatory of Lovecraft's sources and aims.

Lovecraft compares Ibid to Claudius Claudianus (370?–404), whose unfinished *De Raptu Proserpinae* was destined to become greatly influential, even in Lovecraft's day; and Flavius Boethius (480?–524), the philosopher and courtier of King Theodoric, who was eventually put to death by him. He was also the author of the medieval bestseller *De Consolatione Philosophiae*. Lovecraft was well acquainted with classics. We know that he could read Latin well (Greek not so well), and we have major historical works in his private library such as Livy, Cornelius Nepos, and Suetonius

(Joshi and Schultz, *Lovecraft's Library* nos. 574–75, 701, 934). It is, however, difficult to know if Lovecraft had direct access to Claudianus and Boethius. For the occasion, he cited Edward Gibbon, the acclaimed author of one of the Enlightenment's masterpieces: *The History of the Decline and Fall of the Roman Empire* (1776–88). Lovecraft described Ibid with the words that Gibbon had spent on Boethius as "the last whom Cato or Tully could have acknowledged for their countryman" (Gibbon 5.27; I refer to Lovecraft's edition). Cato Uticensis (95–46 B.C.E.) and Tully (Cicero, 106–43 B.C.E.) are first-century B.C.E. politicians, authors, and rhetors involved in the civil wars and continuously exalted as examples of Republican virtues. The magniloquence of a man being the "Last of the Romans" in the sense of one embodying bygone virtues was ingrained in the discourse of the age, so that fifth- and sixth-century authors found more than a few of them around. Modern historians also defined some important personalities of the age as the last of their kind.

The sentence becomes here a hint of Lovecraft's sympathy for Ibid, and of his possible identification with him. We know that Lovecraft greatly admired the ancient Romans; in his fiction, Ibid was an intellectual of this bygone gentry living in a barbaric age, being recognized as a peer by the stoic gentlemen of the past. This was indeed one of Lovecraft's recurrent fantasies, infusing much of his output and being dramatically expressed in the concluding line of "The Outsider" "I know always that I am an outsider; a stranger in this century and among those who are still men" (*CF* 1.272). A further element in Lovecraft's identification with his character may have been Ibid's military background. In the story, we read that the Roman fought a few battles for the Empire, including the dramatic Gothic siege of Rome, on which occasion "he served bravely in the army of the defenders." We know that Lovecraft regretted his failure to serve in the military. In the spring of 1917 he attempted to join the Rhode Island National Guard, but his mother foiled the plan (Joshi, *I Am Providence* 222–23). It was at this time that he bitterly commented to Maurice W. Moe how even a week in military camp would have been fatal to him because of his weak health (*Letters to Maurice W. Moe and Others* 65). Lovecraft alludes to this perceived deficiency in the story "Polaris": "to me

Alos denied a warrior's part, for I was feeble and given to strange faintings when subjected to stress and hardships" (*CF* 1.68).

Lovecraft not only quotes ancient authors, but he also engages the scholarship of his own day and the recent past. The mention of a scholar called only by his (apparent) surname, Littlewit, is significant. Perhaps he is meant to be the same Humphrey Littlewit, Esq., one of Lovecraft's pseudonyms, who also authored "A Reminiscence of Dr. Samuel Johnson," originally published in 1917. The short story shows many parallels with "Ibid," and these must have been deliberate, based on the undeniable resemblance between Ibid's *Lives of the Poets,* as recorded by Moe's student, and Samuel Johnson's *Lives of the Most Eminent English Poets* (1779–81). "A Reminiscence of Dr. Samuel Johnson" deals with a character moving through an inhuman amount of time (Littlewit is 228 years old at the moment he is writing), developing in a much more delightful way the very idea of the man of learning surviving his age. Like Ibid, Littlewit is a relic of the past (the first literally, the second metaphorically), and they both meet historical characters during their journey through history. They both live out of their time at the moment of the story's writing, and are more similar to their spiritual literary fathers than their contemporaries. If Cato and Tully recognized Ibid as one of their own, Littlewit was acquainted with Alexander Pope (1688–1744), John Burgoyne (1722–1792), and others, and he dedicated his "reminiscence" to Samuel Johnson, of whom he was a friend. If in "Ibid" Lovecraft employed a humorous academic style, in "A Reminiscence" he wrote, by his own admission, with a "sort of antique flow" (*CF* 1.59).

Littlewit is not the only scholar recorded in "Ibid." Lovecraft plays with his knowledge of foreign languages (and that of his audience) in order to create further fictional scholars, whose names seem allusive of their (lack of) intellectual capabilities. These names are actually very easy to decipher, demanding a less than basic knowledge of French and German. We meet von Schweinkopf (Pighead) and Bêtenoir (black beast, in the sense of a person or thing detested or strongly avoided). These men seem to be revealing of Lovecraft's opinion of academics, engaged in dusty and useless scholarship (Joshi, *I Am Providence* 1.253–54).

The issues that these historians discuss are entirely outlandish. They debate Ibid's identity, an issue on which their opinions are absurdly divergent, even for a late antique author, stretching from a Visigoth warrior at the beginning of the fifth century (this idea apparently stemmed from the old interpretation of Jordanes as a Goth living on the Danube) to the Ibid to whom we introduced; his actual name, ludicrously long; and even his authorship, with some attributing to him the work of Cf., as mentioned above. Lovecraft also mentions modern scholars' work: von Schweinkopf was the author of the *Geschichte der Ostrogothen in Italien* (the history of the Ostrogoths in Italy), composed in 1797, very important and apparently a watershed on Ibid scholarship; Bêtenoir wrote the *Influences Romains* [*sic*] *dans le Moyen Âge* (Roman Influences on the Middle Ages) in 1877; while Littlewit in 1869 authored *Rome and Byzantium: A Study in Survival* (a similar title was adopted by the real Roman historian Chester Starr). They all were assuredly long treatises: von Schweinkopf's opus was defined as "monumental," and from the footnotes we know that the other two counted at least fifteen and twenty volumes respectively! It is also interesting that, although these intellectuals were apparently European (Littlewit with certainty), their histories were published in the United States in the exotic-sounding Fond du Lac and Waukesha, both in Wisconsin.

We find other academics in Lovecraft's stories. They play important roles in iconic stories such as "The Whisperer in the Darkness," "The Dunwich Horror," and "The Shadow out of Time." Their representation seems to have been mostly ambivalent and probably developed over time. It is perhaps impossible to find a single and recurring pattern. It will be enough to say that on the one side, universities are depicted as the main keepers of knowledge, as in the recurring mentions of Miskatonic University (Pearsall 345–46). It was this institution that financed the Antarctic expedition narrated in *At the Mountains of Madness;* there, we even encounter a comparable pre-human institution in the abandoned stone city that illustrated the deep past of the Elder Ones. It is in that same story that we can grasp the ambiguity of Lovecraft's representation of academics and universities: the emeritus professor of geology William Dyer is represented as a man seeking knowledge (or, in Lovecraft's words, the truth). At the same time, he defended a traditional and false scholarship in the face of the newly revealed cosmic evidence brought by Professor Lake. Therefore, academics are often focused on petty human issues, being blind to the terrible truth of the universe. This trope is deployed on a few occasions, when scholars play small cameos, mostly negative. As in "Ibid," their involvement with human scholarship limits their understanding of the origin and nature of real lore, such as the "celebrated ethnologist" in "Dagon" who was unable to help the story's protagonist because he was "hopelessly conventional" (*CF* 1.58). In "The Call of Cthulhu," when inspector John Raymond Legrasse attended the 1908 meeting of the American Anthropology Society asking for explanations about the idol he found, it was only William Channing Webb among the many scholars gathered at the meeting who showed some familiarity with the strange item (*CF* 2.32–33). The same could be said of the "buffoonlike" Henry Armitage (Burleson, "On Lovecraft's Themes" 148) of "The Dunwich Horror." Nevertheless, "Ibid" is almost isolated in its utterly negative representation of scholars, with the conspicuous exception of Alfred Galpin, whose caricaturized characterization in "Old Bugs" represents, perhaps, the low point of academic vileness.

III.

Acting as a historian himself, Lovecraft is from time to time mistaken. The whole story of Alcuin of York and the transfer of Ibid's skull to England is patchy at its best. Alcuin was buried in Tours (today France), and it is actually unclear why at his death Ibid's remains were shipped to England to his "kinsfolk." Likewise, the idea that in sixth-century Byzantium there was a textbook (Ibid's *Op. Cit.*) that could have been adopted for the empire's schools because of the emperor's command is a gross inaccuracy. In other occasions, we find missed opportunities. Lovecraft states that Ibid, at the height of his powers, received the consulate of 516. Even if Rome was governed by emperors since Octavian Augustus (r. 27 B.C.E.–17 C.E.), consuls were still nominated yearly until 543 C.E. The year of Lovecraft's choice could have been excellent. One of the consulates was not assigned that year, which could have been a convenient spot for placing our Ibid, while the second one went to a certain Flavius Petrus, a man otherwise unknown. Lovecraft was perhaps unaware of this, and instead of Flavius he cited a certain Pompilius Numantius Bombastes Marcellinus Deodamnatus as Ibid's colleague (in the phony Latin we recognize "bombastic" and "goddamned," a rather lame joke).

At the same time, Lovecraft's knowledge of political history and some anecdotes is solid and he may have known the subject as a history undergraduate does. From his letters and fiction, as well as from the books he owned, we know of Lovecraft's love for the Romans, whom he discussed in many occasions and also depicted in a story (or, at least, a dream-account that could have become a story): "The Very Old Folk," written in 1927. We also know that in one of his letters Lovecraft comically traced his own lineage to Azathoth through the imaginary *gens* Viburnia (*Letters to James F. Morton* 317). Marcus Lullius, proconsul of Gaul, clearly an ancient Roman, was the fictional author of "Old Bugs." Lovecraft must have had a better knowledge of the Republic rather than of the Empire, but he was well acquainted also with these later years and Ibid's career offers us insight on Lovecraft's knowledge of the age. The scholar's *cursus honorum* indeed echoed rather closely that of one of the age's greatest intellectuals, Boethius, whom Lovecraft knew well enough, as he showed in the short essay "The Literature of Rome," published in 1918 (*CE* 2.23–33). Ibid's belonging to the *gens* Anicia strengthens the parallelism with Boethius, and an Anician was also Pope Gregory the Great (590–604), a man often thought of as standing on the verge of epochal and dramatic changes, as Ibid was. Even more striking is the similarity between Ibid and Flavius Magnus Aurelius Cassiodorus Senator (485?–585?) who, like Boethius, was a man of King Theodoric's, and like many of his contemporaries found shelter in Constantinople when the Gothic War was raging in Italy, living an incredibly long life.

Lovecraft is skilled also in the mimicry of contemporary historians. His narrator explains that Ibid studied in the school of Athens, adding that "the extent of whose suppression by Theodosius [r. 379–95] a century before is grossly exaggerated by the superficial." The closure of the philosophical school actually happened under Emperor Justinian in 540, almost a century and a half after Theodosius' reign. We do not know if Lovecraft was mistaken or he maintained that such a closure was an exaggeration because it actually did not happen.[1] What is striking here is Lovecraft's use of the bluntly assertive tone of the academics of his day. Further impressions of scholars are frankly brilliant. The story according to which Ibid in his afterlife became a saint is amusing, but in all its oddity finds comparison in actual scholarship. An Italian historian, writing around the same time as Lovecraft, made of the sixth/seventh-century chronicler Secundus of Trento (d. 612), who curiously lived in the same region and epoch as Ibid, a bishop for no reason that we know about (Cessi 613, 618). He is less than a saint, but still impressive. Moreover, the alleged reason for Ibid's sanctity, a military victory against the Lombards through prayers, was a common trope of the Christian empire (Cameron, *Last Pagans* 129), which Lovecraft apparently knew well. It is mostly known for the so-called Alleluja Victory of 429, when St. Germanus of Auxerre (378?–448), together with an army of Britons, defeated a host of pagan Saxons and Picts only by chanting Alleluja three times (Jones 1986).

Odd usage of academic norms, introduced by Ibid's very name, adds insult to injury. Lovecraft transformed the Muratori edition of Jordanes, which Gibbon used for his *Decline and Fall*, into a mysterious Cod. Murat. (perhaps a Codex Muratorianus), which we know nothing about, but which bears hints of Lovecraft's fasci-

---

1. Joshi (personal communication) persuasively suggests that HPL may have mistaken the closure of Athens' schools with the emperor's turn of the screw to the pagan cults since 381, culminating in the following year with his western colleague Gratian (r. 367–83), who ordered the removal of the Altar of Victory from the Roman Curia (see Sheridan). We know that in his youth HPL was romantically mesmerized by Roman paganism (Joshi, *I Am Providence* 1.43), and he mentioned Theodosius' ban on the ancient religion in one of his earliest poems, written in September 1902, when he was only twelve, and collected in his *Poemata Minora: Volume II* (Lovecraft, *Juvenilia* 31). Later in his life, this enduring fascination for the gods of Rome seems to have reflected in his description of the enthroned, "graceful bearded" deities of Sarnath (*CF* 1.127).

nation with fictional volumes.[2] Quoting Procopius' work, Lovecraft recorded the passage x, z, y, which are clearly coordinate (although merely three-dimensional) rather than a reference. The list of horrendous quotations is apparently topped by "Pagi 50–50," which, at first sight, could seem a mannered Latin plural of *page,* referring however to a single location. But it turns out to be once more an indication of Lovecraft's skill. Relying on the trusted device of mixing the fictional and the real, Lovecraft seems to have referred to Antoine Pagi (1624–1699), who wrote a lengthy correction and commentary to Cesare Baronius's gigantic *Annales ecclesiastici,* the *Critica historico-chronologica in universos annales ecclesiasticos,* in four volumes (1689–1705). Lovecraft's reference to Pagi's work does not make too much sense (maybe a fifty-fifty chance of something? The 1915 Clem Easton movie?), but it implies that Baronius and Pagi discussed the figure of Ibid.

It is striking that the meticulousness in the events' discussion, and the reference to ongoing historical debates (fictional and not), are limited to the early centuries. After Ibid's death, the footnotes disappear, and so do the sources, with the narrator becoming omniscient. Here, Lovecraft presents his reader with information very hard to collect for even brilliant researchers (such as the story of Hans Zimmerman getting drunk and losing Ibid's skull), and truly impossible for anybody to acquire, as when the hero's spoils became the object of the prairie-dogs' "dark rites." Who may have recorded this unhuman activity? This plot device was used elsewhere, although in stories quite different in kind, such as "The Haunter of the Dark," where Robert Blake finds a cryptogram written by an equally all-seeing Aklo author (*CF* 3.466); or in von Juntz's *Black Book,* which narrated in great detail happenings in the year of the Red Moon, about 175,000 B.C.E. (*CF* 4.411f.).

As the story became less and less an essay, religion gains salience (because of Ibid's growing importance as a Christian figure) and the narrative increasingly becomes a humorous and iconoclastic pamphlet on faith and belief.[3] The sanctity of Ibid becomes a

---

2. Antonio Muratori (1672–1750) was the great Italian humanist thinker who edited many of the sources for Italian history during the eighteenth century.

3. HPL wrote that there was some confusion between Ibid the saint and Ibid the scholar, and "Not till the appearance of von Schweinkopf's work in 1797 were St.

trigger for more mockery, beginning with the names that Lovecraft gave to the settlers of New England: Read-'em-and-Weep Hopkins, Rest-in-Jehovah Stubbs, and Zerubbabel, the man who brought Ibid's remains to New England and whose name echoes the biblical character who led the Jews' return to Israel, which ended the Babylonian Captivity in c. 537 B.C.E. Recording these oddly named characters, Lovecraft seems to have returned to a beloved topic. In 1915, he had written in his "Department of Public Criticism" (*United Amateur*, September 1915) a review of the amateur periodical, the *Woodbee.* Discussing an article of Irene Metzger called "What Is a Name?," Lovecraft humorously discussed the Puritan habit of naming children, in a passage that deserves to be quoted in full:

> Glancing backward a little through history, Miss Metzger would probably sympathize with the innocent offspring of the old Puritans, who received such names as "Praise-God", and the like. Praise-God Barebones, a leading and fanatical member of Cromwell's rebel parliament, went a step further than his father, naming his own son "If-Jesus-Christ-had-not-died-for-thee-thou-hadst-been-Damned"! All this was actually the first name of young Barebones, but after he grew up and took a Doctor's degree, he was called by his associates, *"Damned Dr. Barebones"!* (*CE* 1.71)

The skull's misadventures among oddly named characters implies

---

Ibid and the rhetorician properly re-identified." This is again a riddle. HPL may have here implied that there were actually two Ibids, but this idea is contradicted by the whole narrative. If, against every single rule of textual analysis, we just ignore this odd sentence, we could then try to draw a line between Ibid the rhetor and Ibid the saint. HPL implies that somebody wrote "Ibidus rhetor romanus" in "Lombardic Minuscule" on his skull, a possible clue that he was not a saint yet. Lombard Minuscule is an alternative name to the more well-known Early Beneventan Minuscule, a script spread in Southern Italy between the eighth and the thirteenth century, which does not looks like the one used by HPL in the narrative (see Loew). However, I suspect that HPL thought the Lombard Minuscule to be the script spread in the Lombard kingdom, in time thereafter previous to Charlemagne's conquest of Italy of 774. As is universally known, Pope Leo III anointed Charlemagne in the year 800: in HPL's fiction he did it from the rhetor's skull. That the bishop of Rome used a skull as vessel is grotesque; however, it seems to suggest that his canonization was, by this time, accomplished.

the incredibly successful afterlife of Ibid, who was apparently known far and wide. We read that William the Conqueror (in the eleventh century) knew of Ibid's legacy, and even the soldiers of Cromwell showed mercy to his remains. The story becomes even more grotesque when the relics finally fell in the hands of Jean Grenier, "whose Popish zeal recognised the features of one whom he had been taught at his mother's knee to revere as St. Ibide." First, we notice that as much as St. Ibid was venerated among the Anglicans as Brother Ibid because of contempt for "all that was Popish" among the French-speaking settlers, he was remembered as St. Ibid*e*. Moreover, we are expected to believe that Jean was able to recognize the osseous features of Ibid because of his mother's tales!

IV.

The reason for this discrepancy in the story's structure lies in Lovecraft's use of his sources. The almost single basis of his narrative is Gibbon's *Decline and Fall,* a long epos covering the imperial centuries between the second and the fifteenth, at the time seen as an irreversible decadence under barbarian pressure, fatally fuelled by the poisonous (in Gibbon's opinion) Christian religion. Gibbon's *Decline and Fall* was at the backbone of the first part of the story "Ibid," as we know that other books massively influenced Lovecraft's stories and novellas. The aforementioned "A Reminiscence of Dr. Samuel Johnson" was indeed almost exclusively based on James Boswell's *The Life of Samuel Johnson* (1791) as well as Johnson's own writings (Joshi and Schultz 225), while Margaret Murray's controversial masterpiece *The Witch-Cult in Western Europe* (1921) had a pervasive influence on "The Dreams in the Which House" (Harms & Gonce 96–97).

Gibbon's work could have charmed Lovecraft for many reasons. He wrote a history that was considered literature; he was keenly critical of religion; and he was an independent scholar, which may have appealed to Lovecraft's sensibility and personal history. Lovecraft confessed that his own writing resembled Gibbon's (and Samuel Johnson's) "Asianic" rhetoric (Joshi, *I Am Providence* 1.241); moreover, his hilarious references may have echoed

Gibbon's mastery in the art of footnotes (Grafton 1–4). Lovecraft's alter ego, Littlewit, even met Gibbon personally at one of the Literary Club gatherings narrated in "A Reminiscence of Dr. Samuel Johnson." Littlewit too, like Lovecraft, claimed to admire his historical work notwithstanding Gibbon's personal rudeness (which was notorious). Reliance on the Englishman's authority is understandable also for more circumstantial reasons. The great share of the historical literature on barbarian Italy was for the most part written in German or Italian, which, we suspect, Lovecraft read only with difficulty ("I am abysmally weak in modern languages, and mathematics, and in certain phases of history" [*A Means to Freedom* 2.580]). Moreover, it was a historiography burdened by contemporary national and nationalistic issues often aimed to nation branding in a roaring age of nationalism (see Evans and Marchal). Nevertheless, a few years before the writing of "Ibid" important works appeared, such as the histories of Thomas Hodgkin (1831–1913) and J. B. Bury (1861–1927), from whose reading Lovecraft could have benefited.[4]

We do know that Lovecraft possessed three of Gibbon's writings; two of them still constitute the canon today. Among his volumes, we find a copy of the monumental *Decline and Fall* in the edition of Henry Hart Milaman (1791–1868), which may have been a concrete inspiration for the absurdly long works of von Schwein-

---

4. Thomas Hodgkin wrote his monumental history of the Italian peninsula under barbarian rule. Like Gibbon, Hodgkin was an amateur historian—an element that could have appealed to HPL. His *Italy and Her Invaders* (1880–99) was an eight-volume work stretching from the fifth to the tenth century, where entire volumes were dedicated to Theodoric and the Lombard invasion and which would have furnish an incredibly rich background for Ibid's adventures (see T. S. Brown; Wood 217–20). J. B. Bury wrote *The Invasion of Europe by the Barbarians,* which was published one year after his death, in 1928. Bury, an Irishman, was an established academic, professor of modern history at Cambridge, and a greatly influential scholar (Wood 210–17). His *Invasion of Europe* was perhaps issued too late for HPL to use for "Ibid," but Bury also wrote different versions of a history of the late Roman Empire since 1889 (one of them has been constantly reissued up to the present day). No volume of Bury or Hodgkin is to be found in HPL's library. HPL does mention Bury's *The Student's Roman Empire* (1893) in a 1936 letter to Fritz Leiber (*Letters to* C. L. *Moore and Others* 304), but it is unclear whether he actually read the book.

kopf and Bêtenoir; his autobiography; and a nineteenth-century abridged version of *Decline and Fall,* called *The Student's Gibbon,* which Lovecraft acquired in 1933, well after having written "Ibid." In "Ibid," Lovecraft explicitly mentioned Gibbon once, but clues of his *Decline and Fall* are scattered throughout the whole story. Examples are few, but highly suggestive. Lovecraft called Jordanes "Jornandes," which by his day was already an antiquated spelling, but he could find it in Gibbon's history. The same is true for other protagonists' names, such as the Lombard king Authari (whom Lovecraft named Autaris), the Emperor Justinian (Justinianus) or Justin (Justinus). Once again, we find these forms are seldom recorded by contemporaries (Bury and Hodgkin did not use them), but we do find them in Gibbon's *Decline and Fall.* Also the anecdote on the Emperor Maurice's origins must have stemmed from Gibbon, but Lovecraft elaborated it in order to obtain a comic result. Gibbon wrote that Maurice's family originated from Rome, although his close relatives lived in Arabissus, a town in Cappadocia, a region of present-day Turkey (Gibbon 5.345). In "Ibid," the emperor becomes a preposterous figure in an age of decadence. Although he prided himself on his Roman origins, he was actually born in the Cappadocian town of Arabiscus [*sic*], which does not exist. In a nutshell, Maurice boasted of Roman origins, but he belonged to the Greeks, whom for Lovecraft and many contemporaries were seen as feminine and irrational (Callaghan 11–18).

One phrase in the story is a further conundrum. As was mentioned, Pope Leo anointed Charlemagne, who on this occasion Lovecraft defined as a "hero-nomad." Another look at Gibbon helps to solve this little riddle. The English historian was not particularly fond of Charlemagne. In his work, the Frank was a sort of one-eyed man in the land of the blind. Introducing him, Gibbon indeed wrote:

> His real merit is doubtless enhanced by the barbarism of the nation and the times from which he emerged: but the apparent magnitude of an object is likewise enlarged by an unequal comparison; and the ruins of Palmyra derive a casual splendour from the nakedness of the surrounding desert. (6.169–70)

This is rather ungenerous of Gibbon, and most modern historians would probably disagree. Nevertheless, the Englishman must have influenced Lovecraft's perception of Charlemagne as truly barbarian.[5] As noted by T. S. Brown, moreover, Gibbon was mistaken about the nomadic nature of the Germans, which he erroneously equated to the Scythians (Brown 138), the riders of the Pontic Steppes. Gibbon was also impressed by Charlemagne's swiftness and freedom of movement. He narrated the Frank's epic rides from one corner of Europe to the other and his ability to cover his vast empire in the shortest possible time. Here, Gibbon made a comparison between the sedentary reader ("The sedentary reader is amazed by his incessant activity of mind and body" [6.170]) and Charlemagne, who becomes in his context a nomad (Roberts 38): it is a contrast that would have delighted Robert E. Howard. Moreover, it is possible that the usage of "hero" was due to Thomas Carlyle's philosophy of history. His *On Heroes, Hero-Worship and the Heroic in History* was published in 1841, and in the first chapter (dealing with Woden) he also discussed Charlemagne's wars against the Saxons. Lovecraft did not apparently possess a copy of the book, but he did possess other works of the Scottish historian. This seems to have been the origin of Lovecraft's peculiar dictum.

From Gibbon's work also stemmed the idea of the skull-cup. In "Ibid," the creation of the cup is associated with an actual historical event: the pillage of Ravenna's port of Classe by the Lombard duke of Spoleto (it is suggestive that Gibbon did not report the duke's name and neither did Lovecraft: Gibbon: "and the suburb of Classe, only three miles from Ravenna, was pillaged and occupied by the troops of a simple duke of Spoleto" [Gibbon 5.346]).[6] Quoting the Lombard Paul the Deacon, who wrote in Latin at the end of the eighth century, Gibbon recorded that king Alboin, having defeated and killed king Cunimund of the Gepids, made a cup out of his skull. He writes: "The bravest of the nation fell in the field of battle; the king of the Lombards contemplated with delight the head of Cunimund; and his skull was fashioned into a cup to satiate the hatred of the conqueror, or, perhaps, to

---

5. Palmyra recurs also in HPL's writings, figuring in the novel *At the Mountains of Madness*. Gavin Callaghan points to the great significance of these passages (234–37).

6. The duke of Spoleto was in fact among the most powerful warlords of early medieval Italy.

comply with the savage custom of his country" (5.334). The skull-cup became among the most precious relics of the Lombard kings—so at least Paul tells us. We do not know the spooky vessel's destiny after the Franks had conquered the Lombard kingdom in 774. Lovecraft tells his readers what happened to Ibid's skull instead.

If we pause shortly on the skull-cup, we have to convey that from ancient times it had became a familiar trope denoting barbarism. Already Herodotus (484?–425? B.C.E.), universally known as the father of history, described it as a custom of the wild Scythians. In some ways, therefore, we could say that the motif of the skull-cup is old as history itself. A few powerful men ended their careers as skull-cups, such as Cunimund and Ibid. The Byzantine emperor Nicephorus (r. 802–11), defeated in battle by the Bulgarians, became a vessel for their lord Krum. Many centuries later, the same thing happened when the Latin emperor of Constantinople, Baldwin of Flanders (r. 1204–5), fell on the field against another ruler of the Bulgarians (and the Vlachs), Emperor Kalojan. Why somebody would carve a cup out of a slain enemy's skull is a matter of conjecture. It seems that Lovecraft's contemporaries, thinking and writing in an age influenced by the works of James George Frazer, may have found the shamanic roots of the practice meant to capture the defeated enemy's strength. Gibbon himself added a footnote (5.334n10) that runs as following:

> It appears from Strabo [l. vii.], Pliny [l. vii. c. 11], and Ammianus Marcellinus [l. xxvii], that the same practice was common among the Scythian tribes (Muratori, Scriptores Rer. Italic. tom. i. p. 424). The *scalps* of North America are likewise trophies of valor. The skull of Cunimund was preserved above two hundred years among the Lombards; and Paul himself was one of the guests to whom Duke Ratchis exhibited this cup on a high festival, (l. ii. c. 28.)

In order to narrate Ibid's skull overlong afterlife, Lovecraft may have enriched Gibbon's comments with the entry on "Cannibalism" that he found in the ninth edition of the *Encyclopaedia Britannica,* which he owned. We know that he used the ninth edition of the same work in order to narrate the sacrifice that we find in "The Horror at Red Hook," where he quoted from the entries "Magic" and "Demonology" (Joshi and Schultz 151).

Reliance on Gibbon, however, is not limited to the recording of historical deeds. Lovecraft must have shared many of the historian's views, such as the aforementioned fascination with the ancient gods of Rome. Moreover, Lovecraft wrote before the publication of Henri Pirenne's (1937) and Peter Brown's (1971) groundbreaking works. These scholars maintained that the fall of Rome in 476 was by no mean a watershed in the life of the Greater Sea, which on the contrary experienced long-lasting continuities. Like many of his contemporaries, Lovecraft saw the years as an age of decline, debauchery, and barbarism, and we may think about his insistence on concepts such as effeminacy and superstition. His great admiration for the German scholar (and Deep-One lookalike) Oswald Spengler (1880–1936) must have strengthened this perspective.

Even Lovecraft's great fascination with the majestic remains of a deeper past may have found roots in Gibbon. Ruins play a pivotal role in the writings of the English historian (Roberts 148–69), being at the very origin of his historical enterprise (I will return to this topic on a forthcoming article). Lovecraft described them in many of his works. Ruins from an age older than humanity are to be found in many of his narratives and constitute one of the most inspired of his tropes (Shershow and Michaelsen). Grandiose examples are scattered in "The Temple," "The Nameless City," and *At the Mountains of Madness.* Lovecraft showed a very early interest in this topic, and it is already evident in the prose poem "Memory," first published in 1919, where he describes gigantic remains looming under the moss long after the extinction of humanity (*CF* 1.86).

V.

This brings us to question the short story's role in the broader context of Lovecraft's literary achievement. Even if in "Ibid" we find no explicit terror or weirdness, the parallels with his more horrific tales are many. The very core of the story, that of Ibid's lengthy life and afterlife, is clearly echoed by the "unwholesome survival" (Burleson, "On Lovecraft's Themes" 140) of the rest of his output. We saw the similarities with "A Reminiscence of Dr.

Samuel Johnson," but the theme was inflected in darker tones in the stories "The Picture in the House" and "The Terrible Old Man." We also encounter Lovecraft's notorious horror for miscegenation, which has been interpreted as structural to his master narrative and perhaps of horror fiction itself (Lévy 32–39; Houellebecq; Simmons; Caroll 102–4; Tyree; Callaghan). It is a trope that recurs often in his writings, particularly in the aftermath of his Brooklyn years as exemplified in the story "The Horror at Red Hook" (Schultz; McRoy).

Indeed, the racial paradigm emerges rather soon in the short story: after a few lines we read that Ibid was a Roman as far as "that degenerate and mongrelised age could produce," and also that *Op. Cit.* was produced "with admirable acuteness, notwithstanding the surprisingly late date at which Ibid wrote." In the latter passage, we can recognize Spengler's conception of cultures as organisms doomed to decline and perish. It was a biological analogy that often tempted Lovecraft, although with some reservations (Joshi, *I Am Providence* 774–75). Even if Ibid still has some of the temper of old Romans, in Lovecraft's day this shine was forever lost and mixed marriages had already turned the stoic Romans into Italians. In "The Haunter in the Dark" we find a description of twentieth-century Italians as superstitious and fearful, and in an infamous letter that Lovecraft wrote to Frank Belknap Long we read of the "Italo-Semitico-Mongoloid" hordes sprawling in New York City, who could not even be "call'd human" (*SL* 1.333–34). This becomes more striking if we remember that in Lovecraft's day the Italian fascist government vigorously pursued the invented tradition of the Italian descent from the ancient Romans, and we also know of the author's initial fascination with Mussolini (Giardina and Vauchez 2000; Joshi, *I Am Providence* 488). Nevertheless, "Ibid" remains loyal to its humorous tone. In an amusing passage, we meet the "conquering Aryan" massacring the prairie-dogs. However embarrassing it may sound, we have to convey that Lovecraft meant to deal with the topic in an amusing way, and some readers will still find themselves able to smile at his humor.

In the same ironic fashion Lovecraft seems to have made references to local names and topography bearing an inside meaning. This is perhaps lost to us and even in Lovecraft's day may have been recognized only by a close circle of his friends and correspondents. It is a feature of many of his writings. We know that in-jokes and references about actual locations and landscapes were also hidden in more serious narratives such as "The Dunwich Horror" and "The Whisperer in the Darkness" (Burleson, *American Allegory* 181–93). Milwaukee, whose topography is described in such detail, was Moe's hometown, and we have seen that the books by Bêtenoir and Littlewit were published in Wisconsin—a state that, in addition to Moe, was also the home state of Alfred Galpin, August Derleth, and Robert Bloch (a later correspondent). In "Ibid" there is no mention of the fictive topography of New England as the place where the familiar meets the darkness (Lévy 49–50), but we do encounter Salem, a New England town with a dark past, universally recognized as the place that inspired the creation of Arkham, and the abode of the Pickman family (Joshi and Schultz 6–7, 204). It was also the place were the last known Greek copy of the *Necronomicon* was lost in a fire (*CF* 2.407).

Also, the last lines of "Ibid," concerning the growth of the town above a deep past, literally rooted below the human settlement, find an echo in many of Lovecraft's stories where we come upon halls and vaults haunted by the darkest secrets of past societies. "The Rats in the Walls" is the most obvious example, but we could find similarities also in "The Festival" and other stories. In "Ibid" we see the scholar/saint's skull being venerated with "dark rites" by prairie-dogs "who saw in it a deity sent from the upper world."[7] Here we risk over-interpreting, but the insignificant inhabitants of a smaller world living by the indifference of the dwellers above them offer further insight. The religious practices ("dark rites") of the animals who worshipped a man's skull could be a mockery (again) of human religion, which is thematized more than once in "Ibid." Moreover, it also points to a relativism of the human role in the cosmos, which is the major theme of

7. The mention of prairie-dogs appears to be an in-joke, given that Maurice W. Moe lived at 2303 Prairie Street in Milwaukee at the time when HPL wrote "Ibid" (see *Letters to Maurice W. Moe and Others* 10). The name of this street was then changed to Highland Avenue, inspiring HPL's statement in the story that "In the roseal dawn the burghers of Milwaukee rose to find a former prairie turned to a highland!" (*CF* 2.416).

Lovecraft's fiction. As we can look amused at the meaningless practices of the prairie-dogs, on a cosmic scale the same is true for human beliefs and religiosity. Thereafter, it could become a hint to what Fritz Leiber called the Copernican revolution of Lovecraft's writings, and Burleson defined his "denied primacy" (Leiber; Burleson, "On Lovecraft's Themes"). Lovecraft even dismissed the little animals as "simple, artless burrowers," which echoes his loathing for cities—an issue that has been debated many times and left traces in many of his stories, particularly the ones stemming from his years in New York (Schultz; McRoy).

Finally, the scholar's masterwork *Op. Cit.*, with all its "undercurrents" of ancient learning, seems to fall into the fictional "library of mythical books of occult lore" that exist in abundance in Lovecraft's narratives (Joshi, *I Am Providence* 643; Carter). The earliest work of forbidden lore to be mentioned is the Pnakotic Manuscripts (or fragments), introduced as early as 1918 in the story "Polaris." However, the most infamous among the books created or simply mentioned by Lovecraft (others were products of authors such as Robert E. Howard or Robert Bloch) was, of course, the notorious *Necronomicon* (Harms 341–59), a grimoire that becomes particularly revealing in this context. The *Necronomicon* needs no introduction: it was first presented in 1922 when it was featured in the story "The Hound" (*CF* 1.343, 344), and it has been iconic ever since so that higher criticism was invoked to return the book to his original meaning (see Price). Here it becomes relevant because the structure of "Ibid" is closely mirrored by "History of the 'Necronomicon'" (*CF* 2.405–9). This is an even shorter work of fiction, which Lovecraft wrote in late 1927, around the same time as the composition of "Ibid." Like "Ibid," it is a mock-scholarly article, although much darker in tone. Like "Ibid," "History of the 'Necronomicon'" mixes reality and fiction. It begins by introducing the book's author: Abdul Alhazred, a Yemenite mad poet "who is said to have flourished during the period of the Ommiade [now we would say Umayyad] caliphs, circa 700 A.D." Abdul lived a century and a half after Ibid in another center of the Mediterranean world of Late Antiquity and, like him, he died a few lines into the narrative, although poor Abdul perished in a much cruder way than his Roman counterpart, echoing the general gloom of the whole story. Afterward, the narrative goes on to record the editorial adventures of his work: the *Necronomicon* moved through space and across the centuries from eighth-century Arabia to twentieth-century New England.

As in "Ibid," in "History of the 'Necronomicon'" we meet a distinctive blend of the fictional and the factual. Imagined (mad) poets or scholars such as Abdul Alhazred and Theodorus Philetas are discussed together with John Dee (1527–1608) and Robert W. Chambers (1865–1933), the author of *The King in Yellow* (1895). Lovecraft also cared to tell his readers how we know about Abdul Alhazred. His life was supposedly a fictional entry in a real collection of biographies, the one of Ibn Khallikan (1211–1282), whom Lovecraft mistakenly dates to the twelfth century (instead of the thirteenth). Further characters, such as Olaus Wormius (Ole Wurm, 1588–1664), are misplaced in time, from the seventeenth century to the thirteenth. Joshi (*I Am Providence* 698–99) convincingly argued that Lovecraft mistakenly believed that Ole and the famous Saxo Grammaticus (1150?–1220?), author of the *Gesta Danorum,* may have been contemporaries. Notwithstanding these minor issues, we see here what we see in "Ibid": Lovecraft maintaining that existing historians mentioned a preposterous character in a real narrative, of course in a nonexistent passage.

The editorial vicissitudes of *Op. Cit.* are by no means as detailed as those of the *Necronomicon,* but we are safe in asserting that it must have been a widely distributed work, copied in medieval manuscripts (recall that Emperor Maurice "adopted" it for the Empire's schools). At least one of these must have reached the authors of the Modern Age, such as Cesare Baronio and Antoine Pagi. Eventually, German, French, and English scholars commented on and perhaps edited his work, and *Op. Cit.* must have become the subject of university classes: students knew Ibid, mentioning him in their "themes," so that we may suppose that modern and easily accessible editions of the work existed, perhaps contained in major university libraries. It is unfortunate that we do not know who published it (Teubner? Oxford? Golden Goblin?). Neither do we know the name of its latest editor.

Lovecraft's imaginary versions of Baronio's and Pagi's great enterprises suggest how *Op. Cit.* is not the only fictional book featured in "Ibid." We know that in the narrative nonfictional works are also apparently different. As noted, Lovecraft stated that Ibid's life had been recorded by the sixth-century authors "Jornandes" and Procopius. Jordanes is the author of two works: the *Romana* and the *Getica.* Lovecraft mentions neither of them, so we cannot exclude the possibility that he created a third, otherwise unattested work where Ibid's deeds were narrated. However, concerning Procopius, Lovecraft quotes his *Bellum Gothicum,* which is the final section of the *Bella,* the historian's major work, dealing with Justinian's wars on the Mediterranean. This means that in the story, Procopius' work was dissimilar to the one we know. This is a point of coherence with much of Lovecraft's output, where we find not only fictional grimoires, but also actual books, which, in the fiction, contain sections and lore that do not figure in the versions we know. A wonderful example is Filippo Pigafetta's *Relatione del reame del Congo* (1591), which in its Latin translation *Regnum Congo* is featured in the story "The Picture in the House." Joshi has exhaustively discussed Lovecraft's use of this volume, noting how his "description of it makes it sound far weirder than it is" (Joshi, *Rise and Fall* 31). Other existing books, such as the ones found by Robert Blake in "The Haunter in the Dark," equally seem to have been much darker than the real ones, containing cosmic teachings that we do not find while reading them, not unlike Ibn Khallikan's narrative on Abdul Alhazred or Procopius' *Bellum Gothicum,* which contained the story of Ibid. Therefore, although a short and amusing story, "Ibid" is apparently touched by Lovecraft's main obsessions, which like tentacles link the tale to his genuinely horrific production. And this brings us to the Dhole in the Room.

VI.

In a letter written to Robert E. Howard in 1932, Lovecraft maintained that in the weird tale humor was "diluting element" that should be avoided (*A Means to Freedom* 429). A similar notion is expressed in "Supernatural Horror in Literature" (1927), where the author was probably concerned with mundane narrative elements in the fiction of cosmic fear (27–28). "Ibid" apparently obeys this genre distinction. It was a distinction in style and themes rather than in message and philosophy: Joshi has on different occasions demonstrated how much of the former reading of Lovecraft's work, which was categorized among different currents (such as New England tales, Dunsanian tales, and, of course, Cthulhu Mythos tales), owe much to August Derleth's pervasive interpretation (*I Am Providence* 643; see also Mackley) and can be now dismissed as wholly artificial. On the contrary, Lovecraft remarked in a now famous letter to Farnsworth Wright, which accompanied the second submission of "The Call of Cthulhu" to *Weird Tales*, that he considered his entire work as structurally unitary. Therefore, while "Ibid" was confined to the humorous style, it also obeyed "the fundamental premise that common human laws and interests and emotions have no validity or significance in the vast cosmos-at-large" (*SL* 2.150).

Considering the broader context, we must state that the months when Lovecraft composed "Ibid" were a momentous time in his narrative production. In 1925 he had in fact completed the synopsis of "The Call of Cthulhu," universally regarded as a turning point toward the cosmicism that increasingly dominated his later output (Joshi, *I Am Providence* 642; Berruti 363; see, however, the recent reading in Callaghan). There is no need to summarize the learned scholarship on one of the most beloved and terrifying of Lovecraft's tales (Joshi, *Rise and Fall;* Harms; Joshi, *Dissecting Cthulhu;* Frenschkowski), but it will be enough to recall that Lovecraft completed "Ibid" after having already conceived and written "The Call of Cthulhu." The great earthquake of 1925 that apparently inspired "The Call of Cthulhu" may have found its way also into "Ibid," where, at the end of the story, the skull of the scholar (now a saint) re-emerges from the depths of Milwaukee. The historical conjuncture was framed by Lovecraft by way of the beloved theme of the past emerging not only metaphorically, but geologically in all its physicality, as we see in "Dagon."

The close synchronicity between "Ibid" and "The Call of Cthulhu" bears further suggestions. In "Ibid," as in "The Call of Cthulhu," we find indeed a clear statement of the author's mechanistic pessimism, and the story is truly a triumph of death as incommensurable compared to human existence. It is significant that even a man as incredibly long-lived as Ibid was alive for just a fraction of his story. It was his skull that endured the most challenging adventures and travels. The disparity between the vicissitudes of Ibid as man and as a relic emphasizes the essence of Lovecraft's (and many others') philosophy. The same trope is delineated in a much darker and weirder way in the story "Out of the Aeons," which shows the horrific torment of T'Yog: "Horribly fixed and prisoned through the ages, and maddeningly conscious of the passage of interminable epochs of helpless inaction till change and time might complete the decay of the petrified shell and leave it exposed to die" (*CF* 4.413). These tropes of Lovecraft's are beloved by mechanist thinkers and authors who also share his cosmic pessimism (see Ligotti). To cite an example, the recorded narrative-devices recur with striking similarities in the *Operette morali* by the acclaimed Italian poet Giacono Leopardi (1798–1837), particularly in the "Dialogo di Federco Ruysch e le sue mummie" and the "Cantico del gallo silvestre" (Leopardi 173–74, 239–44); in the latter *operetta*, the author narrates a time span that crosses beyond the life of every human being to the absolute timeless stillness that will follow the demise of man. Lovecraft, in his turn, explored a similar vision in the dark verses of "Nemesis" (1918): "I have seen the dark universe yawning, / Where the black planets roll without aim; / Where they roll in their horror unheeded, without knowledge or lustre or name" (*AT* 46). In all these fictions, death triumphs with its eternity above the short and purposeless lives of humans. What emerge from "Ibid"'s clumsy sequence of incidents are indeed the insignificance of human history and the irrelevance of the human cultures that followed one another in it.

In this context the sharp but always playful criticism of Christian belief and mythology (which we know Lovecraft saw as puerile and ludicrous) gains a deeper meaning. But, like Christianity, scholarship also emerges as laughable, ephemeral, and superficial because of its anthropocentrism, while the real knowledge is the one of the cosmos and the insignificant position of humanity in it (Joshi, *Subtler Magick* 262), with time itself being a pure human construct (Fawver). This is perhaps the key to understanding how

"Ibid"'s narrator was able to tell episodes that were entirely impossible for him to know. It was their humanity, and perhaps their predictability, that placed them in the sphere of the knowable and pedestrian. History can be subjectively meaningful (and we know how much care Lovecraft invested in discovering his own roots: see Eckhardt 82; Joshi, *I Am Providence* 5), and it is also possible to take an Epicurean pleasure from it, as from folklore or tradition (Evans), but it will not provide any shelter from an indifferent cosmos.

We could, therefore, explain the singularity of "Ibid" with Lovecraft's genre conceptions, as he wrote to Robert E. Howard. Nevertheless, the short story follows Lovecraft's major topics, showing striking coherence with his works of supernatural fiction. I suggest that in "Ibid" we encounter the same blink to man and existence that we find in his broader fiction and philosophy, just from a different (non-Euclidean?) angle. In a rarely used amusing style, Lovecraft communicated what in his most famous fiction was left to the weird and the terror.

*

"Ibid" is an unusual tale, a playful mockery that confirms Lovecraft's wide reading and interest in history, also bearing clues of his humor and kindness all the way through. In a moment when his writing and philosophy embraced a deeper and fully cosmic dimension according to which the humans were relegated to a meaningless position and ceased to possess the intellectual and physical instruments to understand or even describe the otherness that surrounds them, "Ibid" remains a fully human story. Across its few pages, we still move in the kingdom of human word and sense.

The story could, indeed, seem a calm isle of humanity in the vast, cold, and threating Lovecraftian cosmos. But to paraphrase a famous lesson from literary theory: "no text is an island," and if it is binding to analyze "Ibid" in its insight, we should not forget the broader context of Lovecraft's writings. Then we could raise our heads above the island's shorelines, gazing at the "black seas of infinity" that indifferently surround it (*CF* 2.21).

Works Cited

Berruti, Massimo. "H. P. Lovecraft and the Anatomy of the Nothingness: The Cthulhu Mythos." *Semiotica* 150 (2004): 363–418.

Brown, Peter. *The World of Late Antiquity: A.D. 150–750*. New York: Harcourt, 1971.

Brown, T. S. "Gibbon, Hodgkin, and the Invaders of Italy." In *Edward Gibbon and Empire,* ed. Rosamond McKitterick and Roland Quinault. Cambridge: Cambridge University Press, 1997. 137–61.

Burleson, Donald R. "On Lovecraft's Themes: Touching the Glass." In *An Epicure in the Terrible: A Centennial Anthology of Essays in Honor of H. P. Lovecraft,* ed. David E. Schultz and S. T. Joshi. 1991. New York: Hippocampus Press, 2011. 139–52.

———. *Lovecraft: An American Allegory: Selected Essays on H. P. Lovecraft.* New York: Hippocampus Press, 2015.

Bury, J. B. *A History of the Late Roman Empire: From Arcadius to Irene (395 A.D. to 800 A.D.).* London: Macmillan, 1889. 2 vols.

———. *The Invasion of Europe by Barbarians.* Ed. F. G. C. Hearnshaw. London: Macmillan, 1928.

Callaghan, Gavin. *H. P. Lovecraft's Dark Arcadia: The Satire, Symbology and Contradiction.* Jefferson, NC: McFarland, 2013.

Cameron, Alan. "Anician Myths." *Journal of Roman Studies* 102 (2012): 133–71.

———. *The Last Pagans of Rome.* Oxford: Oxford University Press, 2011.

Carroll, Michael Thomas. *Popular Modernity in America: Experience, Technology, Mythohistory.* Albany: State University of New York Press, 2000.

Carter, Lin (with Robert M. Price and S. T. Joshi). "H. P. Lovecraft: The Books." In *Discovering H. P. Lovecraft,* ed. Darrell Schweitzer. Holicong, PA: Wildside Press, 2001. 107–47.

Cessi, R. "Studi sulle fonti dell'età gotica e longobarda II: Prosperi continuatio Hauniensis." *Archivio muratoriano* 22 (1922): 585–641.

Eckhardt, Jason C. "The Cosmic Yankee." In *An Epicure in the Terrible: A Centennial Anthology of Essays in Honor of H. P. Lovecraft,* ed. David E. Schultz and S. T. Joshi. 1991. New York: Hippocampus Press, 2011. 77–100.

Evans, R. J. W., and Guy P. Marchal, ed. *The Uses of the Middle Ages in Modern European States History, Nationhood and the Search for Origins.* Basingstoke: Palgrave Macmillan, 2011.

Evans, Timothy H. "A Last Defense again the Dark: Folklore, Horror, and the Uses of Tradition in the Works of H. P. Lovecraft." *Journal of Folklore Research* 42 (2005): 99–135.

Fawver, Kurt. "'Present'-ly Safe: The Anthropocentricism of Time in H. P. Lovecraft's Fiction." *Journal of the Fantastic in the Arts* 20 (2009): 248–61.

Frenschkowski, Marco. "Lovecraft als Mythenschöpfer." In *H. P. Lovecraft: Von Monstren und Mythen,* ed. A. Kasprzak. Bad Tölz: Tilsner, 1997. 109–81.

Gasparri, Stefano. *I duchi longobardi.* Rome: Istituto storico italiano per il medioevo, 1978.

Giardina, Andrea, and André Vauchez. *Il mito di Roma: Da Carlo Magno a Mussolini.* Rome: Laterza, 2000.

Gibbon, Edward. *The History of the Decline and Fall of the Roman Empire.* Ed. H. H. Milman. 2nd ed. London: John Murray, 1946. 6 vols.

Grafton, Anthony. *The Footnote: A Curious History.* Cambridge, MA: Harvard University Press, 1997.

Harms, Daniel. *The Cthulhu Mythos Encyclopaedia: A Guide to H. P. Lovecraft's Universe.* Lake Orion, MI: Elder Sign Press, 2008.

Houellebecq, Michel. *H. P. Lovecraft: Contre le monde, contre la vie.* Monaco: Rocher, 1991. Tr. Dorna Khazeni as *H. P. Lovecraft: Against the World, Against Life.* San Francisco: Believer Books, 2005.

Jacobsen, T. C. *The Gothic War: Rome's Final Conflict in the West.* Yardley, PA: Westholme, 2009.

Jones, E. M. "The Historicity of the Alleluja Victory." *Albion* 18 (1986): 363–73.

Joshi, S. T. *H. P. Lovecraft: The Decline of the West.* San Bernardino, CA: Borgo Press, 1990.

———. *I Am Providence: The Life and Times of H. P. Lovecraft.* New York: Hippocampus Press, 2010. 2 vols.

———. *The Rise and Fall of the Cthulhu Mythos.* Poplar Bluff, MO: Mythos Books, 2008.

———. *A Subtler Magick: The Writings and Philosophy of H. P. Lovecraft.* San Bernardino, CA: Borgo Press, 1996.

———, ed. *Dissecting Cthulhu: Essays on the Cthulhu Mythos.* Lakeland, FL: Miskatonic River Press, 2011.

Joshi, S. T., and David E. Schultz. *An H. P. Lovecraft Encyclopaedia.* 2001. New York: Hippocampus Press, 2004.

———. *Lovecraft's Library: A Catalogue.* 4th ed. New York: Hippocampus Press, 2017.

Leiber, Fritz. "A Literary Copernicus." 1949. In *Discovering H. P. Lovecraft,* ed. Darrell Schweitzer. Holicong, PA: Wildside Press, 2012. 7–16.

Leopardi, Giacomo. *Operette morali.* Ed. P. Ruffini. Milan: Garzanti, 1984.

Lévy, Maurice. *Lovecraft ou du fantastique.* Paris: Union Générale d'Éditions, 1972.

Ligotti, Thomas. *The Conspiracy against the Human Race.* New York: Hippocampus Press, 2010.

Lowe, E. A. *The Beneventan Script: A History of the South Italian Minuscule.* Oxford: Clarendon Press, 1914.

Lovecraft, H. P. *The Annotated Supernatural Horror in Literature.* Ed. S. T. Joshi. 2nd ed. New York: Hippocampus Press, 2012.

———. *Juvenilia: 1895–1905.* Ed. S. T. Joshi. West Warwick, RI: Necronomicon Press, 1984.

———. *Letters to C. L. Moore and Others.* Ed. David E. Schultz and S. T. Joshi. New York: Hippocampus Press, 2017.

———. *Letters to James F. Morton.* Ed. David E. Schultz and S. T. Joshi. New York: Hippocampus Press, 2011.

———. *Letters to Maurice W. Moe and Others.* Ed. David E. Schultz and S. T. Joshi. New York: Hippocampus Press, 2018.

———. *Tutti i racconti 1927–1930.* Ed. Giuseppe Lippi. Milan: Mondadori, 1991.

———, and Robert E. Howard. *A Means to Freedom: The Letters of H. P. Lovecraft and Robert E. Howard.* Ed. S. T. Joshi, David E. Schultz, and Rusty Burke. New York: Hippocampus Press, 2009. 2 vols.

Mackley, J. S. "The Shadow over Derleth: Disseminating the Mythos in *The Trail of Cthulhu.*" In *New Critical Essays on H. P.*

Lovecraft, ed. David Simmons. New York: Palgrave Macmillan, 2013. 119–34.

McRoy, Jay. "There Goes the Neighborhood: Chaotic Apocalypse and Monstrous Genesis in H. P. Lovecraft's 'The Street,' 'The Horror at Red Hook,' and 'He.'" *Journal of the Fantastic in the Arts* 52 (2003): 335–51.

Pearsall, Anthony. *The Lovecraft Lexicon: A Reader's Guide to Persons, Places and Things in the Tales of H. P. Lovecraft.* Tempe, AZ: New Falcon Publications, 2005.

Pirenne, Henri. *Mahomet et Charlemagne.* Paris: Presses Universitaires de France, 1937.

Pohl, W. "Alboin und der Langobardenzug nach Italien: Aufstieg und Fall eines Barbarenkönigs." In *Sie schufen Europa: Historische Portraits von Konstantin bis Karl dem Großen*, ed. Mischa Maier. Munich: Beck, 2007. 216–27.

Price, Robert M. "Higher Criticism and the *Necronomicon.*" 1982. In *Dissecting Cthulhu: Essays on the Cthulhu Mythos*, ed. S. T. Joshi. Lakeland, FL: Miskatonic River Press, 2011. 88–99.

Roberts, Charlotte. *Edward Gibbon and the Shape of History.* Oxford: Oxford University Press, 2014.

Schultz, David E. "Lovecraft's New York Exile: Its Influence in His Writing." *Crypt of Cthulhu* 30 (1985): 8–14.

Sheridan, J. J. "The Altar of Victory: Paganism's Last Battle." *L'Antiquité Classique* 35 (1966): 186–06.

Shershow, Scott Cutler, and Scott Michaelsen. *Love of Ruins: Letters on Lovecraft.* New York: SUNY Press, 2018.

Simmons, David. "'A Certain Resemblance': Abject Hybridity in H. P. Lovecraft's Short Fiction." In *New Critical Essays on H. P. Lovecraft*, ed. David Simmons. New York: Palgrave Macmillan, 2013. 13–30.

Tyree, J. M. "Lovecraft at the Automat." *New England Review* 29 (2008): 137–50.

Wood, I. N. *The Modern Origins of the Early Middle Ages.* Oxford: Oxford University Press, 2013.

Lovecraft, Aristeas, Dunsany, and the Dream Journey

Darrell Schweitzer

Claudio Foti's article "Aristeas and Lovecraft" (*Lovecraft Annual* No. 11, 2017) contains much of interest. For most readers, the story of the dream-traveler Aristeas of Proconnesus is a revelation. Here we have one of those itinerant miracle-workers with whom the ancient world was replete, very likely a real man whose life has since become encrusted with legend the way a pearl forms around a particle of sand, very much like Simon Magus, Jesus, Apollonius of Tyana, Lucian of Samosata's "Alexander the Quack Prophet," and so many more. What's more, this person actually wrote a long poem, *Arimaspea,* which was known and quoted by the ancients. It is mentioned in the early Byzantine encyclopedia the *Suda;* and Aulus Gellius, the second-century C.E. author of the *Attic Nights,* reports having found a soiled and battered copy in a used-book sale in Brundisium. This Aristeas is not a totally obscure personage. He even has his own Wikipedia entry. The first place I would look for such a reference is Diana Bowder's *Who Was Who in the Greek World* (1982), and sure enough, he's there, described as a hexameter poet, who flourished sometime between 680 and 540 B.C.E.

Of course, the mere fact that Aristeas wrote a book is no proof of his existence. It was common practice in the ancient world (and later) to attribute books to legendary or even imaginary persons. Surely no one today seriously thinks that Hermes Trismegistus ("Thrice-great Hermes," a fusion of the gods Hermes and Thoth) actually wrote the large body of "Hermetic" literature attributed to him. Nor is it likely that the *Key of Solomon* was really written by King Solomon.

Whether or not Aristeas existed in history or whether the stories told about him were accurate is not immediately relevant to our inquiries. What is more to the point is whether or not Lovecraft had ever heard of him. Yes, Lovecraft owned and doubtless read an edition of Herodotus. Yes, he almost certainly read it. But Herodotus tells a lot of fantastic stories, many of which influenced later classical literature and art. The ancient world loved this sort of thing. There is even a term for such stories, coined in the nineteenth century, *paradoxography,* meaning collections of reports of marvels, which might be considered the ancient equivalent of Ripley's *Believe It or Not* or Brad Steiger's *Stranger Than Science,* et al. Very little of this material has survived, as it was (very likely rightly) not considered serious literature, was not used in education, and Christian copyists surely took a dim view of it. One of the few chance survivals is the *Book of Marvels* by Phlegon of Tralles, a freedman of Hadrian (second century C.E.), to which Lovecraft directly alludes in "Supernatural Horror in Literature" as the source of "the hideous tale of the corpse-bride." Lovecraft gives the title as *On Wonderful Events.* He does not seem to have actually read Phlegon, as his work was not published in English until 1996, and Lovecraft's Greek, as we know, was not good. But he did find the corpse-bride tale in L. Collison-Morley's *Greek and Roman Ghost Stories* (1912).

Lovecraft would have been attracted to such tales, and he certainly read his Herodotus, but did he ever make any note of Aristeas and his celebrated journeys and apparent time-traveling? I am not aware that he did. I know of no discussion of Aristeas in Lovecraft's letters or essays.

However, significant evidence in support of Foti's thesis comes on pages 62–63 of *Greek and Roman Ghost Stories,* where Lovecraft undeniably read this passage in the chapter entitled "Apparitions of the Dead":

> Aristeas of Proconesus [*sic;* variant spelling], a man of high birth, died quite suddenly in a fulling establishment in his native town. The owner locked the building and went to inform his relatives, when a man from Cyzicus, hearing the news, denied it, saying that Aristeas had met him on the way thither and talked to him; and when relatives came, prepared to remove the body, they

> found no Aristeas, either alive or dead. Altogether he seems to have been a remarkable person. He disappeared for seven years, and then reappeared in Proconesus and wrote an epic poem called *Arimispea* [variant spelling: Bowder spells it *Arimisapea*], which was well known in Herodotus's day. Two hundred and forty years later he was seen again, this time at Megapontum, and bade the citizens build a shrine to Apollo, and near it erect a statue of himself, as Apollo would come to them alone of the Italian Greeks, and he would be seen following in the form of a raven. The townsmen were troubled at the apparition, and consulted the Delphic oracle, which confirmed all that Aristeas had said; and Apollo received his temple and Aristeas his statue in the market place.
>
> Apollonius tells virtually the same story, except that his version Aristeas was seen giving a lesson in literature by a number of persons in Sicily at the very hour he died in Proconesus. He says that Aristeas appeared at intervals for a number of years after his death. The elder Pliny also speaks of Aristeas, saying that at Proconesus his soul was seen to leave his body in the form of a raven, though he regards the tale as in all probability a fabrication.

We congratulate Pliny on his skepticism. This sort of "simultaneous" story was common in those days. One thinks of the one about Apollonius of Tyana, in Asia Minor, suddenly standing up and cheering on the assassin of Domitian at the very moment the emperor was being murdered in Rome. How could anyone have known, in a world of sundials and water-locks, when the news of might have taken weeks to reach Asia? As a not quite irrelevant, but irreverent, aside, which might well have occurred to Lovecraft, the apparitions of Aristeas after his alleged death sound a lot like those of Jesus after his resurrection, as told in the Gospels. Another recurring legend of a familiar type?

What matters is that we *know* that Lovecraft read this passage. It is therefore unnecessary to speculate whether he read the whole of the elder Pliny. Lovecraft's classicism seems to have been focused on the poets of the Golden and Silver Ages of Latin literature, the very ones so admired and imitated by the writers of his beloved eighteenth century. Did he read Pliny? His interest in ancient science might well have led him to do so. Did he ever read Aulus Gellius? Probably not. *Attic Nights* is a compilation of anecdotes and discussions (often on philosophical or grammatical points), intended as light reading. It is not too much of an exaggeration to say it was the *Uncle John's Bathroom Reader* of antiquity. It is certainly not high on the list of essential Latin classics.

Lovecraft definitely knew about Aristeas. But did he make any note or use of the story of Aristeas? Here we are on less certain ground. Sure, he might have read this passage and it bubbled up in his memory as he was writing the Randolph Carter stories, but there is no proof to that effect. It is just as likely that Lovecraft merely saw the account of Aristeas as one more ancient apparition story. Would it have stood out for him? It could be a matter of whether or not Lovecraft read about Aristeas in Herodotus (who describes the visits to strange lands) or in *Greek and Roman Ghost Stories* (which doesn't).

But, to use a modern phrase, I think we are overlooking the elephant in the room.

The source for Lovecraft's conception of the dream-journey is Lord Dunsany, and not only that, it is the first book by Dunsany that Lovecraft ever read, aptly entitled *A Dreamer's Tales* (1910). One need look no further than the opening paragraphs of "Idle Days on the Yann" wherein the author explains that he has come from "Ireland, which is in Europe," and the captain and crew of the ship *Bird of the River* reply, "There are no such places in all the land of dreams."

The dreamer/author explains quickly redeems himself in their eyes:

> I explained that my fancy mostly dwelt in the desert of Cuppar-Nombo, about a beautiful blue city called Golthoth the Damned, which was sentinelled all round by wolves and their shadows, and had been utterly desolate for years and years, because of a curse which the gods once spoke in anger and could never since recall. And sometimes my dreams took me as far as Pungar Vees, the red walled city where the fountains are, which trades with the Isles and Thul. When I said this they complimented me upon the abode of my fancy, saying that, though they had never seen these cities, such places might well be imagined. (208)

When a curse comes upon the titular city in the story "Bethmoora," we are told that all the Europeans (presumably other dreamers, since this is not a place you can reach via tourist steamer) flee. In the sequel, "The Hashish Man," a drug-user journeys once more to Bethmoora and finds it deserted. There he observes a sailor, who has also foolishly re-entered the accursed place only to be captured by agents of the evil emperor Thuba Mleen, who haul him off to the emperor's court. The hashish dreamer tries to follow, but the strength of his vision fails, and he awakens. Soon after he takes a stronger dose and is propelled, out of his body (which we are told remains behind in London, where he works in an insurance office by day), across "the Desert round the Hills of Hap towards Utnar Vehi," all the way to the court of Thuba Mleen, where he sees the errant sailor hideously tortured. Suddenly the emperor is aware of another spirit in the room, and two of his minions rapidly consume large spoonsful of hashish, so that their spirits can leave their bodies, seize the intruder, and haul him off to even further realms, as far as "those ivory hills are named then Mountains of Madness" (a phrase that very much *did* stick in Lovecraft's brain for later use).

It's all there. We need not go beyond the pages of *A Dreamer's Tales*. If we do, we encounter one of the sequels to "Idle Days on the Yann," "The Shop in Go-By Street" in *Tales of Three Hemispheres* (1919), in which the dreamer, not having visited the lands of dream of late, returns to find that centuries have passed there, and everything he once knew is now a ruin, because time passes differently in dreamland. Lovecraft made a note of this in his commonplace book.

Occam's Razor says that Claudio Foti's attempt to link Lovecraft's dream stories to Aristeas of Proconnesus, and even the *Arimispea/Arimisapea*, to the *Necronomicon* is interesting, but largely unnecessary. Everything can be easily accounted for otherwise. It occurs to me that the story of Aristeas as a dreamer and time-traveler could form the basis of a good novel.

What remains to be examined is how exposure to Dunsany's dream stories influenced Lovecraft's ideas of dream-travel and of the dreamlands.

First we look at "Polaris," which Lovecraft himself noted as being remarkable for its resemblance to Dunsany's work even though it was written before he had ever read a word of Dunsany. Yes, there are similarities, but there is also a key difference. There is no sense of actual travel to another place, as in "The Hashish Man." It is more a case like the famous butterfly paradox of the Chinese philosopher Chuang Tzu. Is the philosopher dreaming he is a butterfly or is the butterfly dreaming it is a man? The protagonist has two such existences, one in the modern world, one in the ancient land of Lomar. He awakens from one into the other, and vice versa. This is nevertheless a very different state of affairs from Randolph Carter's descent down the stairs to the Gate of Deeper Slumber. In any case, Lomar is not located in any dreamland, but in the Earth's remote past. We are led to believe it was near the North Pole, and that the savage Inutos who threaten it are ancestors of contemporary Eskimos.

Another pre-Dunsanian story which deals with dreams is "Beyond the Wall of Sleep." But this is quasi-science fiction. A "degenerate" Catskill mountaineer is receiving visions of fantastic things from afar, which his crude mind and inadequate "patois" cannot describe. It transpires that his body has been possessed by an alien entity, which, upon his death, escapes to wreak some desired vengeance in the vicinity of the star Algol. A nova appearing in that part of the sky indicates success. This is not a Dunsanian dream at all, but a prefigurement of "The Shadow out of Time," complete minds traveling through the ages and a glimpse of "the cruel empire of Tsan-Chan which is to come three thousand years hence" (*CF* 1.83).

Once Lovecraft discovered Dunsany, his writing about dreams and dreamlands changed radically. In "Celephaïs" (1920), the dreamer Kuranes (his dream-name) glimpses and later comes to the city of his dreams, where he will ultimately reign forever as a god, because he created the place by dreaming it. Maybe so, but on the way there he seems to pass through many realms that have an objective existence. Here again there are prefigurements of later stories, including a glimpse of a sinister priest in a silken mask who dwells all along in a monastery (or tower) on the Plateau of Leng. This image is well known to any Lovecraftian. Even more intriguing is the bit where the dreamer grows impatient with "ordinary" dreaming and, like the characters in Dunsany's "The Hashish Man," gives himself a boost with this drug. He overshoots wildly and ends up in:

> a part of space where form does not exist, but where glowing gases study the secrets of existence. And a violet-coloured gas told him that this part of space was outside what he had called infinity. The gas had not heard of planets and organisms before, but identified Kuranes merely as one from the infinity where matter, energy, and gravitation exist. (*CF* 1.189–90)

That is surely the ultimate statement of Lovecraftian cosmicism, and it curiously suggests "The Colour out of Space," with its totally alien, if less communicative gas or plasma entity.

When Kuranes dies in the "waking" world, he is escorted by a retinue of knights off to Celephaïs, where he is to reign forever. It is indeed as if he has escaped into a timeless dream (in the more conventional sense, i.e., something that only exists in his own mind). The story takes its basic form from Dunsany's "The Coronation of Mr. Thomas Shap" (in *The Book of Wonder*), which treats the theme more frivolously and suggests that the dreamer has indeed escaped into his own (subjective) dreams forever, while his body is committed to a madhouse. Lovecraft seems to be trying to have it both ways, but here he is going beyond Dunsany in his conception of what Dreamland is and how you get there.

Then there is *The Dream-Quest of Unknown Kadath*, which is too well known to require any synopsis here. In this novel, Lovecraft ties together all his previous "Dunsanian" stories and even intriguingly draws in "Pickman's Model." Here we see his most clear conception of Dreamland.

It is true that the "sunset city" of Randolph Carter's dreams is no more than a glorified memory of his native Boston, but the dreamscape he adventures through is something else entirely. It is not just an interior experience in the mind of the dreamer, but seems to be a universe or dimension apart, with its own native tribes and species, and its own geography. Aristeas allegedly traveled to remote parts of the earth, but, in theory, for all the way might be long and dangerous, it should have been possible for an ancient Greek to journey to the lands of the Hyperboreans or Cimmerians, by ship or on horseback or however. But the Lovecraftian dreamland can *only* be reached by dreaming or astral travel, with or without the help of drugs, rather the same way Dunsany's cities along the river Yann can be reached. Furthermore, there is some implication that Lovecraft's dreamland exists beyond death, in another realm, though not a conventional heaven or hell. How exactly did Pickman get there? It would seem that he was transformed almost wholly into a ghoul, then accompanied his ghoul friends down into the earth, into depths far below the level of man-made graves or tunnels, until he came to another sort of realm entirely? Did the Outsider, after climbing a tower above a dark forest, only to crawl out of a grave, also emerge from Dreamland? This is not a place that can be reached by any non-mystical means. You can't fly there in a spaceship. Thus it is more remote than a distant galaxy, even though it can be accessed through the simple process of sleep.

Lovecraft clearly built on Dunsany. He took the concept beyond Dunsany. Some subsequent writers, with varying degrees of success, from Brian Lumley to Kij Johnson, have tried to build on Lovecraft; but I don't see Aristeas of Proconnesus in this line of development.

Works Cited

Bowder, Diana. *Who Was Who in the Greek World.* Ithaca, NY: Cornell University Press, 1982.

Collison-Morley, L. *Greek and Roman Ghost Stories.* Chicago: Argonaut, 1968. [A facsimile of the 1912 edition that Lovecraft read.]

Dunsany, Lord. *The Great Book of Wonder.* Rev. ed. Rockville MD: Wildside Press, 2016.

Foti, Claudio. "Aristeas and Lovecraft." *Lovecraft Annual* No. 11 (2017): 73–91.

Hansen, William. *Phlegon of Tralles' Book of Marvels.* Exeter, UK: University of Exeter, 1996.

H. P. Lovecraft—Beacon and Gateway

Donald Sidney-Fryer

During the recent NecronomiCon III held in Providence, Rhode Island, at the Biltmore and Omni Hotels, during 17–20 August 2017, Thursday through Sunday, I could not fail to note several salient phenomena concerning certain things and events Lovecraftian. Along with quite a few others, I had been invited to function as one of the guests of honor, a distinction rarely given me and one to be cherished. Thanks to Derrick Hussey and Niels Hobbs, I appeared at the convention as poet laureate, a post created in accordance with the cultivated literary standards of poet and fictioneer Howard Phillips Lovecraft. I must say that the people who put on the convention had certainly provided a very rich smorgasbord of lectures, panel discussions, and other presentations concerning a wide range of subject and activity involving poetry, storytelling and other prose, as well as film. It resulted in a genuine *embarras de richesses*.

The earnest conventioneer would have had a hard choice to select what to attend when the options included multiple events of equal interest scheduled for the same hour. The convention people had surely arranged a splendid series of fascinating programs and afforded the paying customers a helluva lot for their money, besides assuring the smooth functioning and management of the convention itself, all possible praise to those behind (and before) the scenes. As ever, the vendor rooms with their many books as produced by a variety of publishers, not to mention T-shirts and other novelties, proved eminently stimulating.

I myself had the great good fortune to appear on a number of panels where I had enough ease and expertise that I could make intelligent and intelligible statements about the authors or literature being featured: Ambrose Bierce, Arthur Machen, modern imaginative poetry of the weird and fantastic, et alia. I also discovered or met people who admire some of my own writings, and for whom I signed their copies of my own books—always a gratifying experience, particularly for a relatively esoteric poet and author like myself. But, as always, or as often occurs at conventions, the principal gratification happens while encountering people in the halls and corridors and spontaneously striking up an earnest conversation. Meeting like-minded people fervently interested in the same subjects can often result in considerable pleasure, no less than in beginning new friendships.

Thus H.P.L. (may Cthulhu bless him as a fellow New Englander) had once again provided a wide umbrella to encompass a huge assortment of topics, readers, authors, poets, and what have you. I need not rehearse in any extensive detail, at least not to Lovecraftians, the now well-known known saga of how August Derleth and Donald Wandrei founded Arkham House to give greater permanence to Lovecraft's remarkable stories, poetry, and essays of the fantastic and supernatural by publishing a hardcover series of his collections beginning in the late 1930s and early 1940s. Through Derleth and Arkham House H.P.L. posthumously came to provide a wide umbrella indeed for publishing many other authors and collections, which otherwise might never have found the dignity of hardcover book publication.

In the same way the different conventions honoring Lovecraft, starting at least with the first World Fantasy Convention in 1975 (and in the same Providence), as founded by Kirby McCauley, have come to provide a wide umbrella for many other authors and many other books. All this, done posthumously in Lovecraft's name, appears to myself, among many other authors who have benefited by the same big umbrella, as an extraordinary legacy. As a fellow New Englander I take great pride in that achievement. Lovecraft's name and fame have now spread throughout much of the far-reaching Anglophone world covering much of planet earth; and where unknown in English, he is known in accomplished translation in quite a few languages.

During NecronomiCon III I could not help but reflect on how Lovecraft through his own writings, and through his influence by way of Derleth and Arkham House, as well as the ensuing propagandizing, has become, almost more than metaphorically, a beacon and a gateway not only for critics, readers, and literary connoisseurs, but thus also a beacon and a gateway for many other authors and other types of creators (pictorial artists, sculptors, makers of films and television features). Thus dear H.P.L. has achieved not just cult status but near universal promulgation. For an unassuming antiquarian and (at one time) an obscure mythographer, that represents a deed at once exceptional and colossal, something tremendous. In that sense the pen is mightier than the sword. I venture to say that the more ample opportunity he has created for other and lesser-known authors would give H.P.L. a huge amount of delight and satisfaction. May no negative reaction to this statement emanate from any committed Lovecraftian!

Recently there has come into my hands a fine journal-review, *Dead Reckonings,* the issue for Fall 2017, as ably edited by Alex Houstoun and Michael J. Abolafia, and published by the ever innovative and enterprising Hippocampus Press, as directed by the enlightened owner-editor Derrick Hussey. I have perused this issue deliberately and with great care, not only in regard to the excellent notices given to a variety of books and other materials (unusually extended and sensitive to the authors under review, their intentions and nuances), but especially to the reminiscences by diverse writers apropos of the recent NecronomiCon III. I can only regret that Kirby McCauley can no longer see the later result of what he started in 1975, by having the first World Fantasy Convention take place in the same town, H.P.L.'s own city par excellence.

We can merely mention in passing such extraordinary notices as those by James Machin à propos Joachim Kalka's Gaslight; by Jim Rockhill à propos Zoe Lehmann Imfield's "The Victorian Ghost Story and Theology"; and by Daniel Pietersen à propos Jeffrey Thomas's *Haunted Worlds*. And I don't envy S. T. Joshi having to review an anthology of contemporary weird stories that would seem to be a very mixed bag indeed.

I find myself particularly indebted to the reminiscences of NecronomiCon III by writers other than myself: "A Few Reflections" by Martin Andersson; "Curating Ars Necronomica 2017" by Brian L. Mullen III; "Musings: NecronomiCon 2017" by Dean Kuhta; "Vibrant and Vivid: Necronomicon 2017" by Elena Tchougounova-

Paulson; "A Reflection: Necronomicon 2017" by Dr. Géza A. G. Reilly. These relate to events or phenomena that I could not attend (for whatever reason) in spite of my keen interest. I find fascinating what I discover about the artists John Jude Palencar and Sarah Horrocks, whose art I did not get to see, but which I can glean from the articles on, or interviews with, these artists with accompanying illustrations.

All the above puts me in a better position to continue reflecting on NecronomiCon III, not only as aided and abetted by other writers in attendance thereat, but also as inspired by the general tone and direction of the overall journal relative to H.P.L. himself. As invariably the odd man out (for much of my life, but less these days as a respected senile citizen), my reflections or observations may have some value for other readers.

I notice in many of the articles the near constant reference to the horrors created or inspired by Lovecraft and his tales of *supernatural* horror. I rarely note the use of *supernatural* relative to this horror, but it differs significantly from other kinds of horror such as those enumerated by history in general, so much of which remains a catalogue of horrors and atrocities that actually occurred: the destruction of Bagdad by the Mongols; the destruction of the Roman city of Cremona by a Roman legion; the organized pogroms of the Jews under the latter Tsarist regime; the death camps operated by the Nazis; and, at the end of 2017, the ethnic cleansing of the Rohingya Muslims out of the otherwise eminently Buddhist country of Myanmar, the former Burma.

Obviously Lovecraft in his fiction is dealing with quite a different kind of horror, rather than with pure grue, which did not interest him as a fictioneer. He had a strong sense of aesthetics that guided him in his fictional but serious revelations, no less chilling than pure grue, but infinitely more artistic.

Rather than regarding his novels and short stories as horror stories, albeit of supernatural horror—such a simplification does an artist of his high calibre a grave injustice—I prefer to regard his prose fictions, particularly the longer tales, that is, *At the Mountains of Madness*, "The Shadow out of Time," "The Shadow over Innsmouth," and so forth, as existential parables, or parables of existential unease, to remind us modern rationalists that the scheme of things might be darker, much darker, than what we care to entertain all alone by ourselves. Enlightenment through a glass darkly, as it were!

Briefly Noted

A previously unknown published letter by Lovecraft has come to light—published, of all places, in the *Omaha World-Herald* (21 February 1920): 6. Titled "The Bible as Literature," the letter reads as follows:

> Omaha, Feb. 18.—To the Editor of the World-Herald: All attempts at gaining literary polish must begin with judicious reading, and the learner must never cease to hold this phase uppermost. In many cases the usage of good authors will be found a more effective guide than any amount of precept. A page of Addison or of Irving will teach more of style than a whole manual of rules, whilst a story of Poe's will impress upon the mind a more vivid notion of powerful and correct description and narration than will ten dry chapters of a bulky text book. Let every student read unceasingly the best writers.
>
> It is also highly important that cheaper types of reading, if hitherto followed, be dropped. Popular magazines inculcate a careless and deplorable style which is hard to unlearn, and which impedes the acquisition of a purer style. If such things must be read, let them be skimmed over as lightly as possible. An excellent habit to cultivate is the analytical study of the King James Bible. For simple yet rich and forceful English this masterly production is hard to equal, and even though its Saxon vocabulary and poetic rhythm be unsuited to general composition, it is invaluable for writers. Lord Dunsany, perhaps the greatest living prose artist, derived nearly all of his stylistic tendencies from the scriptures.
>
> H. P. LOVECRAFT.

It is unclear why the letter is stated to have originated in Omaha. It is not known that Lovecraft had any colleagues in Omaha at this time, but he must have had one, and this person must have forwarded the letter to the editor of the newspaper.

The Void: A Lovecraftian Analysis

Duncan Norris

> "If I say that my somewhat extravagant imagination yielded simultaneous pictures of an octopus, a dragon, and a human caricature, I shall not be unfaithful to the spirit of the thing."
>
> —H. P. Lovecraft, "The Call of Cthulhu" (*CF* 2.23–24)

The above epigraph demonstrates the innate difficulty in attempting to translate the literary works of H. P. Lovecraft to the medium of cinema: it simultaneously describes something tangible and yet leaves it largely to the imagination of the reader to flesh out the details. Cinema is a language of image and the explicitly shown, and this is in many ways the antithesis of Lovecraft's style. The half-hidden and shadowy implications drive his work, and even in stories wherein he exposes the monster, such as in "The Call of Cthulhu," it is through the remote eyes of someone reading another's diary. Attentive readers will note Lovecraft never gives a full description of Cthulhu as a being when it actually appears, but relies mainly on use of snippets of emotive adjectives (and of course adverbs) through the paragraphs such as "lumbered slobberingly," "gelatinous green immensity," "flabby claws," and "awful squid-head with writhing feelers."

By his clever use of foreshadowing Lovecraft, when he finally reveals Cthulhu, does not need to spend any significant portion of time in long description of this entity. Rather he has implanted enough information to the reader for a recognition and basic understanding of the appearance of Cthulhu, sprinkling in a few evocative specifics but with enough attendant vagueness that the reader's own preconceptions, fears, and understandings fills in many of the exact details. It is a technique at which Lovecraft is a master, and it can be seen repeatedly throughout his work, culminating in "The Haunter of the Dark," in which the eponymous creature is frightening enough to cause death from shock just to look upon for an instant, but amorphously undescribed enough that its appearance is almost totally unknown save for black wings and a three-lobed burning eye. This categorization, whilst evocative, is not particularly useful as an overall descriptor beyond the alienness it conveys, and is open to the widest possible interpretations.

Thus while there have been any number of attempts to bring Lovecraft to cinema, television, and their various Internet progeny, both as direct adaptations and as thematic interpretations, unfortunately the majority of such enterprises, especially of the larger Hollywood-style variety rather than smaller independent projects, have often been unsuccessful. Like Lovecraft's own writings, cinematic works later acknowledged as classics of their genre such as *The Thing* (1982), were often critical and commercial failures upon initial release, although their reputations have grown immeasurably over time. This is not to lump all such works together as unappreciated or bad, nor to blithely denigrate the ever-increasing number of attempts as without merits or any redeeming features. There are in fact many incredible realizations of artists and creators work based upon Lovecraft across all these media, and this is especially true of the smaller works such as one might find at the H. P. Lovecraft Film Festival or across YouTube. Yet it is undeniable that few, if indeed any, are commercially significant upon a scale that would be noticed by those outside the wider Lovecraftian and horror communities. Those (and here the term is applied extremely loosely) Lovecraftian films that have succeeded are often divorced in story, tone, and ideals from the source material, at best tangentially related, or are connected almost exclusively by thematic connection rather than any adaptation of Lovecraft's actual stories. Thus, with that caveat, we will attempt an analysis of what makes the 2016 horror film *The Void* so immediately Lovecraftian, to try and see if it is possible to exhume and dissect its underlying influences and thus come to a greater understanding of both the film and Lovecraft's ongoing inspiration in the horror film genre.

It would be a rare review of *The Void* that does not make reference to Lovecraft. From the initial promotional posters showing tentacles coming from some otherworldly space via a triangle portal to strange cultists, malign cosmic forces, obsession with overcoming death, and the profoundly weird atmosphere that pervades the film, it feels instantly and remarkably Lovecraftian. Yet it is also a movie with deep connections to a number of aspects of the horror film genre. The multiple influences and deliberate homages to its cinematic ancestors, especially the viscerally grotesque special effects horror films of the 1980s, are equally patent. So, for all that it immediately feels Lovecraftian, is it truly connected to his ideas and aesthetic or merely copying forms, tropes, and superficial connections? The seminal Evil Dead horror film (and eventually television) series begun with *The Evil Dead* (1981) has the *Necronomicon* as the key plot point and connecting object, yet these are not generally considered particularly Lovecraftian horror movies, while the Japanese film *Marebito* (2004), without any direct connection to Lovecraft in plot or references but steeped in Lovecraft's ideations, is (Migliore and Strysik 75–76). The 2012 film in the *Alien* franchise *Prometheus* is very much a straight science fiction/horror film with the traditional accompanying tropes of spaceships, a hostile humanoid race, and amazing technological prowess far exceeding current understandings. Yet it had enough similarities to *At the Mountains of Madness* in its ideas of extraterrestrials creating earthly life according to accepted practises and exterminating that which failed to suit their purposes that noted director of the fantastic Guillermo del Toro reputedly stated that the film had effectively killed his planned adaptation of the Lovecraft novel (Jagernauth). "Lovecraftian" is thus often a matter of taste and interpretation.

The most obvious place to begin our dissection (or vivisection) is with authorial intent. After all, it certainly possible to create something that may feel Lovecraftian simply by an author's parallel but individual and independent vision. In an often distinctly different yet significantly and related arrogation, a work may reference Lovecraft's works, especially the unique names that superficially underlie the Cthulhu Mythos in the less discriminate wider culture. Such terms have often been absorbed via cultural osmosis rather than by direct connection, such as in the aforementioned *Evil Dead*. Popular understanding to the contrary, in the wider series the malefic grimoire that raises the titular demons is not actually called the *Necronomicon* until the second film, *Evil Dead II* (1987), and the name became applied to the book in the first film with retroactive continuity. However, it is worth noting that this sequel is effectively a remake of the original film with a higher budget and played far more as a horror comedy, coming out after the small wave of Lovecraft adaptations following the success of the black horror comedy *Re-Animator* (1985). The Sumerian origins of the demonic entities in *The Evil Dead* further connect it at a remove from Lovecraft. The hoax book commonly known as the *Simon Necronomicon*, published in 1977 and purporting to be the actual *Necronomicon*, is strongly influenced by Sumerian mythology. *Evil Dead II*'s further abstraction from Lovecraft can be seen it the addition of a second title to the film's version of this grimoire, *Necronomicon Ex-Mortis*, which loosely translated becomes the tautological tortured 'A Book concerning he Dead from Death.'[1]

Such a background of vague and unspecified cultural absorption of Lovecraft is not the case with *The Void*. Lovecraft was in the minds of the creators from its inception, and the project is very much both a labor of love and an independent feature film rather than a typical Hollywood creation. Its co-creators are Jeremy Gillespie and Steven Kostanski, who are both writers and directors of the film, and the budget was in large part sourced with crowdfunding via the website Indiegogo. But it is not entirely without connection to the mainstream Hollywood system. Kostanski notes that he and much of the *Void* crew were working on Warner Bros. Pictures' *Suicide Squad* (2016) before a clash of schedules forced them to leave (The Creeping Craig). *Suicide Squad* eventually made some $745 million at the box office and, more significantly, won the Academy Award for Best Makeup (Suicide Squad, *Box Office Mojo*). According to Gillespie's own testimony, he was inspired by the aforementioned del Toro's comments on his plans to create Lovecraft's monsters for the abandoned *At the Mountains of Madness* movie project, which conjured in his mind

1. Translations of the word 'Necronomicon' are notoriously fraught with ambiguity, and it is not the author's intent to offer a definitive version or ignite debate here. Suffice to say that in no common translation does adding 'Ex-Mortis' benefit the elucidation of the contents.

"a vision of what that meant to me . . . an image very key to *The Void*" (Gelmini). He later elaborated: "there are literary influences like Lovecraft, weird fiction and that overall vibe. In terms of film, I'd say *Aliens* and *Alien*" (Saldana). In a like vein Kostanski, responding directly as to which Lovecraft stories inspired *The Void*, replied: "I don't know of any specifics. It was more overall tone that we wanted to capture, because I love stuff that feels Lovecraftian without just being an adaptation of his stories"; his partner agreed, noting that "in a way I would say this is like, not really on the same page since we are very much showing you the things. But definitely his overarching body of works has a tone or a feeling to them that I think was the inspiration" (The Creeping Craig).

A summation of the plot of *The Void* is required. As this may not be a movie familiar to the average filmgoer, it will be of necessity in some depth. The movie starts with a dead body in a house, gunshots, and a triangle symbol painted on a door. Two people flee the house, a man who successfully runs off and a woman who is shot down by another, older man emerging from the house with a rifle. This man and a younger accomplice then proceed to burn the injured woman alive and are evidently intent on tracking the other fugitive. Said fugitive is discovered by the local sheriff, Daniel Carter, who seeing the blood on his clothing takes him to the local hospital. Said hospital is run by a skeleton staff of a single doctor, Richard Powell, two nurses, Allison and Beverly, and nurse-in-training Kim. A fire gutting the lower part of the building has caused the hospital to be in the process of being abandoned. The entire patient roster is thus only a single young man, Cliff, recovering from minor surgery, and a heavily pregnant teen, Maggie, accompanied by her grandfather, Ben, who has accompanied his granddaughter for a check-up.

The fugitive is soon identified as a known junkie named James and appears largely uninjured but in need of sedation. It is clear that the head nurse, Allison, is the estranged wife of the sheriff, and that their relationship apparently did not survive the death of their child in utero. Almost immediately afterward, Daniel discovers that Beverly has gone insane, finding her stabbing Cliff to death and cutting off her own face. Sheriff Daniel is forced to shoot and kill her when Beverly attacks him. Recovering from this emotional shock in the bathroom, Daniel passes out and has weird visions of what we later learn is the Void and its effects. When he recovers, a state trooper, Mitchell, has arrived, apparently already en route after the report of the injured man James due to a "bloodbath" in a house not far distant. The trooper allows Daniel to make the call in to headquarters about the shooting; failing to get a signal on the hospital phone, Sheriff Daniel goes out to his squad car. Here he is attacked by a robed figure in white with a knife, whose hood has a triangular symbol in front over the face. Daniel then experiences a second vision and discovers that the entire hospital has been surrounded by figures in identical garb. These figures, however, are not attacking but rather seem to be keeping those in the hospital trapped, and Daniel retreats inside.

The now awakened James starts screaming and is menaced by the now reanimated and mutating body of Beverly, but is freed of his restraints and rescued by Daniel. Once free, James then grabs the pregnant Maggie as a hostage, using a scalpel to her throat as a threat. In this moment the two men seen earlier burning the woman alive and pursuing James arrive. During the ensuing chaos James stabs Dr. Powell to death but is subdued by Ben even as the Beverly monster appears and drags off the state trooper, Mitchell. The strangers, identified only by their relationship as father and son, assisted by Daniel, attack and kill the Beverly creature. Everyone regroups, but Maggie is now experiencing complications and requires additional medicine. Daniel, the father, and the son go out to the cruiser for a rifle while Allison goes off alone against advice to get medical supplies for the impending birth. The former trio make it back inside despite being attacked by another cultist, but the supposedly dead Powell appears behind Allison in her mission and she fails to return. The returning trio search for her and are disturbed by a ringing phone, coming from the morgue. It is Powell, who is simultaneously revealed to be part of the cult, along with a grimoire of unnamed provenance and Polaroid photographs on his desk, including a photograph of the door shown in the opening shot of the film and various cult figures. One of the pictures is of James.

Under interrogation by Daniel, the father, and the son, James reveals he killed Powell after recognizing him as the head of the cult, in which he is an initiate by coercion as a result of his drug addiction. The four then go into the burnt-out basement, which isn't congruent with the student nurse Kim's memory of it, and apparently contains a previously unknown area. Allison is then shown as upon an operating/autopsy table being lectured by Powell, and in exploring the basement area Daniel has his third vision before a door marked with the triangle symbol. Powell explains to Allison his scheme to end the cycle of birth and death, and his wish to bring back his own dead daughter. His earlier misbegotten experiments populate the horror-filled basement, trying to find ways to die. They attack the interlopers, killing James.

Meanwhile Maggie kills her own grandfather, as it transpires that she is a member of the cult and that Powell is the father of her child, and the cultists finally enter the building. Down in the basement the son and the father have visions of their old home and the family they lost, and the father nearly kills the son until the latter drives the vision away with a flare in the side. Daniel finds Allison on the operating table, but it is a false vision. Seeing the monstrosity she has become, he mercy-kills her with an axe. Daniel then finds himself transported into a sacrificial chamber facing Powell before a huge glowing triangle on the wall that is flanked by two of the cultists. Maggie appears and stabs Daniel, while a thoroughly mutated Powell opens a dimensional gateway. The fetus in Maggie's womb begins to mutate and burst forth, still attached to its mother, as the father and son arrive. They attack it and the father dies, sacrificing himself as he attempts to kill the monster with fire. Daniel attacks Powell with an axe, but to no effect. In return Powell offers him Allison back. Daniel seems to acquiesce but instead pushes himself and Powell through the triangular portal into the Void. The light ceases and the entire area begins to collapse upon itself, with the son barely escaping a closing corridor to find himself back inside a regular section of the hospital. He then discovers Kim, who has killed a cultist and managed to survive. The final shot is of Carter and Allison holding hands in the wasteland expanse of the Void, looking up at a gigantic pyramid.

In seeking Lovecraftian connections, the obvious first step is in names. The list of movies that utilize Lovecraft's creations completely divorced from, and often antithetically aesthetically and thematically opposed to, their original setting and meaning is depressingly voluminous. Likewise, to the same point the list of homages and shout-outs to Lovecraft is a subject unto itself. Nor is this a new trend. *The Mummy's Ghost* (1944), a largely forgettable entry in Universal Picture's original Mummy films, was forced to change the names of the evil priests of Karnak, a real location in Egypt, due to the sensitivities of wartime with the concomitant fears of offending allies or offering potential objects for enemy propaganda: it was replaced with the name Arkham instead[2] (Worland 55). Refreshingly, *The Void* doesn't seek to arrogate to itself some reflected splendor by name-dropping classic Lovecraft creations, such as Cthulhu, the *Necronomicon*, Yog-Sothoth, etc. Rather, it is able to make a suitable homage and reference in a subtle manner that doesn't interrupt the flow of their own narrative. Specifically, the main protagonist is Daniel Carter and the location of the action is centered on the Marsh Hospital, Randolph Cater of course being Lovecraft's author avatar and the Marsh being one of the families that bred with Deep Ones in Innsmouth. In fact, in subtle metatextual foreshadowing, the very name Marsh Hospital is a subtle clue that terrible things with the mixing of the human form are occurring there. Any doubts about the deliberateness of this nomenclature is dispelled by the repeated line of the sheriff to his dispatcher after the first monstrous attack, "This is Carter at Marsh County," which gives a nod of fan-service to Lovecraft without being distracting or overly calling attention to itself. (There is also a mention of the "something calling" the cultists to the hospital, quite conceivably a reference to "The Call of Cthulhu," but this is possibly a case of critical over-interpretation.)

Instead of directly borrowing from Lovecraft, the filmmakers instead go back to the ideas from which he drew and created his fearful tomes and monstrosities. The evil cult is never named, unexplained but menacing in just its presence, and the omnipresence of its triangle motif becomes a great harbinger of fear. The closest the film gets to exposition is in the vague and Lovecraftian ideas of "Things much older . . . older than time.' This is a deliberate choice, as elaborated upon by producer Casey Walker, who stated

2. Lest it be thought that the name Arkham may be a coincidence, it is worth noting that the majority of the film is set in a fictional Massachusetts university town.

that "we had lots and lots of conversations about not getting into the details of what the belief system is. We felt the ambiguity would be a lot scarier" (Saldana). There is a book connected with the cult, which is shown to have more of the triangle motif in its cabbalistic style drawings, but it is not named nor expounded upon. Instead, Polaroid photographs of indistinct yet orgiastic scenes with said book are used to convey the ideas of the forbidden and dark with which Lovecraft surrounds his occult books.

This limited exposition and deeper implications approach, so typical of Lovecraft, is present for much of the movie and adds potentiality to the weirdness. The father and son hunters who are the killers in the first scene are not the typical horror movie Van Helsing-esque experts with demystifying answers readily at hand. They are acting out of a combination of revenge and a desire to stop the evil they have encountered, a cinematic embodiment of the actions of Walter de la Poer, eleventh Baron Exham in "The Rats in the Walls," whose actions in murdering his entire family and leaving his entire privileged life was determined after he was "shaken by some horror greater than that of conscience or the law" (*CF* 1.374). This duo has clearly endured hardship and difficult encounters—hinted at but never explained—before the movie commences. It is shown that the son has a neck wound so severe that he cannot speak, which occurred as a result of his trusting people; but like what Walter de la Poer discovered, how and why this occurred is never fully explained. The fact that the pair never name themselves, even in the credits being merely listed as The Father and The Son, is particularly significant. While such underdevelopment could be seen as indications of their being disposable fodder in a badly made horror film, this is patently not the case here. Instead, such a deliberate choice plays to the Lovecraftian trope of the atmosphere and the events, rather than human beings being key elements of the story.

There are numerous other aspects of the film that are also distinctly Lovecraftian tropes, such as the foreshadowing of dreams and visions, the importance of geometry, and nightmarish immortality. However, such tropes are not unique or intrinsic to Lovecraft, and are common enough motifs in many horror films, although it must be stated that they certainly do add to the weird and specifically Lovecraftian atmosphere. In terms of other, more solid connections to Lovecraft, the descent into the depths of the burnt-out lower levels of the hospital has distinct echoes of Dr. Willett's ventures under Joseph Curwen's old house in *The Case of Charles Dexter Ward,* with its malformed once-human monsters, huge pentagram, and other such esoteric mathematical designs. The final escape of the son through a corridor that disappears behind him reinforces the connection with Willett finding solid concrete in place of the tunnel at the old Curwen farm after his own experiences. Yet this brings us to the other filmic influences that bubble forth throughout *The Void. The Case of Charles Dexter Ward* had been previously adapted to film at least twice, with the more faithful 1991 version by *Alien* co-writer Dan O'Bannon *The Resurrected* (a.k.a. *The Ancestor,* a.k.a. *Shatterbrain*) noted as a "favorite creature feature" by Kostanski (The Creeping Craig). The scene in *The Void* of fighting the imperfect monsters in the unnaturally endless hospital basement owes as much to O'Bannon's interpretation as it does to Lovecraft's original vision, with its hideous creatures formed of imperfect salts each in individual oubliettes. Likewise, the moments of the son's chase and escape is visually similar enough to another cross-dimensional escape, that of Kirsty from The Engineer in Clive Barker's *Hellraiser* (1987), that it not being done deliberately as homage seems unlikely.

The combination of inspiration and homage throughout *The Void* is a great deal of its appeal. Director John Carpenter is one particularly dominant influence, in particular his *Apocalypse Trilogy* (*The Thing, Prince of Darkness,* and *In the Mouth of Madness).* Carpenter's films are openly filled with Lovecraftian story ideas, themes, shout-outs, name-droppings, and even direct quotations as dialogue. *The Thing* (1982), about an isolated Antarctic research base menaced by a shape-shifting, possessive alien, informs much of the visual aesthetic and unknowing paranoia of *The Void* and, at the risk of mixing metaphors, *The Void* is a film that wears this homage on its sleeve. The scene of Allison on the autopsy table deliberately echoes the examination of the burnt body of the partially transformed Thing recovered from the Norwegian camp. The ambiguous yet ominous finale of *The Void* and the downplaying of the romantic subplot, a seemingly mandatory part of the horror movie genre, also harkens back to the bleakness of Carpenter's widely acknowledged classic. *The Thing,* which has no female presence save the voice on a computer chess game, ends with the characters destroying their own base to prevent the Thing from escaping and having the two survivors, whose status as human or Thing is unknown by either characters or audience, sit down to wait and die in the Antarctic cold.

Yet this is not the only connection to Carpenter's filmography. The cultist trapping those inside a soon-to-be-abandoned public building echoes *Assault on Precinct 13* (1976), with its criminals against cops surrounded in a decommissioned police station, and even more so *Prince of Darkness* (1987), with its possessed homeless people keeping the protagonists trapped in the church, or even the less acclaimed combination *Ghosts of Mars* (2001) and its possessed attackers trapping people inside a police station. The inability to escape by natural means, and sudden unexplained physical shifts in location, also echo the third and most blatantly Lovecraftian film in Carpenter's *Apocalypse Trilogy, In the Mouth of Madness* (1994). These three *Apocalypse* films, with their possessive forces changing those forced into proximity with them and blending science with the arcane, is again a major theme inside *The Void.* The scene with Daniel looking into a mirror and seeing the Void is likewise very reminiscent of the mirror scenes in *Prince of Darkness,* which were also featured prominently in the trailer for the latter film. But mirrors as gateways and portents are a popular feature in films, horror and otherwise, while the trope exists far further back into folklore and legendry. It is important to ascribe a not overly Lovecraftian origin to what may be a larger well of wider and older ideas.

To more definitive connections Stuart Gordon's *From Beyond* (1986), extremely loosely based on Lovecraft's story of the same name and a spiritual sequel to his 1985 hit *Re-Animator,* again loosely based on Lovecraft's original work, certainly inform the ideas of extra-dimensional and post-mortem mutation in *The Void* and the subsequent after-effects upon human appearances. Lucio Fulci, the late Italian director whose films were notorious for their high levels of physical gruesomeness and visceral use of violence, is also another who utilized Lovecraftian names and occasionally some of his stories in his works. *City of the Living Dead* (1980; a.k.a. *The Gates of Hell*) is set in Dunwich; *The Beyond* (1981) quotes from the *Book of Eibon;* while *The Curse* (1987) is a (relatively) faithful adaptation of "The Colour out of Space," which Fulci produced and did much of the second unit and special effects upon. The resonance of Fulci's films, in particular the unofficial trilogy of *City of the Living Dead, The Beyond,* and *The House by the Cemetery* (1981), which "are steeped in cosmic dread" (Larned), is present throughout *The Void.* The director infamously used graphic violence unhesitatingly, in particular the stabbing of characters through the eye, which became almost a signature aspect of many of his films, including *Zombi 2* (1979),[3] *The Beyond,* and *The New York Ripper* (1982). Of the last-named film the director jovially commented: "it was fun to do the scene with the eye of the girl ripped by the razor blade" (Lavagini), while an eye-stabbing scene was famously cut from *The House by the Cemetery,* a film described as a "curious mix of Lovecraft, Romero and Freud" (Christopher 2) for not being realistic enough. Just such a brutal stabbing is done early on in the *The Void* when the nurse Beverly kills the recovering patient Cliff, after succumbing to the influence of the Void. The ending with Daniel and Allison hopelessly trapped in the dimension of the Void again echoes the male and female protagonists of *The Beyond* trapped in a supernatural wasteland from which there is no apparent escape.

Other films mentioned by name as particularly influential by the directors include *Alien* (1979), *The Shining* (1980) (Gelmini), *The Blob* (1988), *The Fly I* & *II* (1986 and 1989) (Craig), and *No Country for Old Men* (2007) (Saldana). The Lovecraftian connections thus continue, but in a distanced and distorted fashion. The least likely at first glance is the Oscar-winning modern western, without any hint of preternatural overtones, *No Country for Old Men.* Yet this unrelentingly nihilistic look at society in 1980 without any higher meaning or purpose or morality than merely random happenstances is certainly a very Lovecraftian worldview, even if solely focused on human events. To the other more patently horror films the Blob and shoggoths for examples, while not

3. It has too many alternative titles to mention

definitively lineally connected, emphatically occupy much of the same conceptual space and almost certainly help inform some of *The Void*'s more protoplasmic and amorphous creatures. *Alien*'s iconic creature design by Swiss artist H. R. Giger occurred after his elevation to the notice of director Ridley Scott following his controversial exhibition entitled *Necronomicon*, which certainly needs no elaboration as to its influence. Co-writer Dan O'Bannon later commented that *Alien* was "certainly my most successful venture into Lovecraft turf" (Collis), while Giger and Scott combined to take the Lovecraftian themes of the malignity of the truly alien which man can never understand and placed the hidden fears of tainted births, bloodlines, and miscegenation that weave through Lovecraft's works into the central, unshadowed position of horror in the film. *The Shining* was likewise adapted from the Stephen King novel of the same name, and King both is a Lovecraft fan and counts him as an influence extending from his earliest work like *The Mist* to his more recent, such as *Revival* (2014). The latter is such a clear homage to Lovecraft to the extent that King not only partially dedicated a book to him but in the same book chose Lovecraft's most famous couplet from the *Necronomicon* as an epigraph. It is not hard to mentally squint and imagine King as a pseudo-doppelgänger of Lovecraft: both New Englanders whose merged real and invented milieu is as much a personality as an environment with interlocked artificial mythologies in their works, with King vastly successful in his own time for his excellent characterizations while Lovecraft's alienating cosmic perspective awaited wider discovery by most from beyond his grave. Thus while *The Shining*, both novel and film, are not Lovecraftian, their genesis has common roots that stretch from King's Castle Rock to Lovecraft's Arkham.

The body horror genre to which *The Fly* duo belong, and the bodily horror of *The Blob*, also oddly fit in the Lovecraftian movie tradition. *The Thing*, unarguably one of the best Lovecraftian films yet made, gains much of its power from the masterful combination of mounting paranoia and isolation. Yet its undeniably powerful gore imagery and body horror aspects are equally important aspects of the film, and such aspects have been much taken up by those making Lovecraftian adaptations. This type of extreme violence and gore can be seen early on starting with the more vaguely

Lovecraftian adaptations of *The Beyond, The House by the Cemetery,* and *The Evil Dead,*[4] all films on the infamous "video nasties" list in Britain in the early 1980s (Christopher). An emphasis on horror from one's own body and mind and the mutilation thereof, from within or without, certainly weaves a distinct thread through the corpus of Lovecraft's work. From the idea of tainted bloodlines causing hideous changes in "Facts concerning the Late Arthur Jermyn and His Family" and "The Shadow over Innsmouth" to the loss of human bodily integrity and independence in "The Colour out of Space" and "The Whisperer in Darkness" or the forced transference of the mind into horrid forms strongly prevalent in the latter as well as "The Thing on The Doorstep" and "The Shadow out of Time," these are decidedly Lovecraftian aspects and themes. They are not a totality in themselves, but an inextricable part of a more powerful whole. However, this predisposition toward Lovecraft as a vehicle for bloodletting, mutation, and butchery in cinema was hugely exacerbated by the relative success of the extremely over-the-top gore of *Re-Animator,* which appropriately chose the most blackly comic of Lovecraft's works to make an even darker comedic horror that is regarded as a cult classic and generated two direct sequels. *Re-Animator* in turn spawned such films (often from the same creators and with some of the same actors) such as *From Beyond* (1986), *The Unnamable* (1988), *H. P. Lovecraft's Necronomicon* (1994), and *Dagon* (2001). With the inability to convey Lovecraft's more nebulous conceptions created with his words in the mind of the reader, there was thus created a "Lovecraftian" tendency for gore and grotesquery to replace it in film that has somewhat taken on a life of its own. This is something that the makers of *The Void* fully understood:

> SK: [Of Lovecraft] I also don't really feel like his stories are that adaptable to film anyways; they feel very rooted in their literary origins and the way they are told do not really lend themselves to a visual medium like film. It's so rooted in reading letters and stuff.
>
> JG: Also so much of it is like describing the indescribable, where

---

4. As noted, the film is not generally considered Lovecraftian by purists, but its success bought the *Necronomicon* to a much greater awareness among the wider public, and thus was influential in creating the perception of what an HPL film was.

> it gets to levels of poetry and you can't show that, because to show that is defeating the purpose.
>
> SK: Or it diffuses the fear of that moment, if you know what you're looking at. (Craig)

Thus they have instead opted for the secondary approach, utilizing Lovecraft's concepts in a wider framework and drawing upon the latter traditions of his films in the presentation of the horrors.

It is important to note that Gillespie and Kostanski cite numerous other influences, such as the *Dead Space*, *Silent Hill*, and *Resident Evil* video game series. How honestly Lovecraftian these games are is very much up for debate, especially as by their nature such games need to give the players agency and power over enemies for the game to be enjoyable, an idea antithetical to the Lovecraftian conceptual universe. But many modern horror games are certainly permeated with Lovecraftian influence. *Resident Evil* creator Shinji Mikami openly states that Lovecraft influenced the original game "in terms of look and visual identity" (Kamen), while *Dead Space* has been described as "like Lovecraft's stories, [it] gives the audience a protagonist who is being driven mad by a cosmic abomination" (Wilson), and it even has a minor character called Howard Philips in *Dead Space* 2. Clearly these are more than hints that the Old Gent's tentacles reach into these newer forms of the horror genre, even if muddied by dilution through other renderings, and the subtle reinforcement of Lovecraft in *The Void* continues.

Thus it is that *The Void*'s Lovecraftian feel is neither accidental nor incidental. As a blending of direct absorption of Lovecraft and the ingestion of various diluted, altered, reinterpreted, and distorted and alternative versions touched by Lovecraft's original conceptions, *The Void* can stand up as a genuinely Lovecraftian artefact.

Works Cited

Christopher, Neil. "The Video Nasties Furore: The Prosecution of the DPP's 74." www.hysteria-lives.co.uk/hysterialives/nasties/nastiesmain1.htm.

Collis, Clark. "'Prometheus' Kills Guillermo del Toro's Dream Project." ew.com/article/2012/06/10/prometheus-ridley-scott-guillermo-del-toro-lovecraft/2/.

The Creeping Craig. "Interview: Directors Steven Kostanski and Jeremy Gillespie for The Void." www.nightmarishconjurings.com/interviews/2017/4/7/interview-directors-steven-kostanski-jeremy- gillespie-for-the-void.

Gelmini, Davidde. "Interview: Jeremy Gillespie,. Co-Writer/Director of *The Void*." www.horror-fix.com/interview-jeremy-gillespie-co-writerdirector-of-the-void/.

Jagernauth, Kevin. "Guillermo del Toro Says 'Prometheus has Killed "At the Mountains of Madness" Because They Both Have the Same Final Twist." www.indiewire.com/2012/05/ guillermo-del-toro-says-prometheus-has-killed-at-the-mountains-of-madness-because-they-both-have-the-same-final-twist-252233/.

Kamen, Matt. "Resident Evil Creator Talks Horror Games and The Evil Within." www.wired.co.uk/article/shinji-mikami-on-evil-within.

Larnard, Ben. "Forbidden Tomes. Books to Films. The Literary Influences on Lucio Fulci." dailydead.com/forbidden-tomes-book-to-film-the-literary-influences-on-lucio-fulci/.

Lavagini, Massimo F. "Lucio Fulci Interview." *Draculina* No. 24, www.shockingimages.com/fulci/interview.html.

Migliore, Andrew, and John Strysik. *The Lurker in the Lobby: A Guide to the Cinema of H. P. Lovecraft.* Portland: Night Shade Books, 2006.

Saldana, Mark. "Fantastic Fest 2016 Review and Interview: *The Void*." trueviewreviews.com/fantastic-fest-2016-review-interview-the-void/.

Suicide Squad. *Box Office Mojo*, www.boxofficemojo.com/movies/?id=dc2016.htm.

Wilson, Kristian. "The Resurgence of Lovecraftian Themes in Video Games." the-artifice.com/lovecraftian-themes-in-video-games/.

Worland, Rick. "OWI Meets the Monsters: Hollywood Horror Films and War Propaganda 1942–1945." *Cinema Journal* 37, No. 1 (Autumn 1997): 47–65.

Howard Phillips Lovecraft: Romantic on the Nightside

Jan B. W. Pedersen

Howard Phillips Lovecraft can be viewed as a Romantic based on his lifelong relationship with wonder (see Pedersen). This short essay gathers further evidence of Lovecraft's Romanticism, beginning with a brief exploration of what Romanticism is and then moving on to highlight elements of Romanticism in Lovecraft's poem "Fact and Fancy" (1917). The essay concludes that, as much as Lovecraft can be labelled a Romantic based on his affinity with wonder, he can also be classified as such based on his aversion to the cold light of reason, which to him was an insufficient antidote to the otherwise dreary world in which he found himself.

What Is Romanticism?

Romanticism can be understood as a counter-movement to Enlightenment thought, which gained momentum approximately between 1760 and 1850 in Europe. By and large it was an artistic movement that voiced itself through music, poetry, dance, literature and painting (Murray ix).

The Romantics criticized the core of the Enlightenment, which according to philosopher Isaiah Berlin covers the following three propositions: 1) all genuine questions can be answered; 2) the answers are knowable; and 3) the answers must be compatible with one another (Berlin 21–22). The Enlightenment view was that the means by which natural philosopher Isaac Newton (1642–1727) had mastered the domain of physics could also be used in the realms of ethics, politics, and aesthetics. Questions about how to live, how to build a perfect society, and how to judge something as beautiful or ugly could be answered simply by applying reason.

In other words, there was little if no room for the passions, and therein the Romantics identified what they thought to be the terrible mistake of the Enlightenment thinkers.

To showcase this particular aspect of Romantic thought, let us turn to Romantic poet John Keats (1795–1821), who writes:

> Do not all charms fly
> At the mere touch of cold philosophy?
> There was an awful rainbow once in the heaven:
> We know her woof, her texture: she is given
> In the dull catalogue of common things.
> Philosophy will clip an Angel's wings,
> Conquer all mysteries by rule and line,
> Empty the haunted air, and gnomed mine—
> Unweave a rainbow, as it erewhile made
> The tender-personed Lamia melt into a shade
>
> (Keats 2.229–38)

In Keats's *Lamia*[1] we find evidence of his critical attitude toward natural philosophy, which one might understand as a precursor to modern science. The scientifically inclined will recall that Newton successfully replicated the rainbow in his studies of prisms, thus stripping away its mystery, and to Keats this was nothing short of the destruction of the poetry of the rainbow (Quinn 270). Newton's prism exorcised the wondrous Iris, messenger of the gods in Greek mythology, from the rainbow. It hollowed it out, stripped it of a valuable quality, and reduced it to a vacuum wrapped in colors.

Another Romantic who called into question the disenchanting attitude of the Enlightenment is the mad, bad, and dangerous to know poet Lord Byron (1788–1824).[2] In the satirical poem *Don Juan* he curiously states that he "never could see the very Great Happiness of the Nil Admirari" (Canto V, 100). Now *nil admirari* is a cautionary Latin phrase originating in the writings of Roman

---

1. Lamia is the name of a being from Greek mythology who started out as a woman but became a child-eating monster after the Olympian Hera destroyed her children.

2. The phrase "mad, bad and dangerous to know" was used by Lady Caroline Lamb to describe Lord Byron, with whom she had an affair in 1812.

poet Horace and much used by Enlightenment poet Alexander Pope. It basically urges us not to marvel, wonder, or admire, because being in such a state of mind is distracting, useless, and dangerous to the person of knowledge.[3] The poem continues not merely with a salutation to Horace and Pope but also with a strong counter-argument that disputes the reasonableness of the *nil admirari* mindset. It reads:

> Not to admire is all the art I know
> (Plain truth, dear Murray, needs few flowers of speech)
> To make men happy, or to keep them so;
> (So take it in the very words of Creech).
> Thus Horace wrote we all know long ago;
> And this Pope quotes the precept to re-teach
> From his translation; but had *none admired,*
> Would Pope have sung, or Horace been inspired?
> (Canto V, 101)

What Byron's is telling us is that if we cannot wonder we will never find inspiration, and if Pope never wondered at the poetry of Horace his Horace-inspired poetry would never have seen the light of day. Thus in Byron's view poetry cannot rely on reason alone but must begin in wonder.

Byron's dislike of the *nil admirari* stance points out an important feature of Romanticism—a point that poet William Wordsworth (1770–1850) shared. Wordsworth was not against science, but he warned his readers against the cold detachment associated with it. In "A Poet's Epitaph" he writes:

> Physician art thou?—one, all eyes,
> Philosopher!—a fingering slave.
> One that would peep and botanize
> Upon his mother's grave?
> (Wordsworth 20)

As mentioned, Romanticism can be seen as a counter-movement to Enlightenment thought, and the detached Enlight-

---

3. For more information on *nil admirari* and how this singular phrase relates to Lovecraft, see Pedersen.

enment scientist with her disregard for or belittling of the passions was to the Romantic an absolute abomination. The Romantic revolt resulted in a "Cartesian split" between science and poetry, meaning that science in the name of reason would continue the exploration of *res extensa,* the material universe, while poetry would exercise dominion over *res cogitans,* meaning everything from the heart to beauty, imagination, the good, spirit, and of course wonder—that special feeling associated with the philosophers of ancient times (Plato, *Theaetetus* 155d).

Romanticism in Lovecraft's "Fact and Fancy"

Evidence of Lovecraft's Romanticism can be found in early essays such as *In Defence of Dagon* (1921) and works of fiction including "The Nameless City" (1921) (Pedersen 28). However, Romantic thought is also to be found in Lovecraft's poetry and in particular the poem "Fact and Fancy," which in its entirety reads as follows:

> How dull the wretch, whose philosophic mind
> Disdains the pleasures of fantastic kind;
> Whose prosy thoughts the joys of life exclude,
> And wreck the solace of the poet's mood!
> Young Zeno, practic'd in the Stoic's art,
> Rejects the language of the glowing heart;
> Dissolves sweet Nature to a mess of laws;
> Condemns th' effect whilst looking for the cause;
> Freezes poor Ovid in an ic'd review,
> And sneers because his fables are untrue!
> In search of Truth the hopeful zealot goes,
> But all the sadder turns, the more he knows!
> Stay! vandal sophist, whose deep lore would blast
> The graceful legends of the story'd past;
> Whose tongue in censure flays th' embellish'd page,
> And scolds the comforts of a dreary age:
> Would'st strip the foliage from the vital bough
> Till all men grow as wisely dull as thou?
> Happy the man whose fresh, untainted eye
> Discerns a Pantheon in the spangled sky;
> Finds Sylphs and Dryads in the waving trees,

And spies soft Notus in the southern breeze;
For whom the stream a cheering carol sings,
While reedy music by the fountain rings;
To whom the waves a Nereid tale confide
Till friendly presence fills the rising tide.
Happy is he, who void of learning's woes,
Th' ethereal life of body'd Nature knows:
I scorn the sage that tells me it but seems,
And flout his gravity in sunlit dreams!
(*AT* 121)

The opening bears a resemblance in both mood and contents to the excerpt from Keats's *Lamia* we saw earlier. Both poems criticize the philosophically inclined; but whereas Keats directs his aversion toward the natural philosopher or scientist who in cold blood will clip an angel's wings, empty the haunted air, and unweave the rainbow by rule and line (scientific method), Lovecraft airs his aversion toward philosophy because it wrecks the solace of the poet's mood with its prosy thoughts and negative attitude toward pleasures of the fantastic.

Lovecraft then takes a swing at the "ever sadder" stoic philosopher Zeno (c. 333–262 B.C.E.),[4] whom he claims cares not for the "language of the glowing heart" (poetry) and by focussing on causality reduces "Nature" to a mess of laws. "Nature" clearly has a particular meaning and value for Lovecraft that he feels Stoicism undermines, and this could well be rooted in a deep Romantic wish for the world to be enchanted.

In ancient and Hellenistic times the great god Pan was not only a being in the woods that occasionally scared humans and animals alike or made them "panic," but could also represent the "whole of nature" or "everything," which the word "pan" may also refer to in Greek. In this sense nature is not an empty concept but very much a word that evokes the mysterious and the divine. Now two things are important here:

---

4. None of Zeno's works have survived in their entirety, but we know some of the titles he used and have several fragmentary quotations available in the works of later writers, including Roman philosopher Cicero (106–43 B.C.E.) and biographer Diogenes Laertius (3rd century C.E.).

First we know that Pan was much valued by the early Lovecraft, because his juvenile poem "To Pan" (1902), published in 1919 under the pseudonym Michael Ormonde O'Reilly, celebrates the deity in question and reveals Lovecraft's longing for living in an enchanted world filled with nymphs and satyrs. Likewise the poem "To the Old Pagan Religion" (1902), also published in 1919 under the pseudonym Ames Dorrance Rowley, reveals his affinity for Greek mythology because it opens with the lines: "Olympian Gods! How can I let ye go / And pin my faith on this new *Christian* creed?" (*AT* 31).

"Fact and Fancy" likewise reveals Lovecraft's longing for a world filled with gods away from cold philosophy: in lines 9–10 he states that Stoicism "Freezes poor Ovid in an ic'd review, / And sneers because his fables are untrue." Publius Ovidius Naso (43 B.C.E.–17/18 C.E.), or Ovid as the English-speaking world came to address him, was a Roman poet who ended his life in exile shrouded in mystery. He is particularly known for his magnum opus, the fifteen-book epic (or type of epic) *Metamorphoseon Libri* (books of transformations), which with playful wit covers a vast amount of myths and delivers intricate portrayals of mythic figures—from Minerva and Arachne to Orpheus in the underworld. We know that Ovid had some influence on nineteenth-century Romanticism because the poet Charles Pierre Baudelaire (1821–1867) [5] wrote an essay on his life and exile, thus giving rise to the idea that Ovid was a misunderstood genius,[6] an important theme in Romantic thought (Cartmill 118–19). That the polytheistic world of the ancients was important to the gentle poet of Providence also emerges in lines 19–20 of "Fact and Fancy," where Lovecraft writes: "Happy the man whose fresh, untainted eye / Discerns a Pantheon in the spangled sky."

The second important thing is that although Stoics like Zeno operated with a notion of the divine, they never evoked mysterious entities like Pan or Iris but thought of them in the abstract

5. Evidence that Lovecraft enjoyed reading Baudelaire can be found in his short story "Hypnos" (1922), which opens with a passage from Baudelaire. Additional greetings to Baudelaire can be found in the short story "The Hound" (1922).

6. The notion of the misunderstood genius is to some extent explored by Lovecraft in his dreamland stories involving the mystic, scholar, author, and dreamer extraordinaire Randolph Carter.

Necronomicon: The Reef. 2007. Courtesy of Les Edwards, www.lesedwards.com

and as something "absent" from our daily lives. For Zeno, the cosmos as a whole was a living thing and God a corporeal and immanent living fire or heat with a development plan moving the world toward a fiery cataclysm followed by rebirth. Though still pantheistic, this is far from the enchanted world Lovecraft dreamed about because, as he writes toward the end of "Fact and Fancy": 'Happy is he, who void of learning's woes, / Th' ethereal life of body'd Nature knows."

That learning is the bringer of woes is a recurring theme in many a Lovecraft story, including "From Beyond" (1920) and "The Call of Cthulhu" (1926). Here a hitherto unseen "horror-world" is brought before the protagonist with destructive consequences, either by marvelous machinery or the art of "piecing together."

In "Fact and Fancy" the horror of learning is altogether different in color and suggestion because it does not so much add a dimension to the ordinary understanding of things but rather takes one away. No inky jellyish monstrosities suddenly fill the blue sky, nor is one all of a sudden confronted by eldritch contradictions of all matter, force, and cosmic order. Instead, in Lovecraft's view one is bereaved as the Stoic takes the ethereal poetical element out of nature, thus reducing it to nothing but a bundle of soulless laws bereft of wonder and the fantastic. Lovecraft's Zeno is what the observing physician and slavish philosopher are to Wordsworth and what the *nil admirari* supporter is to Byron. He is the destroyer of worlds enchanted, the enemy of Romanticism and what the smell of fish was to Lovecraft: utterly insufferable!

Speaking of fish, "Fact and Fancy" ends in Romantic revolt not unlike the ending of the Mythos story "The Shadow over Innsmouth" (1931), where protagonist Robert Olmstead, filled with renewed vigor, refrains from killing himself upon discovering that he will turn into a fish-frog (*CF* 3.230). "I scorn the sage that tells me it but seems / And flout his gravity in sunlit dreams" is a surprisingly uplifting rally to fancy and a wholesomely defiant stance from Lovecraft. It bears witness to the fact that he not only detested the philosophy of the Stoic sage as Byron detested the philosophy of Pope, but that his use of fancy, imagination, or the "poet's eye" is a means to dispel the gravity of the wise and unhappy. As much as poetry can convey a particular message, it is also transformative, and the ending of "Fact and Fancy" bears witness to Lovecraft's poetic acumen. In two lines he re-installs the dimension the learned Stoic took away, and we are left with an impression of Lovecraft as a jovial and positive fellow—a person we can look to for comfort when darkness is closing in.

Thus Spoke Lovecraft the "Poe"-et

Based on the above analysis, I think that "Fact and Fancy" testifies to Lovecraft's Romanticism. The resemblance between Keats's *Lamia* and Lovecraft's "Fact and Fancy" is striking, and it is likely that Keats's poem was a source of inspiration to the gentleman of Providence. Lovecraft definitively knew about *Lamia* because it is mention in his singular essay "Supernatural Horror in Literature" (1927) (*Annotated Supernatural Horror in Literature* 33). That he was aware of other works by Keats is also evident, because the opening epigraph of the short story "The Outsider" (1921) is an excerpt from Keats's narrative poem *The Eve of St. Agnes.*

Now it is a well-established fact that Lovecraft was a great admirer of Edgar Allan Poe. In 1916—a year before he published "Fact and Fancy"—Lovecraft wrote in a letter that Poe was his "God of Fiction" (*SL* 1.20), and early tales of the macabre such as "The Tomb" (1917) and "The Statement of Randolph Carter" (1919) convey a positively Poesque atmosphere. Poe's poem "Sonnet—To Science" bears a curious resemblance to Keats's *Lamia* because whereas Keats laments that the cold touch of philosophy has put the awful rainbow in the dull catalogue of common things, Poe laments that science, "whose wings are dull realities," preys on the poet's heart (Poe 45). This equals Lovecraft's statement that philosophy wrecks the solace of the poet's mood by reducing nature to laws, and thus it may be speculated that "Fact and Fancy" is inspired only indirectly by Keats's *Lamia* and more directly by Poe's "Sonnet—To Science." Whether this is true or not, "Fact and Fancy" is a Romantic poem as much as *Lamia* and "Sonnet—To Science" are, and it leaves us with the impression that Howard Phillips Lovecraft, at heart, was a Romantic deeply at odds with the cold light of reason, which was an uninspiring and inadequate antidote to the dreary world in which he was situated. He was a Romantic that, in light of his immense contribution to weird fiction, is perhaps best addressed as a Romantic on the "Nightside."[7]

Works Cited

Berlin, Isaiah. *The Roots of Romanticism.* Princeton: Princeton University Press, 2001.

Byron, George Gordon, Lord. *Don Juan.* In *The Works of Lord Byron.* London: John Murray, 1833.

Cartmill, Matt. *A View to a Death in the Morning: Hunting and Nature through History.* Cambridge, MA: Harvard University Press, 1996.

Keats, John. *Lamia.* In *The Complete Poems of John Keats.* Ed. John Bernard. 3rd ed. London: Penguin, 1988.

Lovecraft, H. P. *The Annotated Supernatural Horror in Literature.* Ed. S. T. Joshi. New York: Hippocampus Press, 2012.

Murray, Christopher John. *Encyclopedia of the Romantic Era: 1760–1850.* Volume 1. New York: Fritzroy Dearborn, 2004.

Pedersen, Jan B. W. "On Lovecraft's Lifelong Relationship with Wonder." *Lovecraft Annual* No. 11 (2017): 23–36.

Plato. *Theaetetus.* Tr. H. N. Fowler. Cambridge, MA: Harvard University Press, 1989.

Poe, Edgar Allan. *The Complete Poetry of Edgar Allan Poe.* New York: Signet, 2008.

Quinn, Dennis. *Iris Exiled: A Synoptic History of Wonder.* Lanham, MD: University Press of America, 2002.

Wordsworth, William. *Wordsworth's Poetical Works.* Ed. William Knight. Volume 2. Edinburgh: William Paterson, 1896.

---

7. I have borrowed the term "Nightside" from Frank Belknap Long's 1975 memoir, *Howard Phillips Lovecraft: Dreamer on the Nightside.*

How to Read Lovecraft

A Column by Steven J. Mariconda

Number 2

When we last saw Lovecraft, he was up on a hassock—mohair, no doubt, complete with fringe and clawed feet. His fellow amateur journalists, knowing his fondness for re-enacting theatrical scenes from Shakespeare down through the popular theater of the day, had somehow cajoled the solemn newcomer from Providence into donning a hoop skirt, bonnet, and parasol. He was declaiming a little comedic number popularized by female impersonator Julian Eltinge:

> Now listen, now listen,
> It's a secret, don't repeat it . . .
> I've read a lot of books, I found a book on looks,
> One that tells you what to do, when eyes so true,
> Gray or blue , smile on you—
>
> Now listen, now listen,
> To the many, many strange things
> Any little girl can do,
> With a come-hither look in her eyes,
> That signifies, "I kind of like you . . ."

It seems that Lovecraft, despite the typical image of him as a shy and reticent personality, was something of a "ham." He enjoyed reading his stories aloud with great verve and liked to sing and emote in company—especially his favorite scene from *Richard III.* Our thesis here is that Lovecraft's fondness for histrionics and his playful sense of humor informed his fiction, and that it is essential for us to understand these elements to fully comprehend the work.

We can see from Lovecraft's letters that he was extremely playful—that is, he had a predisposition to frame (or reframe) a situation in such a way as to provide amusement or entertainment, manifested with spontaneity and positive affect. In the last column, we discussed Lovecraft's penchant for creating outdoor dioramas using packing cases wheelbarrows and other odds and ends, and went so far as the landscape these play areas. Initially, the play took place inside Lovecraft's carriage house on a tabletop using fire engines and villages, but eventually Lovecraft took the operation outdoors on to the large property of his home at 194 (later 454) Angell St. When his family lost that house due to financial problems, the fourteen-year-old Lovecraft re-created an even more extensive set-up (which he called "New Anvik" after a place in a favorite story) in a vacant lot next door to his new home at 598 Angell St. When Lovecraft was using the props of his New Anvik, he created a kind of a tableau. He would then enact scenarios that went on for upwards of three or four weeks. With the tableau, exploits would be played out that might involve detective work, arctic exploration, or other adventures.

In the year 1907, Lovecraft realized he was growing too old to be conducting this type of play in public and turned over his outdoor stage to a younger boy. However, Lovecraft never really abandoned the concept of setting up a tableau and then manipulating the props it, creating scenarios that encompassed extended durations of time. In future columns, we will examine how the unique way Lovecraft played as a juvenile and as a teenager was perpetuated in the way he approached his "serious" adult fiction. For now, it is well to establish some foundational concepts and definitions.

The characteristics of play all have to do with motivation and mental attitude, not with overt behavior. There have been many attempts to define "play"; the definitions seem to have the following elements in common. First, play is imaginative, non-literal, and mentally distinct from reality. It is activity that is self-chosen and self-directed, and that is undertaken with an engaged yet unstressed mindset. Play has structure or rules created by the participants, rather imposed by necessity, and in play the means are more valued than the ends.

My proposal is that the Lovecraft Mythos was the young

Lovecraft's New Anvik writ large. It was based on similar concepts. Sociologists who have conducted research and analysis on the concepts of play, learning, and behavior can provide some pointers as to how Lovecraft's manner of playing as a youth affected the way he implemented his artificial mythology in his mature literary work.

The first play-related concept helpful in our understanding of Lovecraft is the idea of the "prop." A prop (short for stage property) is an inanimate object used in staging a play. Props are large movable items not built into the set; they may form part of the scene or background. Different kinds of theater use props in different ways; but the props generally provide a dramatic focus bringing greater interest to a performance. Props are the supporting details that flesh out a setting for the characters in a play, facilitate the progress of the story being enacted, and bridge the characters on stage and the reality of life objects.

Props help create a context or "frame" for the action that will happen in the story, and create an implied set of boundaries or rules for the types of action that can take place. American theorist Kendall L. Walton put it this way: "Props are generators of fictional truths, things which, by virtue of their nature or existence, make propositions fictional. A snow fort is a prop. It is responsible for the fictionality of the proposition that there is a (real) fort with turrets and a moat" (37–38).

Walton continues with remarks that are relevant to the way in which other authors subsequently adopted and expanded Lovecraft's fictional play-world:

> Imagining is easily thought of as a free, unregulated activity, subject to no constraints save whim. . . . So it may seem, but it isn't quite so. Imaginings are constrained also; some are proper, appropriate in certain contexts, and others not. . . . [A] fictional truth consists in there being a prescription or mandate in some context to imagine something. . . . . Agreements which participants in a collective daydream make about what to imagine can be thought of as rules prescribing certain imaginings. Anyone who refuses to imagine what was agreed on refuses to "play the game" or plays it improperly. He breaks a rule. These rules are categorical. (39)

Lovecraft's literary truths are therefore "true in [the] fictional world" of the Mythos that he created as a frame for his narratives. Consistent with the findings of academicians who have studied play, the props of the Lovecraft Mythos—the gods, alien races, imaginary towns, and geographical/temporal epochs—became a kind of frame or set of boundaries within which Lovecraft could create his own reality. This reality has its own set of rules or laws and internal logic.

With his New Anvik, Lovecraft created what scholars call a "paracosm"—defined as "a prolonged fantasy world developed by children" that may include "definite geography, language, and history" (Konkin). Research studies of children at play established the following criteria for a paracosm: 1) the child must perceive the activity as imaginary; 2) it must maintain the child's interest over multiple years; and 3) the child must feel a sense of inspiration, importance, and desire in its creation and maintenance. In creating the Lovecraft Mythos, he created a paracosm to succeed New Anvik—one that would secure his place in world literature.

Of interest relative to Lovecraft is another aspect of the paracosm. Researchers see the use of the paracosm not only as a creative mechanism but also as a coping mechanism. Theories assert that the paracosm results from childhood unhappiness, and that the creation of such an imaginary world may be a defensive and compensatory act of self-care. Given the circumstances of Lovecraft's childhood, his unusual approach to play may have been an escape from unpleasant events and circumstances beyond his control (e.g., his father's insanity, confinement, and death). Lovecraft's paracosms (New Anvik, later the Lovecraft Mythos) served to help him cope with traumatic events by dissociation, with the author removing himself not only psychologically but also (as in tales such as "The Whisperer in Darkness" and "The Shadow out of Time") physically. Brian Sutton-Smith, developmental psychologist and leading researcher on the topic, expressed this as follows: "Play was always intended to serve a healing function whether for child or adult, making it more worthwhile to defy the depressing and dangerous aspects of life. . . . But play also includes . . . reaching for triumphant control and happiness and pride . . . [and is] a major method of becoming reconciled with our being within our present universe."

The play-based nature of Lovecraft's fictional work became apparent while he was still actively writing, as Lovecraft's fellow authors gravitated to the game. It became further apparent when the Lovecraft Mythos became an immense franchise for imaginative writers in general, and then spread progressively into other media—most significantly, role-playing games. The popularity of products from Chaosium and its successors shows that Lovecraft's approach to literary creation had much in common with concepts of play, and further highlights the importance of these concepts in understanding the work.

To summarize, we have learned several things. First, from a very young age, Lovecraft had a unique approach to play. Second, when he turned to literary creation, he perpetuated the same type of posture or approach in his written work. That is, he created a "frame" that included setting, objects within that setting (i.e., props) and certain explicit and implicit rules or boundaries—and then undertook to formulate the adventures that took place within those boundaries. The events that occur in the Lovecraftian universe thus seem to be "fictionally true" within it.

The most accurate description of the Mythos is in one of Lovecraft's letters to composer Harold S. Farnese:

> In my own efforts to crystallise [a] spaceward outreaching, I try to utilise as many as possible of the elements which have, under earlier mental and emotional conditions, given man a symbolic feeling of the unreal, the ethereal, & the mystical—choosing those least attacked by the realistic mental and emotional conditions of the present. Darkness—sunset—dreams—mists—fever—madness—the tomb—the hills—the sea—the sky—the wind—all these, and many other things have seemed to me to retain a certain imaginative potency despite our actual scientific analyses of them. Accordingly, I have tried to weave them into a kind of shadowy phantasmagoria which may have the same sort of vague coherence as a cycle of traditional myth or legend—with nebulous backgrounds of Elder Forces & transgalactic entities which lurk about this infinitesimal planet, (& of course about others as well), establishing outposts thereon,. . . . Having formed a cosmic pantheon, it remains for the fantaisiste to link this "outside" element to the earth in a suitably dramatic & convincing fashion.

> This, I have thought, is best done through glancing allusions to immemorially ancient cults & idols & documents attesting the recognition of the "outside" forces by men—or by those terrestrial entities which preceded man. [*SL* 4.70–71]

As we will see in the next installment, the term "phantasmagoria" is of especial interest. The word was coined as the name for an exhibition of optical illusions produced chiefly by means of the magic lantern, first shown in London in 1802. An ancillary definition, by extension, is that of a shifting series or succession of imaginary figures called up by the imagination. Surrealist Jean Schuster said that "The activity of play, in surrealism [. . .] gives to the principle of pleasure form and power, what it needs to face dialectically the principle of reality" (*La Brèche,* September 1962; cited in Morel). Insight into Lovecraft's playful approach to writing, his use of a "paracosmos," and his penchant for histrionics, all act together to form a useful foundation for understanding how to read him.

Works Cited

Gwen Gordon. "What Is Play? In Search of a Universal Definition" (March 2017). gwengordonplay.com/pdf/what_is_play.pdf. Retrieved 5/2018.

Konkin, Serena F. "Between Worlds: Paracosms as Imaginal Liminality in Response to Trauma." Master's thesis, Pacifica Graduate Institute (March 2014). www.researchgate.net/ publication/ 301802659_Between_Two_Worlds_Liminality_and_Late-Stage_Cancer-Directed_Therapy. Retrieved 5/2018.

Morel, Jean-Paul. "Les Jeux Surrealistes" (March 2004). melusine-surrealisme.fr/site/astu/Morel_Jeux.htm. Retrieved 5/2018.

Sutton-Smith, Brian. "Play Theory: A Personal Journey and New Thoughts." *American Journal of Play,* Vol. 1, No. 1 (Summer 2008). www.journalofplay.org/issues/1/1/article/play-theory-personal-journey-and-new-thoughts. Retrieved 5/2018.

Walton, Kendall L. *Mimesis as Make-Believe: On the Foundations of the Representational Arts.* Cambridge, MA: Harvard University Press, 1990.

Reviews

H. P. LOVECRAFT. *Letters to Maurice W. Moe and Others.* Edited by David E. Schultz and S. T. Joshi. New York: Hippocampus Press, 2018. 620 pages. $30.

H. P. LOVECRAFT AND CLARK ASHTON SMITH. *Dawnward Spire, Lonely Hill: The Letters of H. P. Lovecraft and Clark Ashton Smith.* Edited by David E. Schultz and S. T. Joshi. New York: Hippocampus Press, 2017. 800 pages. $75. Reviewed by Steven J. Mariconda.

David E. Schultz and S. T. Joshi have issued two more volumes in their series of Lovecraft's letters through Hippocampus Press. Like icebergs that break off from Arctic glaciers into the North Atlantic, these volumes periodically hove into view—huge, previously unknown chunks of content that drift into the path of unsuspecting Lovecraftians.

But unlike icebergs, these items are not to be avoided; they are essential to understanding Lovecraft's creative process and make for enjoyable reading in the bargain. We have here the correspondence to and from weird author Clark Ashton Smith and, in the other volume, the correspondence to Maurice W. Moe, Samuel Loveman, Bernard Austin Dwyer, and Vincent Starrett.

However, caveat emptor: the books are 800 and 620 pages of text, respectively, and may cause orthopedic injury if dropped. The initial reaction upon seeing them is a kind of panic regarding where one might find the time to read them. The second reaction is a kind of disbelief regarding where Lovecraft might have found the time to write them. A third reaction is a kind of astonishment regarding where the editors have found the time to edit and publish them.

These considerations are only the tip of a much larger and more complex matter—a thing that is difficult to understand or even conceptualize: over about twenty years, Lovecraft wrote enough letters to fill approximately 500 volumes. Joshi's estimate is five to ten letters per day; at some point Lovecraft had as many as 100 correspondents concurrently. How any person could have written a correspondence of this magnitude and have been able to undertake the fundamental activities of everyday life ranks with the greatest mysteries described in Lovecraft's weird fiction.

Schultz estimates that a total of 4.5 million words of Lovecraft correspondence survives to be published. This amounts to the equivalent wordage of the totality of: *Les Misérables,* the seven-volume *À la recherche du temps perdu,* the entirety of Shakespeare, *The Lord of the Rings* (including *The Hobbit*), *War and Peace,* and *Crime and Punishment* (twice). And that does not include the portions of Lovecraft's correspondence that was lost. In total, the Joshi/Schultz juggernaut is now more than halfway through publishing Lovecraft's extant correspondence, with another 700,000 words staged to go to press this year.

Maurice W. Moe became acquainted with Lovecraft through their mutual involvement with amateur journalism. Moe was a high school English teacher in Appleton and Milwaukee, Wisconsin. After Lovecraft's death, Moe wrote that "if there is ever a survey to determine the greatest letter writer in history the claims of Lovecraft deserve close investigation. It is hard to conceive of an individual who has put more words on letter paper in 30 years with so little inanity."

Lovecraft called Moe a "brilliant sage," but at this distance it is somewhat difficult to understand why he assumed such an important place among Lovecraft's correspondents. The editors facilitate the attempt by providing a remarkable amount of material about the obscure Moe. He did post-graduate work in classics at the University of Wisconsin and was an expert in Greek, Roman, and biblical literature. He worked as a high school English teacher, one deeply interested in pedagogy, and wrote and sold numerous tests for English teachers to use in class.

Though Lovecraft was something of a militant atheist, Moe was not averse to apprising Lovecraft of his continued adult Bible study or to defending his religious viewpoints. But as Lovecraft noted, the exchanges with Moe always remained more than amicable despite their difference of opinion, and they remained friends for life. Elsewhere Lovecraft called Moe "a man of kindness and virtue"; the two met in person only twice (1923 and 1936).

In 1927 Moe conceived the idea of a pedagogic textbook to be called *Doorways to Poetry*. Lovecraft became involved in an advisory capacity and provided potted metrical examples to illustrate specific points Moe wished addressed. (Moe's book never saw print.)

In his brief memoir of Lovecraft, Moe cites his favorite parts of the correspondence to him: the poems written specifically for him, discussions of the evolution of classical and colonial architecture, and the travelogues. But mostly it is the technical discussions of poetry that dominate these letters; as here, for example, where Lovecraft expounds on classical metrics:

> In this line, certain words of importance chanced to fall in places perfectly coinciding with the theoretical position of the ictus in a classical dipodick trimeter iambick line of the same number of syllables.

The literary banter shows that Lovecraft unexpectedly held many iconoclastic authors (artists with new ways of thinking and writing—"modern," if you will) in high regard. Whitman and Melville are touted as artists that jettisoned Victorian artistic baggage, and even Joyce, Eliot, Proust, Frost, Sandburg, Conrad Aiken, Virginia Woolf, and Edwin Arlington Robinson come in for praise. (Rereading Robinson hard on the publication of Schultz's outstanding edition of *Fungi from Yuggoth: An Annotated Edition* [Hippocampus Press, 2017] convinces me that he was in fact an influence on the sonnet-cycle, and the mention of Robinson here seems to support this.)

In addition to the extensive and detailed discussion of poetry, the letters to Moe are distinguished by a phenomenon found in letters to very few other correspondents. During a letter, Lovecraft occasionally will break off the narrative and reminisce about the years of his early adolescence—say, 1900 through 1906. These reminiscences take the very strange form of a long series of phrases separated by ellipses. These passages of phrases contain a remarkable breadth and depth of information about the period in question, ranging from major events of the day, to popular songs and shows, to the most hermetic and trivial details of the day. Lovecraft's memory is virtually eidetic. It is almost as if he is casting his mind back to the year in question and putting himself into a quasi-hypnotic state:

> . . . . . Peter F. Dailey at the Opera House in "Hodge, Podge, and Co." . . . . . Copeland's Livery Stable . . . . . cake-walks . . . . . "Oh, Oh, Miss Phoebe" . . . . . Gilmore's Band . . . . . Life's Gibson Calendar for 1902—-a Handsome Gift or Souvenir. . . . . Edison Phonographs . . . . . the new gramophones that use at discs . . . . . T. & C. pyrography outfits, $1.80 . . . . . Braun's Carbon Prints . . . . . Famous Fasso Corsets . . . . . Studebaker Carriages and Wagons . . . . . Angelus Pianola . . . . . the new cat book by Agnes Repplier . . . . . Hand Sapolio, just on the market . . . . . "Good Morning! Have you used Pears' Soap?" . . . . . Mt. Pelee . . . . . Chauncey Olcott . . . . . new strike in the Klondike . . . . . "Ale that is Ale, from the Highland Spring" . . . . . Anti-Imperialism . . . . . "The Riddle of the Universe". . . . . Nova Persei . . . . . disturbing works on sociology by that fellow Lester Ward . . . . . the Sunday sermon . . . . . Sweet Caporal . . . . . Egyptian Deities. . . . . these new houses with colonial gambrel roofs . . . . . McClure's Magazine . . . . . Lincoln Steffens . . . . . "The Shame of Minneapolis" . . . . .moral purpose . . . . .

Some of the references are so obscure that Lovecraft must explain them to Moe in subsequent letters. One example is when Lovecraft drops the phrase "rearward seating" into one of the sequences. Apparently, there was a comedic song called "Go Way Back and Sit Down," written by one Al Johns, that was popular in 1900. The title became something of a smart-aleck all-purpose catchphrase and apparently mutated into the phrase "rearward seating." Moe had no idea what Lovecraft was referring to until Lovecraft explained it to him. Examples could be multiplied—infinitely. Each of these passages is a veritable gold mine not only relative to Lovecraft's mentality (I used the word advisedly) regarding his youth, but also for those interested in what might be termed micro-history. The editors have bravely attempted to annotate the items in these passages, but the lists still provide hours of Google pleasure for the curious and/or lonely.

These passages are like the "stream of consciousness" passages found in tales such as "The Lurking Fear" (1922), "The Colour out of Space" (1927), "The Haunter of the Dark" (1935), and notably the conclusion of *At the Mountains of Madness* (1931). In his fiction, these passages act as a verbatim transcript of the chaotic thoughts of a character. The rational, self-possessed voice of the narrator breaks down into a grammatically fragmented discourse recording the dissociated contents of his mind. Lovecraft found this technique useful because his wonders were of a uniquely alien type that would leave an individual totally stunned. It was a perfect way to reflect such a mental state. The stream-of-consciousness passages typically occur at a high point in the narrative, after an intrusion from outside has taken place and sent the character's mind reeling, to show just how profound a shock he has received. Lovecraft also exploited these techniques as powerful atmospheric devices.

Moe was unique among Lovecraft's correspondents in that he inspired or instigated many memorable Lovecraft works, including "Ibid" (1928), "Observations on Several Parts of America" (1928), "Travels in the Provinces of America" (1929), "Some Causes of Self-Immolation" (1931), and others. Also, as the editors note in the introduction, Lovecraft's involvement with *Doorways to Poetry* may have been a factor in the composition of *Fungi from Yuggoth* (1929–30).

One notable item is an "An Epistle to the Rt. Honble [*sic*] Maurice Winter-Moe, Esq., of Zythopolis ["beer-town"], in the Northwest-Territory of His Majesty's American Dominions" (July 1929). Lovecraft spontaneously spun off this 212-line set of rhymed couplets full of reminiscences of 1904 (the year of Moe's graduation). These passages are like the stream-of-consciousness prose reminiscences in letters 30, 32, 39, and 64. Due to Lovecraft's fondness for the rhymed couplet form and his apparent practice in it during his "blank period" of 1908–13, he was extremely facile with it and was able to create some very humorous effects by playing the sound against the sense. Here, for example, he surveys the prospective publishers of Moe's *Doorway's to Poetry* (Kenyon Press, based in Wauwatosa Wis., had previously published some booklets by Moe):

Macmillan sure would prove a brainless dolt
Did he not vie in eagerness with Holt—
But be their sense of judgment more or less,
You need not care—for you've the Kenyon Press,
Nurse of the arts—hail, Mater Gloriosa!
The press that carry'd fame to Wauwatosa!

Note how ge uses the placement of the caesura (pause), the marginally warped departure from the metrical scheme, and the outrageously "unallowable" rhymes to spring his "punch lines." He wraps it up with a line about his annoying revision client, Adolphe Danziger De Castro:

A brief recess—now back to art's dim last row,
To doctor that curst junk by old De Castro!

"Last row/De Castro." Art, indeed!

To the Maurice W. Moe correspondence are appended letters to Moe's son Robert (14 letters, mostly trivial), Samuel Loveman (9 letters, very good content), Vincent Starrett (5 letters, somewhat formal but interesting), and Bernard Austin Dwyer (12 letters, very good content).

Lovecraft and Clark Ashton Smith, together with Robert E Howard, became known as the "Three Musketeers" of *Weird Tales*. Lovecraft's correspondence with Smith and Howard was among his most extensive. (The combined letters to Smith and Howard almost triple the word count of the 500-page Dumas namesake tome.)

The editors provide both sides of the Lovecraft–Smith correspondence. This is a treasure trove for scholars of imaginative fiction and popular magazines of the 1920s and '30s. It is, however, remarkably superficial considering that we are dealing with two of the twentieth century's supreme imaginative authors. Smith and Lovecraft did not seem to connect on an emotional level; from Lovecraft we do not find the deep philosophical ruminations, finely spun arguments, comedic forays, and personal revelations present in his best letters (e.g., those to James F. Morton). On reflection, this is not surprising given how different the two men were personally—Smith flamboyant and given to the melodramatic, Lovecraft self-effacing and reserved. The Lovecraft–Smith letters are mostly shop-talk about the pulp magazine market and current work, providing a virtual diary of goings-on in the fantastic fiction pulp and fandom realm of the day.

There is at the beginning of the correspondence some enlightening discussion of Baudelaire and other Symbolist poetry, with ongoing intermittent references as Smith undertakes to translate more poems from the French. It reminds us what a significant influence Baudelaire was on Lovecraft, and how we would do well to read him as a Symbolist in the line of influence from Poe through Baudelaire and the Symbolists and then onward into the Surrealists.

One gets a sense that Lovecraft, even as he consistently praised Smith to other correspondents and to the author himself, ultimately soured on him. In a letter to Moe of March 1927, even as he talks up Smith's work, Lovecraft remarks: "He [Smith] is inclined to be discontented because of his inadequate public recognition." Lovecraft was completely uninterested in such matters beyond getting his work into hard covers.

At some point in the early '30s, Smith began to have stories published five or six times a year in *Weird Tales*, while Lovecraft typically was only able to place one. Smith spends quite some effort attempting to convince Lovecraft that the latter could temper his efforts by adding a more commercial slant, thus being more successful in selling work to the pulps. Lovecraft, however, wanted none of it, refusing to add more action to his plots or to blunt the subtlety to his concepts. By November 1931 he was telling Smith curtly: "As for compromise work—possibly it can be done but not by me." Lovecraft consistently praises Smith, both to his face and to other correspondents, but periodically some negative sentiment leaks out. In response to a direct statement by Robert Bloch, for example, Lovecraft had to "fess up":

> You are right in saying that Clark Ashton Smith produces too much. That is the tragedy of economic necessity—he knows that much of his stuff is hack junk yet has to keep grinding it out for the sake of the cash. (Lovecraft to Robert Bloch, 9 May 1933)

Similarly, Lovecraft would make only vaguely positive remarks to Smith as the latter churned out story after story. But to another correspondent he could write: "'Vulthoom' [*Weird Tales*, September 1935] has its moments, but falls a bit beneath Klarkash-Ton's best level. I fear the pulp editors have subtly harmed Smith" (Lovecraft to Donald A. Wollheim, 20 September 1935). Lovecraft does not comment directly on the story to Smith himself.

Lovecraft seems more in tune with Bernard Austin Dwyer (1897–1943), an aspiring horror writer, than he does with Smith. Lovecraft sent Dwyer an account of his "Roman dream"; the only other correspondents known to have received this are Frank Belknap Long (who incorporated it verbatim into his short novel *The Horror from the Hills* [*Weird Tales*, January & February/March 1931) and Donald Wandrei. The Roman dream is a fantastic example of Lovecraft at work, at the top of his game—it is an account of a dream that he had in which he was the primary actor. It includes incredible historical detail, but more importantly it features prose that ranks with some of the best that Lovecraft wrote in his highly polished fiction.

The editors' introduction does an excellent job of outlining Lovecraft's important and problematic relationship with Samuel Loveman (1889–1976). As a neophyte amateur journalist, Lovecraft stumbled across Loveman's poems in archival material and became an admirer of his poetry. A mutual acquaintance put the two men in contact, and they became best friends. Loveman was, in part, responsible for Lovecraft leaving the nest of his home in Providence. He accepted an invitation to visit Loveman and Alfred Galpin in Cleveland in 1922—his first real "road trip." Eventually, Loveman came to visit New York City, and by the collocation of various amateur journalists there including Lovecraft's future wife Sonia Greene, Lovecraft undertook frequent trips to New York City. He eventually moved to New York and married Greene, actions that would have been considered out of the question ten years prior, during Lovecraft's sequestration.

Lovecraft was devoted to Loveman and praised him highly. He dedicated "Hypnos" (1922) to "S. L." The story appears to feature Loveman as a character. Lovecraft gifted Loveman with the manuscript of the story. "Hypnos" became something of a credential in Lovecraft's early career. When he visited Cleveland in 1922, the story was read and admired by some heavyweight local Modernists. Later, Lovecraft wrote that "Loveman veritably throws fits over this bit of cheerful morbidity, & vows he'll bring it to the attention of a publisher's reader" (Lovecraft to Lillian D. Clark, 29 November 1924). The editors tell us that that "Hypnos" was earmarked as one of the eight greatest short stories ever written by a literary club in Cleveland, as recounted by a columnist in a March 1923 edition of the *Cleveland Plain Dealer.*

Sadly, Loveman had some serious character flaws and became increasingly eccentric (and possibly clinically demented) as he grew older. He turned against Lovecraft, apparently because of the latter's anti-Semitic comments in posthumously published letters to others. However, as noted in the introduction, Loveman could not have praised Lovecraft any more highly based on their extensive personal interactions.

Loveman claimed that he "lost" some of his correspondence from Lovecraft, and that the remainder was "destroyed." How it might have been destroyed remains a mystery—probably they were thrown out by a landlord when Loveman moved and left them behind. The items to Loveman here are interesting but serve mainly to make us wish for the ones that were lost. Loveman was central to Lovecraft's interest French Symbolist poetry and was a link to Hart Crane and a wider world of Modernist writers and painters.

Vincent Starrett (1886–1974) is a unique case among Lovecraft's epistolary relationships. Starrett was a "borderline" acquaintance of whom Lovecraft was aware through Samuel Loveman. Starrett, known for popularizing Arthur Machen in the United States, was also a potential bridge to a broader artistic community. Loveman apparently put Lovecraft in touch with Starrett to get Lovecraft's work in front of a wider audience. Unfortunately, not much came of this relationship.

In summary, these volumes contain a vast quantity of highly interesting information and insight. As publications, they are of outstanding quality on every dimension. They meet or exceed the Modern Language Association of America's Guidelines for Editors of Scholarly Editions in terms of rigor and add a bevy of other features that add tremendous value. Each book includes outstandingly complete and helpful front and back matter—introduction with much new data, chronology, glossary of frequently mentioned names, bibliography, and index. The appendices are remarkable in their extent. The items by Maurice W. Moe include "Why I Am Not a Freethinker," "The Church and the World," "Life for God's Sake," "Looking Backward," "Once an Amateur, Always an Amateur," "First Steps in the Appreciation of Poetry," "Maurice W. Moe on Amateur Criticism," "Through the Eyes of the Poet," "Imagism," "Literary Appreciation," "From 'Poem Comments,'" "From *Imagery Aids*," "Introduction to Poetry," "In a Sequestered Churchyard Where Once Poe Walked," "Edwin and the Red Knight," and "Seven O'Clock." The items by Bernard Austin Dwyer include "Ol' Black Sarah," "Beautiful Night," "Fairies," "The Snake-God," "Letters to *Weird Tales*," and "Letter to *Strange Tales*." In the Smith collection, the appendix includes related items by Smith ("[Fantasy and Human Experience]," "[On 'Garbage-Mongering']," "[Realism and Fantasy]," "[On the Forbidden Books]," "The Tale of Macrocosmic Horror," "[Crossword Puzzles]"), by Lovecraft (review of Smith's *Ebony and Crystal*), Clifford Gessler's "Treader of Obscure Stars," and several others. Lovecraftians should obtain another plank and cinderblock to accommodate these items on their "five-foot shelf" of Lovecraft.

SCOTT CUTLER SHERSHOW and SCOTT MICHAELSEN. *The Love of Ruins: Letters on Lovecraft*. Albany: State University of New York Press, 2017. xi, 193 pp. $80.00 hc; $22.95 tpb. Reviewed by S. T. Joshi.

This book was apparently published with relatively little fanfare, and for good reason. It is one of the most pretentious, bombastic, and just plain silly treatises on Lovecraft ever written. It demonstrates conclusively why so much academic criticism has become a parody of itself: based on inadequate research, full of impenetrably opaque conclusions and puffed up with authorial preening, it unwittingly provides more illumination on the authors' own biases and presuppositions than on the literary work it purports to be analyzing.

The book is not a straightforward treatise but a series of letters—ranging from as little as two pages to as many as eight—back and forth between the two Scotts; and, because each of them signs himself "Scott," it becomes impossible to tell which Scott wrote which letter. All this is inane enough; the authors maintain that they have adopted this practice because Lovecraft himself was such a voluminous letter-writer, and one whose "daily life revolved around correspondence"; but the upshot, in their case, is a scattershot, almost free-associationist approach that fails to explore certain subjects comprehensively while harping at tedious length upon others.

The authors repeatedly stress their "love" of Lovecraft, and their enthusiasm does shine through at random moments. But there is reason to doubt their credentials in writing a book of this sort, however unorthodox its structure. Both are professors of English, but Shershow has published a book on the "right-to-die debate" and Michaelsen has co-written one on anthropology. Neither of them seem particularly well versed in the history of weird fiction before and during Lovecraft's lifetime, and they do not even appear to be familiar with the totality of Lovecraft's literary texts (fiction, poetry, essays), as my discussion will reveal.

The book does not get off to a good start. One Scott points to a passage in "The Call of Cthulhu" whereby Francis Wayland Thurston, after concluding his narrative, states, "Let me pray that, if I do not survive this manuscript, my executors may put caution before audacity and see that it meets no other eye" (*CF* 2.55). This leads Scott to wonder if Lovecraft really was the "card-carrying atheist and enemy of religion" that much modern scholarship has claimed he was. Why would a Lovecraft character "pray" if Lovecraft was so hostile to religion? (This Scott is probably the same one who confesses that he first read Lovecraft in the 1980s in the course of various occultist studies of the Kenneth Grant sort.) But it apparently doesn't seem to dawn on this Scott that, even though Lovecraft really was a "card-carrying atheist," his characters may not have been; or (even more relevantly) that they are uttering "pray" with a less than literal signification.

I suppose it was to be expected that *The Love of Ruins* harps on Lovecraft's racism, although it at least does not use this issue to denigrate Lovecraft's achievement. Like Michel Houellebecq and others (see my article in this issue), these two Scotts seem at times to regard racism as central to Lovecraft's literary work; but they can only make this argument by ambiguity, conjecture, and equivocation. "Race," in this context, can only refer to sub-groups within a given species; it is careless and illegitimate—and, I would argue, disingenuous—to extend this idea to members of different species. It is as if one were to assert that the "race" of dogs are prejudiced against the "race" of cats, or that human beings are prejudiced against mosquitoes. And yet, that is in effect exactly what the two Scotts do. They grudgingly acknowledge that the Old Ones of *At the Mountains of Madness* and the Great Race (a term used in precisely the same way as "human race" is used in regard to *Homo sapiens*) of "The Shadow out of Time" ultimately become admirable and not horrifying; but the Scotts still assert that these entities exhibit some kind of racial animus against their opponents—the shoggoths and the Elder Things, respectively. They stubbornly maintain that "one must take the racism [in Lovecraft's stories] as irreducible and inescapable." But it seems to me that the Old Ones and the Great Race have every good reason to hate and fear the shoggoths and the Elder Things. This is a conflict between *species* and not between *races*. Fritz Leiber seemed to be far more on target when he pointed out this same dichotomy and noted: "the authors shows us horrors and then pulls back the curtain a little farther, letting us glimpse the horrors of which even the horrors are afraid!"[1]

The authors engage in arid discussions about the putative readership of Lovecraft's stories in his time, which they maintain "was (and mostly remains) very white." I do not know how the authors came to this conclusion. Given that *Weird Tales* was a pulp magazine deliberately designed for "the masses," it is likely that at least some people of color—who at the time were certainly in the lower reaches of the American socioeconomic order—read the magazine. But this whole conjecture is simply beside the point, for it fails to take into consideration that Lovecraft's primary (and perhaps only) audience was himself. In 1921 (admittedly before the founding of *Weird Tales*) Lovecraft wrote: "There are probably seven persons, in all, who really like my work; and they are enough. I should write even if I were the only patient reader, for my aim is merely self-expression" (*CE* 5.53). Perhaps those seven

1. "A Literary Copernicus" (1949), in *H. P. Lovecraft: Four Decades of Criticism*, ed. S. T. Joshi (Athens: Ohio University Press, 1980), 57.

persons were all white, as Lovecraft certainly was; but he was a lot of other things as well. The two Scotts compound their folly by even more vapid speculations about what a "politicized person of color" might think when reading Lovecraft. Since these authors are self-admitted white folks, I am not sure how or why they have any authority to talk of such things. (Anyway, isn't this a classic instance of cultural appropriation?)

I will counter with an assertion that is not based in idle conjecture: there is not the slightest evidence that any significant number of Lovecraft's readers—either in his own time or in the decades that followed—displayed any response at all to the purportedly racial content of his stories. Hostile critics like Edmund Wilson and Colin Wilson found plenty of things to criticize in Lovecraft's work (and even in his character)—but racism wasn't one of them. The fulminations about Lovecraft's racism are an extremely recent phenomenon, and seem to be fueled by certain writers who are determined to seize on this one aspect of Lovecraft's life and thought as a way of knocking him down a few pegs in critical esteem. This may not be the two Scotts' motivation, but they have succumbed to the perceived need to debate this issue at tedious length, as a dog worries a bone. And yet, the letter columns of *Weird Tales* were full of encomiums of "The Horror at Red Hook" (including one by Robert Bloch), and no discussions of "The Shadow over Innsmouth" except in very recent years have cited its supposedly racist substratum. And I also maintain that, if we did not know of Lovecraft's racial views, it would occur to very few of us to see a racist element in any but a small number of Lovecraft's tales. Even some of those that do know of his views have still come to that conclusion, as when the British philosopher John Gray wrote: "Fortunately, the core of [Lovecraft's] work has nothing to do with his social and racial resentments."[2]

Now it is remotely possible that all such readers were and are simply blind and oblivious; but it strikes me as more likely that, in our hyperpoliticized climate today, we are all too quick to see racial elements in every bit of writing that passes before our eyes.

---

2. John Gray, "Weird Realism: John Gray on the Moral Universe of H. P. Lovecraft," *New Statesman* (24 October 2014) [https://www.newstatesman.com/culture/2014/10/weird-realism-john-gray-moral-universe-h-p-lovecraft].

This phenomenon has particularly afflicted academic criticism, where it is now the fashion to examine literature largely—and perhaps solely—through the lenses of race, class, and gender. To my mind this perspective seriously disfigures the import of a good many literary works, and at a minimum results in analyses that are more like sociology tracts than literary criticism. But I suppose I am a fossil in this regard.

The authors engage in random discussions of "He," which is held up as one of the stories we are now meant to deprecate because of its racism; but they (along with many others) have incredibly failed to see that a careful—or, in actual fact, fairly obvious—reading of this story shows it to be *anti-racist*. For all Lovecraft's lamentations about the contemporary environment of New York, the story is a straightforward supernatural-revenge narrative in which the spirits of Native Americans—whom the English squire had poisoned and whose land he subsequently claimed for his own—dispatch that preternaturally aged gentleman in a particularly pungent manner; and the narrative tone of the story clearly suggests that the Englishman got his just desserts.

The authors take up the racism issue later in the book, focusing chiefly on "The Shadow over Innsmouth." It is here that the two Scotts suddenly and belatedly come to a conclusion that any sane and unbiased reader should have arrived at without any assistance from learned commentators:

> I will venture to suggest that the most keen and vivid sense of horror that erupts from Lovecraft's pages involves neither race nor class nor indeed any mode of sociality at all. On the contrary, the ultimate Lovecraftian horror is the sheer insignificance of humanity as a whole; the terror of absolute spatial and temporal finitude in a vast, empty, and indifferent universe. This horror, however, as we have both suggested in different ways, must at least take us beyond or even before any conceivable idea of "race."

Brilliant, my dear Watson!

And yet, the authors, in their infinite wisdom, take occasion to question whether Lovecraft is on target in regard to another issue—one that elucidates the otherwise perplexing title of their book. They wonder whether Lovecraft really did have a "love of the ancient & the permanent" (*SL* 1.110), since "his stories are set in a universe where absolutely nothing is permanent"; therefore, in at least one of the two Scotts' opinion, "one might venture to suggest a revision to Lovecraft's own schema and speak of a love, not of the ancient and the permanent but of the ancient and the *ruined*."

My only response to this is: *sigh.* Are not the authors aware of how diligently Lovecraft sought out ancient towns up and down the Eastern Seaboard, from Quebec to St. Augustine, and gloried in the fact that in many of these places the centuried structures (both public buildings and private residences) were still being utilized in accordance with their original functions—and, more pertinently, that the inhabitants were preserving their traditional folkways even in the face of abrasive modernity? Have they not read the many letters where Lovecraft bitterly denounces the destruction of colonial buildings in his hometown? The passages from his essays and letters on these topics are too numerous for citation here.

Where the two Scotts have erred—here as in other aspects of their book—is in regarding Lovecraft's fiction as some kind of simple and straightforward guide to his beliefs and opinions. They forget that Lovecraft *is in fact writing fiction.* They habitually attribute the opinions of Lovecraft's characters to himself, and commit analogous errors in critical analysis. I would advise them, and all potential commentators on Lovecraft, to ponder the following passage (from a letter to James F. Morton, [1 April 1930]) that I believe to be the essential key to understanding the interrelationship between Lovecraft's philosophical thought and his fiction:

> I get no kick at all from *postulating what isn't so,* as religionists and idealists do. That leaves me cold [. . .] My big kick comes from *taking reality just as it is*—accepting all the limitations of the most orthodox science—and then permitting my symbolising faculty to *build outward* from the existing facts; rearing a structure of *indefinite promise and possibility* whose topless towers are in no cosmos or dimension penetrable by the contradicting-power of the tyrannous and inexorable intellect. But the whole secret of the kick is *that I know damn well it isn't so.* (*SL* 3.140)

Lovecraft is not only writing fiction; he is writing *weird fiction.* The purpose of weird fiction is to frighten, to terrify. He knew that, in order to terrify others, he must first need to terrify himself. What would be more terrifying to Lovecraft than to contemplate, for the duration of a tale, the refutation or subversion of his cherished beliefs—atheism, materialism, and, yes, "love of the ancient & the permanent"? It is this act that constituted, for him, a gesture of imaginative liberation—an attempt to "achieve, momentarily, the *illusion* [my emphasis] of some strange suspension or violation of the galling limitations of time, space, and natural law which for ever imprison us and frustrate our curiosity about the infinite cosmic spaces beyond the radius of our sight and analysis" (*CE* 2.176). But *he knew damn well it wasn't so.* He knew he was writing fiction: in postulating various "gods" (most of them really space aliens) in his fiction, he was not undermining his atheism, but confirming it; in suggesting that the laws of matter do not apply in certain corners of space or to certain entities of his own imagination, he was confirming his materialism; and in depicting ancient ruins (usually constructed by alien species), he was confirming his love of the ancient and the permanent. Got that, people?

Much of the two Scotts' book is devoted to a meandering, unfocused, and at times frivolous discussion of "The Shadow out of Time." I really don't know that there is much profit in speculating on what would happen if a mind from the Great Race occupied the body of Buster Keaton or the contemporary stand-up comic Stephen Wright. But amidst all this verbiage there is exactly one point that I found of some interest. The authors wonder why the Great Race built their immense and indestructible library in the depths of the Australian desert, when they themselves abandoned it (and knew they were going to abandon it) by leaving their cone-shaped bodies and entering "the bulbous vegetable entities of Mercury" (*CF* 3.400). This is an intriguing paradox or ambiguity in the story, and the authors have no explanation for it—perhaps there is none. And yet, even here their discussion goes off the track on certain points, especially in their insistence that the Great Race's enemies (the blind creatures who have harnessed great winds) are nameless. But the authors themselves on two occasions quote passages from the story in which these creatures are plainly called the "Elder Things"! Does this not count as a name?

The enthusiasm of the authors cannot conceal the fact that

they are novices to Lovecraft and Lovecraft studies, as an array of small but embarrassing mistakes indicates. One of them states that "No Lovecraft protagonist, so far as I'm aware, chooses suicide" at the end of a tale. This plainly false statement is immediately qualified by a footnote pointing out that the narrator of "Dagon" unequivocally indicates his intention to dispatch himself after telling his story. But the authors seem to have missed the final line of "The Hound," where the narrator confesses that "I shall seek with my revolver the oblivion which is my only refuge from the unnamed and unnamable" (*CF* 1.348). (My ears still echo to Roddy McDowall intoning these words in the old Caedmon recording of this story.) Have the two Scotts even read this story? It does not appear so, for their readings of Lovecraft's fiction are apparently restricted to the tales in the Library of America edition (2005), one of my corrected Arkham House editions (*At the Mountains of Madness* [1985], which the authors misdate to 1986), and the lesser tales included in *Miscellaneous Writings* (1995). Alas! "The Hound" is not in any of these books. And yet, one would not imagine that this text is terribly hard to find.

The authors tie themselves in knots trying to figure out the significance of Lovecraft's statement, in the second chapter of "Supernatural Horror in Literature," about an actual medieval "cult of nocturnal worshippers whose strange customs [. . .] were rooted in the most revolting fertility-rites of immemorial antiquity" (*CE* 2.85). Even though the authors have consulted *Collected Essays*, Volume 2, they apparently overlooked my footnote indicating that this conception was derived from Lovecraft's infatuation with the now exploded theories of Margaret A. Murray as found in *The Witch-Cult of Western Europe* (1921). The authors engage in an unsound and misleading discussion of Lovecraft's late conversion to moderate socialism—a result, perhaps, of their failure to read Lovecraft's several trenchant essays on the subject as found in *Collected Essays*, Volume 5, even though they cite that book in their bibliography.

The authors seem to have all manner of difficulties getting names right. They refer consistently to the "god" Shub-Niggurath as Shug-Niggaruth. They refer to *The Dream-Quest of Unknown Kadath* as "Dreamquest" or "Dream Quest." They cite Lovecraft and E. Hoffmann Price's sequel to "The Silver Key" as "Beyond the Gate of the Silver Key." They once refer to Frank Belknap Long as Belnap. David E. Schultz is once cited as Schulz. Henry Wentworth Akeley in "The Whisperer in Darkness" is cited as William Akeley. Some of these errors, you would think, could and should have been detected by an astute copy editor; but it appears that nowadays copy editing in the academic press is just as shoddy as copy editing among commercial publishers and small presses.

I do not doubt that the two Scotts have enjoyed swapping these letters back and forth; but I think they would have done everyone a favor if they had kept their correspondence private.

www.ingramcontent.com/pod-product-compliance
Lightning Source LLC
Chambersburg PA
CBHW072342100426
42736CB00044B/1698
* 9 7 8 1 6 1 4 9 8 2 2 9 6 *